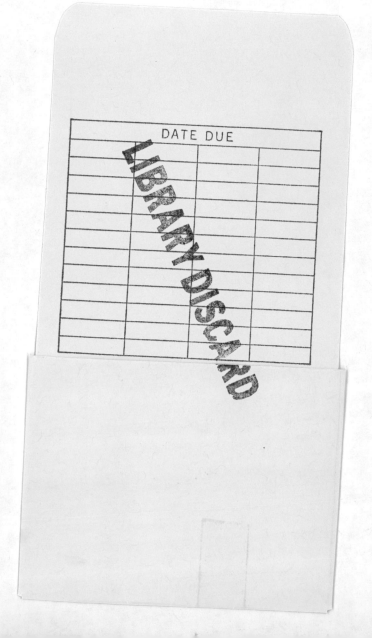

DATE DUE

LIBRARY DISCARD

POLITICS and FORCE LEVELS

Desmond Ball

POLITICS and
FORCE LEVELS

The Strategic Missile Program
of the Kennedy Administration

University of California Press

Berkeley · Los Angeles · London

University of California Press
Berkeley and Los Angeles, California

University of California Press, Ltd.
London, England

1 2 3 4 5 6 7 8 9

Library of Congress Cataloging in Publication Data

Ball, Desmond.
  Politics and force levels.

  A revision of the author's thesis   Australian
National University.
  Bibliography: p.
  Includes index.
  1. United States—Military policy. 2. Strategic
forces—United States. 3. Intercontinental ballistic
missiles. 4. United States—Politics and government
—1961–1963. I. Title.
UA23.B275 1980   355'.033'073   78-57302
ISBN 0-520-03698-0

For my parents

Contents

Tables and Figures

Acronyms and Abbreviations

ABM	Antiballistic Missile
ACDA	Arms Control and Disarmament Agency
AFB	Air Force Base
ALBM	Air-launched Ballistic Missile
AMSA	Advanced Manned Strategic Aircraft
ASW	Anti-submarine Warfare
BMD	Ballistic Missile Division
BNSP	Basic National Security Policy
BoB	Bureau of the Budget
CEP	Circular Error Probability
CNO	Chief of Naval Operations
DDR&E	Director, Defense Research and Engineering
DIA	Defense Intelligence Agency
DoD	Department of Defense
DPM	Draft Presidential Memorandum
EWO	Emergency War Order
FBM	Fleet Ballistic Missile

FCDA	Federal Civil Defense Agency
F/Y	Fiscal Year
ICBM	Intercontinental Ballistic Missile
INR	Intelligence and Research Bureau, State Department
IOC	Initial Operational Capability
IRBM	Intermediate-range Ballistic Missile
ISA	International Security Affairs
J-2	Air Force Intelligence
JCS	Joint Chiefs of Staff
JSCP	Joint Strategic Capabilities Plan
JSOP	Joint Strategic Objectives Plan
LCF	Launch Control Facility
LLTI	Long-lead-time Items
MMRBM	Mobile Medium-range Ballistic Missile
MRBM	Medium-range Ballistic Missile
Mt.	Megaton(s)
NESC	Net Evaluation Subcommittee (of the National Security Council)
NIE	National Intelligence Estimate
NOA	New Obligational Authority
NSC	National Security Council
OSD	Office of the Secretary of Defense
PSAC	President's Science Advisory Committee
PSI	Pounds per square inch (blast overpressure)
R&D	Research and Development
RAND	Research and Development Corporation
SAC	Strategic Air Command
SALT	Strategic Arms Limitation Talks
SAMOS	Satellite and Missile Observation System
SAMs	Surface-to-air Missiles
SRF	Strategic Retaliatory Forces
SIOP	Single Integrated Operational Plan
SLBM	Submarine-launched Ballistic Missile
SMS	Strategic Missile Squadron
SSBN	Strategic Nuclear Ballistic Missile Submarine
SST	Supersonic Transport
TAC	Tactical Air Command
USIB	United States Intelligence Board
WSEG	Weapons Systems Evaluation Group

Preface

The strategies pursued by the United States and the Soviet Union in the development and deployment of their respective strategic nuclear forces are quite different. The Soviets have chosen an evolutionary approach to force development, advancing qualitatively by means of many relatively small steps involving successive modifications. The United States, on the other hand, has proceeded by means of relatively large generational leaps.

The United States is currently preparing for another such leap forward. In 1980–81, the first of a new generation of fleet ballistic missile (FBM) submarines will become operational. These Trident submarines will each carry 24 submarine-launched ballistic missiles (SLBMs), each of which will carry some 10 to

17 multiple independently-targetable reentry vehicles (MIRVs), a truly awesome capability. A decision will also have to be made within the next two or three years regarding the deployment of a new generation of intercontinental ballistic missile (ICBM), designated the MX, a missile more than twice as large as the current Minuteman III, designed to deliver some 10 MIRVs with extraordinary accuracy, and capable of being deployed in some mobile mode. A decision is also imminent regarding the future of bombers and air-launched missiles as part of the American triad; this decision could result in the deployment of several thousand air-launched cruise missiles (ALCMs) aboard the 120 long-range bombers and cruise missile carriers allowed under the SALT II constraints.

These developments have been prompted by the technological obsolescence and perceived increasing vulnerability of the current U.S. strategic nuclear forces—the 1,000 Minuteman and 54 Titan II ICBMs, the 41 FBM submarines carrying 656 SLBMs, and the B-52 long-range bomber force. These current strategic force levels were decided upon during the last major generational leap, in the early 1960s, largely during the administration of President Kennedy.

When the Kennedy Administration took office on 20 January 1961, the United States was just entering the missile age. Only a dozen ICBMs were operational and, although the Eisenhower Administration had programmed about 1,100 strategic missiles, only some 800 of the ultimate U.S. force were to be the strategically viable, second-generation Polaris and hard-silo Minuteman missiles. By the time of President Kennedy's assassination in November 1963, however, this figure had been doubled to the current level of over 1,700 strategic ballistic missiles. Whereas the Eisenhower missile program is reasonably explicable—the post-Sputnik fears of a "missile gap," congressional and military pressures[1]—the Kennedy missile build-up has still to be convincingly explained. Yet this was a build-up of an unprecedented rate and scale, and one which has had momentous consequences for American society, the strategic arms race, and international relations in general.

1. See Edmund Beard, *Developing the ICBM.*

This book consists of a political and strategic analysis of the missile programs undertaken by the Kennedy Administration. It covers that period in U.S. public and defense policy from the so-called "missile gap" to the imposition of a quantitative ceiling on the U.S. strategic missile forces, approximately 1958 to 1965, although the focus of the analysis will be on the Kennedy-McNamara years.

In September 1967, when the U.S. strategic nuclear forces had reached their current levels, Secretary McNamara stated that the United States' "current numerical superiority over the Soviet Union in reliable, accurate and effective warheads is both greater than we had originally planned and in fact more than we require."[2] This book is therefore centered around this question: why, in 1961–62, did the Kennedy-McNamara Administration deploy (or program for deployment) such an unnecessarily large strategic deterrent? But the wider intent of the study is to shed light on the development of national strategic postures and policies (as representations or rationalizations of those postures) in a period of rapid military-technological change. It should also explain something of the nature and dynamics of the Soviet-American strategic relationship.

The study is intended to have both theoretical and policy import. It is a contribution to the current debate among students of national security policy as to how to explain foreign and defense policy decisions and events. Indeed Part III is explicitly concerned with explanation. Over the years in which I have been researching, thinking, and writing about the Kennedy Administration's missile decisions, the orientation of my general argument has altered substantially. Earlier drafts of this work argued along lines similar to that which has since become publicly identified with the "bureaucratic politics" school of, in particular, Graham Allison and Morton Halperin. The present argument does not accept so crude a bureaucratic determinism. Rather, it sees the decision-making process as complex, the key relationships being those between McNamara and Kennedy, and between them and the military and Congress.[3]

2. Robert S. McNamara, "The Dynamics of Nuclear Strategy," p. 445.
3. For a fuller critique of "bureaucratic politics" theory, see my "The Blind Men and the Elephant," pp. 71–92.

The field of weapons-system procurement programs and national strategic and public policy not only allows enormous scope for genuine disagreement, with decisions issuing more from adversary processes than from rational calculations,[4] but actually attracts special pleading and emotionalism. In order to elucidate, to the extent possible, the roles of the various factors which affected the decision-making process and its outcome, I have adopted the following approach in the writing of this book.

Parts I and II describe in detail the successive strategic missile decisions of the Kennedy Administration from 1961 to 1965, and set out necessary background data upon which the later analysis and criticism is based. For those who may not fully accept my critique of the Kennedy-McNamara missile build-up, the body of historical and descriptive material on which my arguments rely, separately assembled in these sections, remains to be reinterpreted. Most analyses, including even those in pure history, involve reducing the historical evidence to some lower epistemological status; this approach has been adopted in an attempt to avoid such loss of information.

The analysis of the strategic and political factors involved in the strategic missile decisions of the early 1960s has great relevance for contemporary policy issues. There are undoubtedly many lessons which should be applied in the current decision making leading to a forthcoming generational leap in U.S. strategic nuclear force development. Perhaps the most important of these is to avoid being precipitate; the nature of the bureaucratic-political factors in national security decision making creates a strong tendency to overreaction. Moreover, if it can be shown that the decision making which produced the current force levels was in some sense irrational, then the case for the replacement of these strategic forces (at least at the same levels) becomes questionable.

This project has been in gestation for several years; the debts incurred during this period were considerable. I am especially

4. See William T. R. Fox, foreword to Michael H. Armacost, *The Politics of Weapons Innovation*, p. vii.

grateful to Professor Warner R. Schilling of the Institute of War and Peace Studies, Columbia University, for advice and guidance at the initial stages of the research.

Some of the material in this book was first written up in the form of a doctoral dissertation, in the Department of International Relations, Australian National University. I am indebted to my supervisors, Geoffrey Jukes and Professors Hedley Bull and Arthur Lee Burns, who gave continuous aid and advice throughout the writing of the dissertation.

Revision of the doctoral dissertation into publishable form was begun at the Center for International Affairs, Harvard University; I owe a great debt to Professor Robert L. Jervis for his advice on that initial revision.

Various drafts of the manuscript were read by Hedley Bull, James L. Richardson, Geoffrey Jukes, Arthur Lee Burns, and Harry Gelber in Australia, and Bernard B. Brodie, Albert J. Wohlstetter, Morton H. Halperin, William W. Kaufmann, W. T. R. Fox, Robert L. Jervis, James R. Kurth, Robert J. Art, Alfred Goldberg, Richard Fryklund, and Daniel Ellsberg in the United States. Their comments, criticisms, and suggestions were instructive.

During July and August 1970, December 1972, January and February 1973, and October 1975, I interviewed some fifty former senior officers and civilians within or associated at first-hand with the Kennedy-McNamara defense establishment. Their names and relevant former positions are listed in the bibliography. My debt to them all is tremendous. I wish, however, particularly to thank Richard Fryklund, Marvin Stern, Daniel Ellsberg, Morton Halperin, Major General Robert P. Lukeman, Albert J. Wohlstetter, and George Pugh for assistance beyond the interview.

This book was completed while I was a Senior Research Fellow in the Strategic and Defence Studies Centre, Australian National University. I am grateful to the support staff of the centre for the typing and proofreading of the manuscript, and to the head of the centre, Dr. Robert O'Neill, for the facilities and assistance provided me during those final stages of the project.

Desmond Ball
December 1978

Introduction

John F. Kennedy was elected to the presidency of the United States on 8 November 1960, in one of the closest contests in the history of the country, and was inaugurated as thirty-fourth president on 20 January 1961. During his three years in office, he and his secretary of defense, Robert S. McNamara, the chief architect of the defense policies and posture of the Kennedy Administration, built up "the most powerful military force in human history." It was, according to Theodore C. Sorensen, special counsel to the late president, the largest and swiftest military build-up in the peacetime history of the United States, costing some $17 billion in additional appropriations. It provided President Kennedy, as he himself put it, with a versatile arsenal "ranging from the most massive deterrents to the most subtle influences."[1] The most massive deterrent was the U.S. strategic nuclear force.

In a speech given by McNamara to the Economic Club of New York on 18 November 1963, just four days before President Kennedy was assassinated, the secretary of defense summarized "the current status of the balance of strategic forces":

> The U.S. force now contains more than 500 operational long-range ballistic missiles—Atlas, Titan, Minuteman, Polaris—and is planned to increase to over 1700 by 1966. There is no doubt in our minds and none in the minds of the Soviets that these missiles can penetrate to their targets. In addition, the U.S. has Strategic Air Command bombers on air alert and over 500 bombers on quick reaction ground alert. By comparison the consensus is that today the Soviets could place about half as many bombers over North America on a first strike. The Soviets are estimated to have today only a fraction as many intercontinental missiles as we do. Furthermore, their submarine-launched ballistic missiles are short-range and generally are not comparable to our Polaris force.[2]

In the speech that President Kennedy had proposed to deliver in Dallas the day of his assassination, he had outlined what his administration had done in regard to the U.S. strategic nuclear forces during the previous three years:

> The strategic nuclear power of the United States has been so greatly modernized and expanded in the last 1,000 days, by the rapid production and deployment of the most modern missile systems, that any and all potential aggressors are clearly confronted now with the impossibility of strategic victory—and the certainty of total destruction—if by reckless attack they should ever force upon us the necessity of a strategic reply.
>
> In less than three years, we have increased by 50 percent the number of Polaris submarines scheduled to be in force by the next fiscal year—increased by more than 70 percent our total Polaris purchase program—increased by 50 percent the portion of our strategic bombers on 15-minute alert—and increased by 100 per-

1. Theodore C. Sorensen, *Kennedy*, p. 672. The presidential citation accompanying the Distinguished Service Medal which was awarded to Secretary McNamara on 29 February 1968 said: "He has built our Nation's forces to a pinnacle of new strength and efficiency."
2. Cited in William W. Kaufmann, *The McNamara Strategy*, p. 304.

cent the total number of nuclear weapons available in our strategic alert forces.[3]

Moreover, less than one-third of the programmed U.S. missile force had by this time actually been deployed. The heights of the Kennedy-McNamara strategic missile build-up would not become apparent until later years.

The U.S. strategic missile force reached its present level of 1,000 Minuteman ICBMs, 54 Titan II ICBMs, and 41 FBM submarines carrying 656 Polaris missiles during the last half of 1967; the development of each of these missile systems was begun under the Eisenhower Administration, but the decisions as to force levels, strategic mix, type of deployment, associated strategy, and so on, were made by the Kennedy Administration. Only a dozen of the primitive first-generation Atlas D ICBMs and two Polaris FBM submarines had been deployed when the Kennedy Administration took office.

Although McNamara continued as President Johnson's secretary of defense for a further four years after Kennedy's assassination, virtually all the strategic missile decisions which related to numbers of strategic missiles had been taken before 22 November 1963. Only 50 new Minuteman missiles were programmed for the U.S. missile force after 1963, but even the decision to deploy these was probably made before President Johnson took office. There were, certainly, some very important and consequential missile decisions made after 1963, but these were largely qualitative improvements to the Minuteman and Polaris missile force; responsibility for the numerical build-up of the U.S. missile force can be located fairly and squarely with the Kennedy Administration.

As the chief executive, ultimate responsibility for this build-up must rest with the late President Kennedy. But within the broad policy guidelines laid down by the president, the chief architect of the build-up was his secretary of defense, Robert S. McNamara. The president and his defense secretary worked together so closely and so well that it would, at least in most cases, be arti-

3. Ibid., p. 315.

ficial to delineate their respective contributions to the missile build-up. William Kaufmann, a close observer of and contributor to the defense policies of Secretary McNamara, has written that

> the collaboration between Kennedy and McNamara was a close one. The President allowed his Secretary of Defense remarkable latitude in the development of specific plans and programs while McNamara, for his part, sought consistently to attain the objectives that Kennedy had defined even before acceding to the Presidency. In so doing, McNamara actively solicited and received the President's final decision on every major defense issue. The Secretary and the Joint Chiefs proposed; the President disposed. For McNamara, the right was Kennedy's as much out of the wisdom of the President as out of the authority of the Presidency. Yet so linked were their thoughts that Kennedy rarely found it necessary to overrule his Secretary. Typically, when McNamara prepared a major address on defense policy, Kennedy not only reviewed the draft, but contributed to the drafting. When McNamara spoke, it was for the President in a very literal sense.[4]

I have therefore adopted, as shorthand expressions, the terms *Kennedy-McNamara strategic missile build-up* and *Kennedy-McNamara Administration* to refer to the joint program undertaken by President Kennedy and his secretary of defense from 1961 to 1963.

Notwithstanding the radical changes to U.S. defense policies and posture which the election of Kennedy to the presidency predestined, the strategic-force decisions of Kennedy and McNamara were not, and could not have been, taken in a vacuum. Despite the enormous powers of initiative which the president has in matters of defense and foreign policy, he is necessarily circumscribed by numerous factors which he can only partly, if at all, influence and modify. The size, character, and rate of production and deployment of the Soviet missile program were the factors which Kennedy could affect least of all. Within the United States, he faced certain historical constraints. Decisions and events which had taken place before 1961 not only determined in part the environment in which he had to operate as president,

4. Ibid., p. 300.

but even shaped *his* perceptions and committed him to a certain range of decisions and policies with regard to the strategic missile program. The missile-gap controversy of 1958–61, the sophisticated strategic analyses of the late 1950s, the strategic missile programs which had been initiated and put into production by the Eisenhower Administration, all in some way—ideologically, politically, or technologically—constrained the Kennedy Administration. These factors, which constitute the historical background and the pre-1961 contributions to the 1961–63 strategic missile build-up of the Kennedy-McNamara Administration, are outlined in Part I.

The U.S. defense policy-making establishment can be viewed as a collection of quasi-sovereignties, consisting of the military services and other bureaucratic entities, which act as institutional interest groups whose lobbying activities are directed toward the achievement of larger budgets, more extensive roles and mission assignments, and additional weapons systems.[5] These quasi-sovereignties limit the freedom of action, in the political sense, of the chief executive; hence the positions on the question of the U.S. strategic missile-force requirement which were adopted by the Air Force and the Navy, and by other participants in the defense policy-making process, are also included in Part I.

Finally, Part I contains a detailed chronological account of the build-up of U.S. intercontinental and submarine-launched strategic ballistic missiles from 1959 to 1967, and of the public and official demise of the missile gap during 1961. This provides the necessary background data from which analysis and criticism can later be developed.

Part II consists of a description, with a minimum of analysis, of the successive missile decisions made by the Kennedy Administration from January 1961 to November 1964. It is arranged chronologically to allow one to see the unfolding of the various decisions, and it especially makes explicit the fact that the most critical decisions were made very early in the Kennedy Administration. Each decision is described in detail; the official

5. See Michael H. Armacost, *The Politics of Weapons Innovation*, especially the conclusion, pp. 250–93.

rationale is spelled out, as often as possible in the words of the relevant officials; and the various proximate background factors are explained. My own comments and judgments are limited to those places where they are immediately called for—deeper analysis is postponed to Part III.

Part III of the book examines various attempts to explain the rate and scale of the Kennedy-McNamara missile build-up. The explanations all accept McNamara's admission of 18 September 1967 that U.S. missile forces at the conclusion of the Kennedy-McNamara missile build-up were "both greater than we had originally planned and in fact more than we require."[6] In that same speech, Secretary McNamara stated that the strategic missile build-up "was necessitated by a lack of accurate information" about Soviet intentions; in hedging against a possible Soviet missile build-up, the United States procured and deployed an unnecessarily large strategic missile force.[7] This remains the only official explanation of the Kennedy-McNamara missile build-up; it is examined in chapter eight.

The new management procedures introduced into the U.S. defense establishment by Secretary McNamara have been acclaimed as "a scientific" commitment to a rational organization discourse.[8] One implication of this acclaim is that McNamara established a direct connection between national strategic policy and strategic-forces procurement. Chapter nine examines the relationship between developments in (officially accepted) U.S. strategic policy from 1961 to 1965–66 and the programming of the missile build-up during those years.

Another implication of the alleged rationality of the McNamara defense establishment is that force programs were decided on a cost-effectiveness basis, involving trade-offs among alternative weapons systems. These trade-offs, however, can also be interpreted as exercises in bureaucratic bargaining, a process involving various groups within or related to the U.S. defense policy-making establishment, each with power-political bases of

6. Secretary McNamara, "The Dynamics of Nuclear Strategy," p. 445.
7. Ibid.
8. Paul Y. Hammond, *Resource Limits, Political and Military Risk Taking, and the Generation of Military Requirements*, p. 24.

their own from which they pressed to have their respective roles, missions, positions, budgets, profits, and so forth, enhanced. Part III also looks at these factors in the Kennedy-McNamara strategic missile build-up.

All these explanations of the missile build-up are, in one sense or another, official or semi-official. McNamara's 1967 argument that the build-up was a consequence of a lack of adequate information about the Soviet missile program remains the only official explanation of the build-up as a whole. But in early 1963 McNamara and other members of the administration offered the cancellation of the Skybolt air-launched ballistic missile program as an explanation for part of the increase in the U.S. missile force. The arguments that the missile build-up was necessitated by *political factors* have semi-official standing. Arthur M. Schlesinger, Jr., special assistant to President Kennedy, and other members of the White House staff explain the build-up in terms of a political *quid pro quo* for the Air Force and its industrial allies and powerful lobby in Congress for the discontinued production of the B-52 and B-58 manned bombers, the rapid phaseout of the B-47s, and the refusal to produce the B-70 as an operational weapons system.[9] Other former members of the administration, such as Jerome Wiesner, see the build-up as a consequence of a bargaining process with the military, but particularly the Air Force, over the U.S. (quantitative) missile requirement.[10] Ralph Lapp, a Kennedy campaign adviser and occasional adviser to the new administration, has argued that Kennedy was obliged to expand the missile force because of the commitments which he made during the 1960 presidential campaign.[11]

Several of these explanations warrant special analysis because they have become accepted as conventional wisdom by the international-relations fraternity and others interested in questions of defense, strategy, and foreign policy. That the high quantitative level of the U.S. missile force was simply an overreaction to fears of a missile gap favoring the Soviet Union, occasioned by

9. Arthur M. Schlesinger, Jr., *A Thousand Days*, p. 438.
10. Jerome B. Wiesner, "Arms Control," p. 6.
11. Ralph E. Lapp, *The Weapons Culture*, pp. 60, 184.

a lack of adequate intelligence about the Soviet missile program, is such a piece of conventional wisdom, accepted in numerous books and articles. Various approaches to the study of defense policy making in the United States which command widespread acceptance in the fields of international relations and political science also offer conventional explanations—for example, that of bargaining with the military in a bureaucratic-political process, and that of military industrial capitalism.

The purpose of the relatively long conclusion is to weigh these explanations and to present a balanced and integrated account of the strategic missile build-up of the Kennedy-McNamara Administration. Any case study on questions of national strategic and military policy should also say something about the various theories, concepts, and notions which are current in the strategic-studies community. The analysis comes down in favor of that approach to the study of public policy which interprets the Kennedy-McNamara strategic missile build-up in terms of intramural bureaucratic bargaining, in which internal political factors and the strategic perceptions of the key decision makers primarily shaped the outcome. Within this framework, the section is written to allow the conclusions which have wider relevance to stand out. The contributions this study makes derive as much from its value as a case study as from the answers it provides to the questions posed at the outset.

part one

The Background of the Kennedy-McNamara
Strategic Missile Build-up

1 The Political- Strategic Background, 1957–1960

Decisions in international relations, defense, and national security policy are usually best seen as a process—they are rarely made without cognizance, either explicit or implicit, of the many preceding actions, events, and decisions which are almost invariably relevant, and they are rarely self-contained or discrete. That is, of course, particularly the case if the decisions relate to issues which are complex, important, and consequential, as were those decisions responsible for the strategic missile build-up undertaken by the Kennedy-McNamara Administration of 1961–63. President Kennedy made a deliberate (and undoubtedly successful) attempt to contrast his own position on defense and national-security policies—and after January 1961, that of his administration—with the defense and national-security policies of the Eisenhower Administration. Despite this effort—in fact, at least in part, because of it—the strategic missile decisions of the Kennedy Administration cannot be understood properly without reference to events, actions, and decisions which took place before 1961.

The factors which precede actual decisions and strongly influence the outcome include sources of information; the framing of the questions at issue; and the choices of values, objectives, and means. The most important of these factors arise from the domestic environment, for decision makers in defense and national-security policy are much more intimately connected, and concerned, with their domestic than with their foreign environment. This conditioning may take subtle forms—the internalization of domestic values, participation in the national culture and partaking of national characteristics, and constant exposure to influences and pressures in the play of domestic politics. Decision makers in defense and national-security policy are "actually part and parcel" of the domestic environment.[1] Or the influences can be rather more obvious—the nature of the sources of information, the selection of aides and advisers, the choice of questions of import and concern.

This chapter deals with the domestic political and strategic background which preceded the Kennedy-McNamara strategic missile build-up of 1961–63. The most proximate of these political and strategic factors can be dated from about 1957. For ease of exposition, the chapter is divided into three principal sections.

First, the "missile gap" controversy, which dominated the defense and national-security policy debate of the late 1950s and 1960. This controversy arose from a fear, widespread after 1957–58, that the Soviet Union would possess a commanding superiority in ICBMs over the United States three or four years hence. This illusion of a missile gap was created, nurtured, and maintained by the numerous Americans who feared that the Soviet superiority would lead to a devastating attack on U.S.

1. See Joseph Frankel, *The Making of Foreign Policy*, p. 70; also Henry A. Kissinger, *American Foreign Policy*, chap. 1.

retaliatory forces. It was in response to the same forces and factors which were responsible for the belief in the missile gap that the Eisenhower Administration increased the U.S. strategic missile program during 1957–60.

Second, Kennedy in 1960. Throughout the period of the missile-gap controversy, but especially in 1960, Senator Kennedy was a major protagonist and a major critic of the defense and national-security policies of the Eisenhower Administration. Kennedy's presidential campaign of 1960, and his actions during the interregnum, are abstracted from the overall discussion of the missile-gap controversy because they focus attention on matters of more particular import to the later analysis—the fact that Kennedy was forced to articulate and justify a position on U.S. defense and national-security policy, and that he made various commitments relating to the U.S. defense posture of varying specificity, which may reasonably be expected to have figured in the deliberations and decisions of his administration; and the fact that many of his aides and advisers during 1960 later became important officials and consultants in his administration.

Third, this chapter includes an outline of various strategic studies and analyses conducted in the period before 1961 which had an impact beyond their contribution, both public and confidential, to the missile-gap controversy. Several of these studies and analyses, both through their substantive content and their authors and sponsors, figured prominently in the decisions which were responsible for the strategic missile build-up of the Kennedy-McNamara Administration after 1961. They therefore deserve relatively detailed description.

THE "MISSILE-GAP" CONTROVERSY

The unpleasant surprise produced by the Russian Sputniks in October and November 1957 inaugurated a long period of alarm in the West.[2] In the United States at this time, interservice

2. For a comprehensive chronological study of the "missile gap" controversy, see Edgar M. Bottome, *The Missile Gap*. The first part of this chapter relies heavily upon the work of Professor Bottome.

rivalry within the military was intense, and a debate was in process over the comparative military strengths of the United States and Soviet Union. And the period following the Sputniks was, not surprisingly, characterized by additional confusion and an increase in the number of different evaluations, available to the public through the mass media, of comparative military strengths. The debate became much more directly political, and the Eisenhower Administration came under attack for allegedly allowing the Soviet Union to attain superiority in what was already recognized as the decisive weapon of the next decade, the long-range ballistic missile.

In the fall of 1957, the Preparedness subcommittee of the Senate Armed Services Committee, under Lyndon B. Johnson, began a "searching inquiry" into the United States' defense posture.[3] These hearings provided a forum for the opposing forces in the defense debate.

The administration's position, as defined by Secretary McElroy, was that the basic military posture of the United States was sound. The significant strategic-weapons system at the time was the long-range bomber force, and the significant strategic question was the ability of this force to deliver nuclear weapons over the Soviet Union even after absorbing a surprise bomber attack by the Soviets. At the end of 1957, the United States had about 1,600 to 1,700 heavy and medium combat jet aircraft (and 2,000 to 3,000 other aircraft, including fighter-bombers capable of carrying megaton-range thermonuclear weapons to the Soviet Union), and Russia only 100 to 200 intercontinental bombers (though many officers within the U.S. Air Force believed at the time that Russia had more like 500). With such a limited comparative capability, the Soviet Union would be highly unlikely to risk a first strike at the United States. On the specific question of the missile race, McElroy was much more vague. He stated that he had no positive view as to whether the United States was ahead of or behind the Soviet Union in missile development, but

3. See U.S. Congress, Senate, Armed Services Committee, Preparedness subcommittee, *Hearings*, 85th Cong., 1st and 2nd sessions (25 November to 17 December 1957 and January 1958). [Henceforth *Hearings* will be cited by name of committee, title and date only.]

that the United States "must accelerate our programs in order to stay ahead if we are ahead, and to get ahead if we are not ahead."[4]

The attacks on the administration's position were led by Democratic Senators Johnson and Symington, and elements of the Air Force. Johnson's position was that the Russians were ahead of the United States in missile development, that the lack of national leadership had caused this weakness, and that the United States had a "record of under-estimation of [Soviet] military progress." Speaking for his subcommittee, Senator Johnson stated flatly that the United States was behind the Soviet Union in ballistic missile development, and that Russia was rapidly narrowing the lead in manned bombers that the United States had held in the past. The subcommittee advocated large increases in all U.S. bomber and missile programs.[5]

The controversy over the comparative military strengths of the United States and the Soviet Union tended to focus public attention on alleged U.S. intelligence estimates. In the summer of 1958, the first of many public attempts was made to estimate the future comparative missile forces of the United States and Russia. A leading newspaper columnist, Joseph Alsop, predicted the following future U.S. and Soviet ICBM numbers:[6]

	1959	1960	1961	1962	1963
United States	0	30	70	130	130
USSR	100	500	1,000	1,500	2,000

These figures apparently approximated fairly closely to the National Intelligence Estimate (NIE) projections at that time. However, the administration succeeded in allaying the fears of the American people. The Department of Defense indicated its belief that the strategic military posture of the United States was

4. See Bottome, *Missile Gap*, pp. 56–59.
5. *New York Times*, 6 November 1957, 11 November 1957, 23 November 1957, and 24 January 1958.
6. Cited in Thomas R. Phillips, "The Growing Missile Gap," *The Reporter*, 1 August 1959, p. 11. The series of articles in which these projections were made, accompanied by very severe charges against the Eisenhower Administration, was followed on 14 August by a speech in the Senate on the missile gap by Kennedy which reflected these charges. See George E. Lowe, *The Age of Deterrence*, pp. 181–84.

second to none, and while it acknowledged that the Soviet Union had the capacity to build a substantial number of missiles, it did not believe the Russians would necessarily use that capability.[7] There was no evidence that the Soviet Union was producing long-range missiles at this time. In fact, available evidence indicated that the Soviet Union was experiencing difficulties in its ICBM development program.[8]

However, the debate resumed, and at a much more intense level, early in January 1959. This was initiated by a "secret background briefing" given by McElroy, in which he allegedly stated that in 1961–62 the Soviet Union would have a three-to-one advantage in missiles over the United States. This assessment was presumably based on CIA estimates, which looked something like this:[9]

	U.S. ICBMs	USSR ICBMs
1959	10	10
1960	30	100
1961	80 to 100	100 to 300
1962	100 to 300	500

In testimony before the Preparedness subcommittee of the Senate Armed Services Committee, Secretary McElroy stated that U.S. intelligence estimates did not indicate that the Soviet Union was ahead in missile development, but did concede that the Soviet Union could catch up with and surpass the United States if it used its full missile production capability. In any event, he said, "It is not our intention or policy to try to match missile for missile in the ICBM category of the Russian capability in the next couple of years"; the United States would rely instead on "our diversified capability to deliver the big weapon."[10]

In spite of the various predictions for the future, most observers agreed that at this time (early 1959) the military security of

7. Library of Congress, Legislative Reference Service, *United States Defense Policies in 1958* (Washington, D.C.: Government Printing Office, 10 July 1959), p. 8.

8. See Hanson W. Baldwin, *The Great Arms Race*, p. 84.

9. Bottome, *Missile Gap*, pp. 87, 103.

10. Senate Armed Services Committee and Committee on Aeronautical and Space Science, *Joint Hearings, Missile and Space Activities* (1959), pp. 46, 49, 52, and 54.

the United States was assured. Neither side as yet had an operational ICBM, but the United States had about 1,800 long-range and medium-range nuclear-armed bombers stationed within range of Russia, while Russia had only 150 long-range bombers capable of reaching the United States. These bombers would, however, be vulnerable to a surprise missile attack. At this time, the Strategic Air Command (SAC) had only about 44 major air bases, with 29 of them overseas, and since it was assumed that it would take two to six Soviet ICBMs to destroy the effectiveness of an air base, it looked as though SAC could be negated by a surprise Soviet missile attack in the period of "maximum danger," 1962–63.[11]

In 1959 two sets of National Intelligence Estimates (NIE) were prepared: the first was based on the premise that the Soviet Union would pursue an "orderly" ICBM production program; the second assumed that the Soviet Union would pursue a highly accelerated or "crash" program.[12] For mid-1963, the projections were 350 and 640 ICBMs respectively.[13]

During 1959 a series of reports indicated that the Soviet Union had run into difficulty in its ICBM testing and development programs. There were also indications that the Russian missile program had placed a serious strain on the Soviet economy.[14] These reports presaged the second major downward revision of intelligence estimates of projected Soviet missile strength. This revision occurred early in 1960, when Thomas Gates, the new secretary of defense, stated that the Russians had in fact engaged in an "orderly" missile production program, and that earlier estimates had been too high.[15] In the 1960 NIE, the "low" estimate for mid-1963 was reduced to 200 ICBMs.[16]

11. See Bottome, *Missile Gap*, pp. 103–5.   12. Ibid., pp. 127, 184.
13. *Statement of Secretary of Defense Robert S. McNamara before a Joint Session of the Senate Armed Services Committee and the Senate Subcommittee on Department of Defense Appropriations on the Fiscal Year 1965–69 Defense Program and 1965 Defense Budget, 3 February 1964*, p. 37 (declassified 1975).
14. See statement of Secretary McElroy, *Newsweek*, 13 July 1959, p. 52.
15. Testimony of Secretary Gates, Senate Armed Services Committee and Committee on Aeronautical and Space Sciences, *Joint Hearings, Missiles, Space and Other Major Defense Matters* (1960), pp. 441–42.
16. *Statement of Secretary of Defense Robert S. McNamara on the 1965 Defense Budget, 3 February 1964*, p. 37 (declassified 1975).

In presenting the new intelligence projections to the House Appropriations subcommittee, Secretary Gates stated:

> Heretofore we have been giving you intelligence figures that dealt with the theoretical Soviet capability. This is the first time that we have an intelligence estimate that says, "This is what the Soviet Union probably will do." Therefore, the great divergence, based on figures that have been testified to in years past, narrows because we talked before about a different set of comparisons—ones that we based on Soviet capabilities. This present one is an intelligence estimate on what we believe he [the Soviet Union] probably will do, not what he is capable of doing.[17]

The revised intelligence estimates and the new formula for arriving at them came under immediate attack by key Democratic political figures. Senator Lyndon Johnson declared that the new intelligence formula was "incredibly dangerous," and stated that "the missile gap" could not be eliminated by a mere stroke of the pen. Senator Symington charged the administration with issuing "misinformation" about the missile gap, and claimed the Eisenhower Administration had changed "the ground rules for evaluating the facts." Symington also declared vehemently that "the intelligence books have been juggled so the budget books may be balanced."[18]

In testimony before the Senate Armed Services Committee, Admiral Arleigh Burke, the chief of naval operations (CNO), attempted to clear up the administration's position. He stated that the new U.S. intelligence estimates were based on Soviet missile production rather than on the maximum capacity of the Soviet Union to produce missiles. Admiral Burke contended that U.S. intelligence estimates had been revised because the intelligence community had more accurate data on existing Soviet missile programs. He concluded: "It was obvious Russia wasn't exercising her maximum capability."[19]

17. House Appropriations Committee, *Department of Defense Appropriations for 1961*, part 1, p. 23.

18. See *New York Times*, 24 January 1960 and 28 January 1960; and *Aviation Week & Space Technology*, 1 February 1960, p. 31.

19. Testimony of Adm. Burke, CNO, Senate Armed Services Committee and Committee on Aeronautical Sciences, *Joint Hearings, Missiles, Space and Other Major Defense Matters* (1960), pp. 293–94.

Much of the confusion was apparently caused by the chaotic situation within the U.S. intelligence community in 1960. This was produced by three factors.[20] First, in spite of the continued downward revision of projected Soviet missile strength, several individuals within the administration apparently continued to accept the earlier, more pessimistic projections; second, the existence of at least two official sets of figures within the NIE ("orderly" versus "crash" Soviet missile programs) until 1960 gave some spokesmen the supposed option of accepting either the "high" or the "low" set; and third, the fact that the military services continued to produce their own estimates of future Soviet missile strength gave rise to at least two additional possible sets of figures—one from the Air Force and one from the Army-Navy coalition. The CIA also produced its own estimates. This meant about half a dozen possible sets of figures in 1960 purporting to be the projected number of Soviet missiles for a given year. And, moreover, some top administration officials, including Secretary Gates, sometimes appeared to be basing their testimony on *none* of these.

The question of the strategic vulnerability of U.S. retaliatory power was debated in this atmosphere of uncertainty over intelligence figures on future Soviet missile strength. This debate was intensified by a speech by General Thomas S. Power, commanding officer of SAC, before the Economic Club of New York on 19 January 1960. General Power claimed that the 100 U.S. nuclear launching installations (ICBM bases, bomber bases, and IRBM sites in Europe, etc.) could be virtually destroyed by a force of only 300 ballistic missiles (IRBMs and ICBMs), and that the Soviet Union could accumulate this number before the United States had developed an adequate warning system against missile attack.[21]

This speech aroused a tremendous amount of doubt and controversy in the United States, and became one of the major ele-

20. Bottome, *Missile Gap*, p. 190.
21. Text of Gen. Power's speech before the Economic Club of New York, 19 January 1960, in Senate Armed Services Committee and Committee on Aeronautical and Space Sciences, *Joint Hearings, Missiles, Space and Other Major Defense Matters* (1960), pp. 4–5.

ments of controversy discussed in the United States Senate *Joint Hearings* which began in early February and were concluded on 16 March 1960. Some of the key military and civilian personnel in the U.S. government once again disagreed on the basic requirements for future U.S. security. General Power believed that for the moment SAC was "the most powerful military force in the history of the world." He declared, however, that he was not satisfied with the progress being made by the United States to ensure the future adequacy of its deterrent force.[22]

The strongest defense of the United States' existing and future deterrent posture that was made during the congressional hearings in 1960 came once again from Admiral Burke. In the midst of what appeared to be an incredibly complex and confusing situation, Admiral Burke bluntly challenged General Power's thesis that 300 Russian missiles could destroy U.S. retaliatory forces. He pointed out the significant fact that since it was extremely difficult in this stage of missile development to get even one missile to fire at a specific time, it was impossible to launch a salvo of 300 missiles that would arrive at designated targets at the same time (even if the Soviet Union had 300 missiles). He stated in the most forceful terms possible the present and future adequacy of the deterrent posture of the United States, saying, "We have the ability now, right now, to destroy any enemy that wants to attack us or does attack us, regardless of what it (the enemy) does, or when it does it, or how it does it or anything else."[23]

This apparent lack of decisiveness and the contradiction within government circles immediately stimulated a lively exchange between the Republican supporters of the administration's defense policies and the critical Democrats, including three of the potential Democratic presidential candidates in the 1960 election (Senators Symington, Kennedy, and Johnson). On the Democratic side, Senator Johnson characterized the conflicting statements before the joint committee as "baffling," and contended that Russian ability to launch ICBMs was "increasing instead of decreasing" as some administration spokesmen had

22. Ibid., p. 23.   23. Ibid., pp. 313–20.

contended. The most vehement critic of the Eisenhower Administration's military policies, Senator Stuart Symington, accused the president of misleading the American people and stated: "Above all, they [the American people] are entitled not to be misled by false information."[24]

The Republicans (especially Senators Dirksen and Saltonstall) accused the Democrats of leaking national-security information, of giving the American people a distorted picture of the U.S. defense posture, and of "assisting the Communist propagandists" by their charges of inadequacy in U.S. national defense programs, and argued the adequacy of the administration's "mixed forces" concept of bombers and missiles in an attempt to forestall criticism.[25] President Eisenhower himself expressed amazement "about all this business of catching up," called the charges that he had misled the American people "despicable," and in an address to the nation on February 22 assured the American people that the United States had forged an "indestructible force of incalculable power."[26]

Once the congressional hearings for the Fiscal Year (F/Y) 1961 were completed in March 1960, however, the leaders of both parties appeared to lose interest in the controversy, and little was said on the missile question until the 1960 presidential campaign got fully underway in the summer.[27]

But before the nominating conventions in July could set the campaign in full swing, an event occurred that proved very relevant to the missile-gap controversy. On 1 May 1960 the Soviet Union shot down one of the high-flying U-2 reconnaissance aircraft that had been carrying out photographic and electronic intelligence missions over the Soviet Union since the middle of 1956. During these four years about thirty extended penetrations of Soviet air space were made, and the then CIA director,

24. *New York Times*, 7 February 1960, 15 February 1960, and 20 February 1960.
25. *New York Times*, 10 February 1960, 11 February 1960, 20 February 1960, and 24 February 1960.
26. *New York Times*, 22 February 1960. Later President Eisenhower charged in his book *The White House Years*, p. 390, that the "missile gap" crisis was a "useless piece of demagoguery" and that it disappeared a month after his successor took office.
27. See Bottome, *Missile Gap*, p. 134.

Allen Dulles, was later to consider the U-2 the most useful intelligence tool of the 1950s.[28] In June 1960 President Eisenhower defended the U-2 flights on the grounds that, "These flights had given us information of the greatest importance to the Nation's security. In fact, their success has been nothing short of remarkable."[29]

The U-2s became involved in monitoring Soviet missile launchings and flights soon after the U.S. electronic surveillance and radar network first detected the Soviet missile testing program.[30] Following the beginning of Soviet ICBM testing and the launchings of Sputniks I and II, the number of U-2 flights was further increased. In early 1958, however, there began a drastic reduction in overflights—from then until April 1960, there were "almost none." But then, with the direct and explicit approval of the White House, two flights were scheduled for April 1960.[31] In the early spring of 1960, reports from Western agents inside the Soviet Union and electronic eavesdropping had deepened suspicions that the Soviet Union was building its first operational ICBM base. On 9 April a U-2 flew within surveillance range of Plesetsk, in northwest Russia, and its findings added further evidence to American suspicions.[32] The 1 May flight was to pass directly over Plesetsk,[33] but the aircraft was shot down by Soviet air defenses near Sverdlovsk.

28. Francis Gary Powers, *Operation Overflight*, p. 52; Charles J. V. Murphy, "Khrushchev's Paper Bear," p. 227; and David Wise and Thomas B. Ross, *The U-2 Affair*, p. 57.

29. President Eisenhower, TV and radio address, 25 May 1960, in the Department of State *Bulletin*, 6 June 1960, p. 900.

30. Murphy, "Khrushchev's Paper Bear," p. 227. According to Murphy, "the U-2 camera actually looked down on the first Soviet ICBM on its launcher" some weeks before the first test.

31. Powers, *Operation Overflight*, pp. 63, 70, 229, and 374. The lull in flights between early 1958 and April 1960 presumably reflected the temporary cessation of ICBM tests by the Soviet Union in April 1958. See Joseph Alsop in the *International Herald Tribune*, 22 March 1959.

32. Wise and Ross, *U-2 Affair*, p. 10; *Newsweek*, 13 June 1960, p. 15; interviews with Roger Hilsman, 12 June 1970, and Herbert Scoville, 9 February 1973.

33. Interviews with Jerome Wiesner, 20 February 1973, and Herbert Scoville, 9 February 1973. According to Dr. Wiesner, "the U-2 [Powers's] was going for Plesetsk—the first operational missile base—when it was shot down." And according to Dr. Scoville, "there is no question but that one of the major objectives of the last flight [Powers's] was to look for missile sites around Plesetsk." The planned route on the 1 May flight is described by Powers, *Operation Overflight*,

It was largely on the basis of the U-2 program that President Eisenhower was able so confidently to answer the charges that his administration was permitting the Soviet Union to surpass the United States in missile strength.[34] The May revelations of the U-2 flights should have strengthened the credibility of the administration's intelligence estimates and defense policies, and increased the acceptance of their validity in the eyes of the American public. That the missile gap remained an issue during the summer and fall of 1960 was due primarily to the political partisanship of the presidential election campaign.

KENNEDY IN 1960—THE PRESIDENTIAL CAMPAIGN
AND THE INTERREGNUM

In his years as a senator, Kennedy showed a great personal interest in matters relating to peace, defense, and foreign policy, and in 1960 he forged these into a central issue in his presidential campaign. His policies and actions throughout 1960, during the campaign, and up to the inauguration became, as one would expect, major factors in the defense decisions of the Kennedy Administration in 1961.

The Campaign. Senator Kennedy officially announced his candidacy for the presidency on 2 January 1960. He had begun running for president at least as early as the beginning of 1959, however, and perhaps from about 1956. During his years as a senator, Kennedy had achieved recognition as a major national spokesman on matters relating to defense and foreign policy. In February 1958, for example, he made an important speech in which he called for a new set of national priorities and a new national effort to meet the challenge of Soviet competition in science and technology. The Sputnik series of satellites in 1957 had demonstrated Russian superiority in space exploration, and Kennedy had no hesitation in drawing the conclusion that "the

pp. 72–74. A map of the flight plan is given in "Francis Gary Powers Tells His Story," by Francis Gary Powers, p. 36. Plesetsk is about 130 miles south of Archangel.

34. Interview with Dr. James R. Killian, 16 January 1973; see also Wise and Ross, *U-2 Affair*, p. 263; and Bottome, *Missile Gap*, pp. 135–36.

future is very dark indeed."[35] In the Senate on 14 August 1958, he took up the missile-gap issue; it was an extraordinary speech, and undoubtedly remains the most comprehensive and reasoned discussion of the subject. "We are rapidly approaching that dangerous period which General Gavin and others have called the 'gap' or the 'missile-lag period,'" Senator Kennedy stated. "In the years 1960–64," he argued, "the deterrent ratio [will] in all likelihood be weighted very heavily against us." It was not a "scare speech," but one in which he made reasoned proposals to "reverse the complacency" and "fix a course for the future that would restore American superiority."[36] And in a speech in Wisconsin in November 1959, he stated that "we have fallen behind the Soviet Union in the development and production of ballistic missiles—both intercontinental and those of intermediate range," and called for an effort to put the "eight gray years" of the Eisenhower Administration, the "years that the locusts have eaten," behind.[37]

From the very beginning of his campaign, Kennedy projected the theme that the United States had suffered an unnecessary slowing of progress under Eisenhower. In fact, the day before he formally announced his candidacy, Kennedy made a dramatic and challenging speech, the main purpose of which was to make a call for action, to "get the country moving."[38]

A more concrete critique, which Kennedy stressed throughout 1960, was the U.S. position vis-à-vis the Soviet Union in the field of strategic missiles. He spoke positively and without equivocation as early as 23 January 1960, when he said that the United States had become "second in space—second in missiles."[39] In the Senate on 29 February 1960, Kennedy made a prepared speech in support of the Senate's attempt to add $1.3 billion to the administration's F/Y 1961 budget request. He ar-

35. Cited in Edmund S. Ions, ed., *The Politics of John F. Kennedy*, p. 24.

36. John F. Kennedy, *The Strategy of Peace*, ed. Allan Nevins, pp. 61–63. Gen. Gavin later became a close Kennedy campaign advisor on military affairs.

37. Ibid., chap. 26.

38. See speech by John F. Kennedy, Washington, D.C., 1 January 1960, in Ions, ed., *The Politics of John F. Kennedy*, pp. 32–35.

39. Cited by Congressman Gubser, *Congressional Record, House*, 11 April 1962, p. 6392.

gued that while in 1960 the United States' mix of strategic forces might be superior to those of the Soviet Union, "it is indisputable that we are today deficient in several areas—and that in one of those areas, ballistic missiles, our deficiency is likely to take on critical dimensions in the near future." He refrained from fixing either dates or numbers to the missile gap, "for whichever fig- ures are accurate, the point is that we are facing a gap on which we are gambling with our survival." In order "to do something about it," he recommended major changes in the F/Y 1961 de- fense budget, including increased funds for the Polaris and Minuteman development programs and accelerated production of Atlas missiles "to cover the current gap as best we can." Say- ing that he could not find any stronger words with which to support his recommendations, he concluded with a quotation from Gibbon on the Romans: "They kept the peace—by a con- stant preparation for war."[40]

Speaking before a Veterans of Foreign Wars' convention on 26 August, Kennedy said that "the missile gap looms larger and larger ahead."[41] In San Diego on 12 September, he said that the United States needed "a policy which will keep America the strongest country in the world."[42] Two days later, in New York City, he stated: "We must step up crash programs to provide ourselves with the ultimate weapons—the Polaris submarines and Minuteman missiles—which will eventually close the missile gap."[43] A week later he declared: "The next President must promptly send to Congress a special message requesting the funds and authorization necessary to give us a nuclear retalia- tory power second to none."[44] And in a letter to *Missiles and Rockets* on 10 October 1960 he detailed specific requests which, if elected, he pledged to send to Congress in January; again, accelerating "our Polaris, Minuteman and other strategic missile programs" headed his list.[45]

40. Speech by Senator Kennedy, *Congressional Record, Senate*, 29 February 1960, pp. 3801–8.
41. *Aviation Week & Space Technology*, 5 September 1960, p. 29.
42. *Congressional Quarterly Weekly Report*, 13 January 1961, p. 32.
43. Ibid.   44. Ibid.
45. *Missiles & Rockets*, 10 October 1960, p. 13.

On 18 October, three weeks before the presidential election, Kennedy made his principal campaign speech on defense. He told an American Legion convention in Miami Beach that the United States was moving into a period where the Soviet Union would be outproducing it "two to three to one" in missiles, and blamed this "dangerous deterioration" in U.S. military strength on the Republicans. In support of his indictment, he cited such documents as the Gaither Committee report and the Rockefeller Brothers' report. And, in order to improve the U.S. defense effort he proposed (a) that SAC be provided with a continuous airborne alert capability, (b) that the Atlas base-building program be stepped up, and (c) that the Polaris and Minuteman programs be accelerated.[46]

Senator Kennedy was nominated for the Democratic candidature for the presidency on 13 July, and in his acceptance speech he endorsed the Democratic platform which had been adopted by the convention the day before. This platform pledged that:

> The new Democratic administration will recast our military capacity in order to provide forces and weapons of a diversity, balance and mobility sufficient in quantity and quality to deter both limited and general aggressions.

It charged that under the Republican administration the United States had lost its position of preeminence, and that:

> the Communists will have a dangerous lead in intercontinental missiles through 1963—and that the Republican administration has no plans to catch up. . . . our military position today is measured in terms of gaps—missile gap, space gap, limited war gap.

It called for:

> 1. Deterrent military power such that the Soviet and Chinese leaders will have no doubt that an attack on the United States would surely be followed by their own destruction.
> 2. Balanced conventional military forces which will permit a response graded to the intensity of any threats of aggressive force.
> 3. Continuous modernization of these forces through intensified research and development, including essential programs now

46. *Aviation Week & Space Technology*, 24 October 1960, p. 21. The Gaither and Rockefeller reports are described later in this chapter.

slowed down, terminated, suspended, or neglected for lack of budgetary support,

and for a "strong and effective civil defense."[47]

Together with this critique of America's defenses, Kennedy continually attacked the Eisenhower Administration for imposing arbitrary budget ceilings on defense expenditure, and for its "willingness to place fiscal security ahead of national security."[48] Under Eisenhower, according to Kennedy, the "narrow-minded men at the Budget Bureau" had consistently overridden the requests of the service chiefs, whereas it was his policy to base defense spending solely on the security needs of the nation.[49]

Kennedy refused, however, to put a specific money figure on his own policies. This reluctance was perhaps partly due to the fact that increasing costs for current programs would, by themselves, amount to about a $2 billion increase in the F/Y 1962 defense budget.[50] More probably it was due to the view that committing oneself to specifics would not be politically sensible. Kennedy did say that his proposed changes would not exceed the $4.2 billion budget surplus anticipated for F/Y 1961,[51] and most of the public estimates of "what Kennedy will do" ranged from $2 to $4 billion.[52]

It is unclear from the public record exactly what access Kennedy had to intelligence material before his election on 8 November 1960. Richard Nixon has stated on President Eisenhower's authorization that instructions were given that Kennedy be as fully briefed on defense, including U.S. intelligence activities abroad, as was Nixon.[53] According to newspaper reports, Kennedy was visited by CIA representatives three times during the campaign, the first occasion being on 23 July 1960, when he

47. *Congressional Quarterly Almanac*, 1960, p. 776.
48. Kennedy, *The Strategy of Peace*, p. 68.
49. *Congressional Quarterly Weekly Report*, 13 January 1961, p. 32. See also *Missiles & Rockets*, 10 October 1960, p. 13.
50. See *Missiles & Rockets*, 17 October 1960, p. 7.
51. Senator Kennedy, *Congressional Record, Senate*, 29 February 1960, p. 3802.
52. See, for example, *U.S. News and World Report*, 21 November 1960, p. 42; *Congressional Quarterly Weekly Report*, 5 August 1960, p. 1364; and *Aviation Week & Space Technology*, 25 July 1960, p. 25.
53. Richard M. Nixon, *Six Crises*, p. 381.

was given a two-and-a-half hour briefing on intelligence at Hyannis Port.[54] There is no indication as to whether the relatively few CIA briefings reflected a low interest on Kennedy's part or the number of offerings made by the CIA.[55] Kennedy complained during the campaign, however, that he was being denied information concerning progress in missile development relative to the USSR,[56] and in February 1961 Senator Symington charged on the floor of the Senate that there had been "a calculated and deliberate effort on the part of the previous administration to prevent the now President of the United States from obtaining adequate information as late as last fall about the security of the United States."[57] And Sorensen has explicitly stated that none of the U-2 evidence was ever made available to Kennedy before his election.[58] Eisenhower himself made no attempt at personal contact with Kennedy during the campaign.

Late in August 1960, Kennedy flew to SAC Headquarters in Omaha for a day-long briefing by top Air Force officers arranged by the administration. According to Sorensen, "almost immediately it became apparent that he was not to be given a

54. Laurin L. Henry, in Paul T. David, ed., *The Presidential Election and Transition, 1960–1961*, p. 210. However, Pierre Salinger, press secretary to President Kennedy, stated on 20 March 1962 that "Senator Kennedy received two briefings from Mr. Allen Dulles of the CIA, the first on 23 July 1960 and the second on 19 September 1960." See Harold W. Chase and Allen H. Lerman, *Kennedy and the Press*, pp. 210–11. These two visits by Dulles have been widely reported. I have been unable to confirm whether or not a third meeting with other CIA representatives ever took place. Senator Lyndon B. Johnson, the Democratic vice-presidential candidate, was given one briefing by the CIA on 27 July 1960.

55. See Henry, in David, ed., *Presidential Election and Transition*, p. 210. One possibility is that Kennedy might have wanted only a few briefings on selected issues, so as to leave him more freedom in his indictments. According to Henry Trewhitt, for example:

During the campaign a Navy intelligence captain flew to Hyannis Port, Massachusetts, to caution John Kennedy that the national intelligence estimates did not support the frightening calculations of Soviet strength. Kennedy would not accept the figures; he was, after all, a politician just short of the greatest prize the nation could offer.

See Henry L. Trewhitt, *McNamara, His Ordeal in the Pentagon*, p. 6.

56. John J. Harrigan, "Foreign Affairs and the Presidential Election of 1960" (Ph.D. diss., University of Chicago, 1962), p. 25.

57. *Congressional Record, Senate*, 9 February 1961, p. 1966.

58. Theodore C. Sorensen, *Kennedy*, p. 676; see also the same author's *The Kennedy Legacy*, p. 69.

full-scale top-secret fill-in on Soviet-American missile and bomber strength," and "somewhat angrily Kennedy insisted that he had had more access to information merely as a member of the Senate Foreign Relations Committee."[59] What he was told was apparently incredibly "rosy," on the order of top Pentagon civilians acting on Nixon's call for a "truce" on all campaign material which would tend to indicate that the United States was weak.[60]

As a member of the Senate Foreign Relations and Armed Services Committees, Kennedy was entitled to material of a very high level of classification. But he attended very few hearings in 1960. According to Congressman Gubser (Republican, California), information was made available to the Armed Services Committees of both Houses of Congress during 1960,

> which showed CIA, Air Force, Army and composite intelligence estimates of each Russian capability. . . . [A] missile gap did not exist . . . [but] 1960 was a busy year for Senator Kennedy. He may not have found time to attend his committee hearings.[61]

From 27 May to 2 June 1960 the Senate Foreign Relations Committee held an inquiry into the U-2 affair to find out, inter alia, what the CIA was looking for in the Soviet Union that was so important. The inquiry was conducted with extraordinary secrecy and restraint, with all testimony taken in executive session. All of Allen Dulles' five-and-one-half hour presentation to the committee "which included elaborate maps, charts, and U-2 photographs" was deleted from the heavily censored version of the hearings which was made public, and stenotyped tapes of the proceedings were destroyed. Senator Kennedy attended none of the sessions.[62]

Whether Kennedy was honest in his charges and claims about U.S. prestige abroad and military strength, particularly on the missile-gap issue, still remains a question. On the one hand, McNamara (for example) has stated that those who discussed the

59. Sorensen, *Kennedy*, p. 676.
60. *Missiles & Rockets*, 3 October 1960, p. 9; *Newsweek*, 12 September 1960, p. 11.
61. Gubser, *Congressional Record, House of Representatives*, 11 April 1962, p. 6392.
62. Wise and Ross, *U-2 Affair*, pp. 172–74.

missile gap in 1960 "were speaking . . . in good faith";[63] on the other hand, Republicans have charged that it was wholly a "big lie" fabricated by Kennedy and other Democrats for the 1960 election.[64] It is of course possible to be highly critical of the political use which Kennedy made of the issue without impugning his personal integrity. For while the issues of deteriorating U.S. strength and prestige were deliberately stressed by Kennedy for the campaign, they were not completely artificial; Kennedy was probably sincere in his themes, but he undoubtedly exaggerated the issue for electoral reasons. He did have a great personal predilection for a strong United States, superior to the USSR, and he received his campaign support and the material for his critiques from people who wanted a much greater U.S. defense effort. It would not have been a very great step from there to being selective in his choice of the widely conflicting information available, and hammering away with exaggerated critiques of the U.S. defense posture, in order to increase his vote in the November election.

The Interregnum. In 1960, both before and after his election, Kennedy made an important innovation in U.S. presidential transitions by appointing twenty-nine task forces, which were asked to report to him on a wide variety of domestic and foreign policy problems in the period immediately preceding and following his inauguration. Headed by Adlai Stevenson, the first of these task forces, on foreign-policy problems, was appointed by Kennedy on 29 July 1960, about two weeks after his nomination. A week later, Kennedy asked Senator Symington to prepare a report on defense organization, and on 31 August he announced the appointment of Paul H. Nitze to prepare a report on national-security policy for use in the transition period.[65]

In setting up these committees, Kennedy said he envisaged the groups' responsibility as a post-election effort to make sure that,

63. McNamara, Senate Armed Services Committee, *Military Procurement Authorization, Fiscal Year 1963*, p. 50. One would not, of course, expect McNamara to say otherwise, but his assurance was apparently accepted by the Senate Armed Services Committee, perhaps naively, without question.
64. *Congressional Record*, 21 March 1962, p. 4701.
65. *Congressional Quarterly Weekly Report*, 7 April 1961, pp. 620–23.

if he was elected, the months of January, February, and March 1961 could be used most effectively by the incoming Democratic administration to initiate changes and new programs.[66]

The Symington committee submitted its report on 5 December; it referred to "the lag in U.S. weapons systems development versus that of the Soviets," and recommended a drastic reorganization of the Defense establishment.[67] The Nitze committee submitted its report on 5 November; its contents have never been released, but Schlesinger has written that the report "provided an incisive analysis of the case for a more diversified defense posture."[68]

The Nitze task force attempted to survey all the defense and foreign-policy issues which might be expected to confront the Kennedy Administration when it assumed office. One of the issues, of course, was what to do with the strategic forces. The task force considered both the alternatives of pure deterrence, backed up by "massive retaliation," and an actual strategic nuclear-war fighting capability. It judged the former to be inadequate for many situations, and the latter to be not technically feasible. Hence it suggested something in between, but no numbers were cited. During the interregnum, Nitze continued as Kennedy's principal adviser on national-security policy problems. No other task forces were appointed on matters relating directly to defense or national-security policy, and the Nitze report presumably remained the basic defense document for the new administration. According to Nitze, for example, "this was the starting point for the strategic policies of the Kennedy Administration."[69]

One other task force, however, did say something about the

66. Henry, in David, ed., *Presidential Election and Transition*, p. 210; *Aviation Week & Space Technology*, 5 September 1960, p. 29.

67. Public Affairs Press, *New Frontiers of the Kennedy Administration*, p. 14.

68. Schlesinger, *A Thousand Days*, p. 142.

69. Interview with Paul H. Nitze, 7 February 1973. In other work for the Democrats during the campaign, Nitze argued very strongly for large increases in expenditure on strategic forces. For example, he was a major author of the Democratic Advisory Committee report titled "The Military Forces We Need and How to Get Them," which called for an additional expenditure of about $4 billion more a year on U.S. strategic forces. He later became assistant secretary of defense for international security affairs in the Kennedy Administration.

U.S. ballistic missile program. On 11 January Jerome Wiesner submitted a report on the American space effort, in which he stated:

> The nation's ballistic missile program is lagging. The development of the missiles and of the associated control systems, the base construction and missile procurement must all be accelerated if we are to have the secure missile deterrent force soon that the country has been led to expect.
>
> While additional funds will undoubtedly be required to accomplish this, we believe that re-establishing an effective, efficient, technically competent management for the program is the overriding necessity.[70]

The Symington and Wiesner task forces had no access to classified material during the preparation of their reports. While the Nitze committee had no official access, Nitze himself had served on the Gaither Committee and had taken an active personal interest in national-security issues in the late 1950s, and had informal contacts with, for example, the RAND Corporation.[71] But the information which officials of the Kennedy Administration have said was not available to Kennedy during the campaign (especially the U-2 evidence) most assuredly would not have been known to Nitze.

Kennedy himself began receiving daily intelligence summaries soon after his election, and on 18 November Allen Dulles journeyed to Palm Beach to give him a personal report on the international situation. During the week after the election, Clark Clifford began a series of liaison meetings with General Persons, Eisenhower's military assistant. Clifford and Sorensen also conferred with the director of the Bureau of the Budget (BoB) and received a stack of briefing memoranda prepared by that agency.[72] McNamara began to work full time at the Pentagon from 3 January 1961, getting acquainted with his new position and planning the transition.[73]

70. Public Affairs Press, *New Frontiers*, p. 3.

71. He was, for example, aware of the highly classified "no-cities" strategy study being undertaken by the Air Force and RAND in 1960 (interview with Paul Nitze, 7 February 1973; see also Richard Fryklund, *100 Million Lives*, p. 31).

72. Henry, in David, ed., *Presidential Election and Transition*, p. 214.

73. Gen. Lemnitzer, House of Representatives Appropriations Committee, *Department of Defense Appropriations for 1962*, part 3, p. 29.

Kennedy had his first meeting with Eisenhower on 6 December, and a much more extensive meeting on 19 January, the day before the inauguration. At the second he was accompanied by Rusk, McNamara, Clifford, and various other aides, and defense and foreign-policy problems were discussed. Later on the same day, Kennedy had a long conference with the chairman of the joint chiefs of staff (JCS), which was described as covering "procedural matters" pertaining to the responsibilities as commander in chief that Kennedy would assume the following day.[74]

Thus, when Kennedy became president of the United States on 20 January 1961, the direction in which he would move on issues of defense and national-security policy was to some extent predictable, even determined. Laurin L. Henry has summarized some of the main influences:

> On policy matters, Kennedy did not start with a completely clean slate. In the background were legislative proposals carried over from the previous Congress, platform and campaign commitments, the earlier pronouncements of the Democratic Advisory Council, and staff work done for Kennedy as Senator. Fresher ingredients included the reports commissioned during the campaign, staff memoranda available from the Budget Bureau, and the advice pouring in from all sides on many subjects.[75]

SOME STRATEGIC STUDIES

During the period between the middle of 1957, when the particular defense debate of the late 1950s was initiated, and the election of John F. Kennedy to the U.S. presidency in November 1960, which resolved that debate, perhaps a dozen or so official and unofficial inquiries and studies of the U.S. defense effort were made, which to varying extents significantly influenced the national-security decision-making process under both the Eisenhower and Kennedy Administrations. These studies ranged from those of the Gaither and Rockefeller Committees, which took as their scope the whole range of defense problems facing the U.S., through studies of alternative strategies, negotiating

74. *New York Times*, 10 January 1961 and 20 January 1961; Schlesinger, *A Thousand Days*, p. 147; and Henry, in David, ed., *Presidential Election and Transition*, p. 234.
75. Ibid., pp. 215–16.

postures, etc., to relatively technical analyses of weapons-systems requirements. However, five studies especially stand out, and will be discussed here: the Gaither Committee report of November 1957; the Rockefeller Brothers' report of January 1958; the work on the development of the "no-cities" counterforce strategy; the Weapons Systems Evaluation Group's report No. 50; and the RAND Corporation studies on the requirements for effective "deterrence."

In the broadest sense, the Gaither and Rockefeller studies set the terms of reference for much of the defense debate of the late 1950s. They posed the question of the vulnerability of U.S. strategic forces; they put the argument for a large expansion of these, and especially of U.S. missile programs; and they figured prominently and explicitly in the 1960 presidential election campaign. The explication of the "no-cities" version of the counterforce nuclear-war fighting strategy by the Office of the Assistant for Co-ordination within the Air Staff and by members of the RAND Corporation in 1959 and 1960 increased the number of alternative strategies available to the United States, widened the scope of the strategic debate, and provided an attractive strategic theory for many of the defense civilians in the Kennedy Administration. The WSEG study No. 50 provided the Defense Department with a systematic analysis of alternative weapons systems and defense measures, which the new administration could draw again upon. And the RAND Corporation studies proposed, in classified form, many of the major changes made in the U.S. strategic force by the Kennedy-McNamara Administration, such as the substitution of less vulnerable strategic delivery vehicles and the establishment of a more responsible and protected control of this strategic force.

The members of the Kennedy Administration all entered office with basic preconceptions, however rudimentary and however rigidly held, about U.S. defense requirements and nuclear strategy, and about the defense decision-making process—or at least a view of the world, of the role of the U.S. defense establishment, and of the nature of "security."

President Kennedy himself, for example, accepted the general conclusions of the Gaither and Rockefeller studies. Several of the top civilian officials of the Kennedy Administration had worked in the preparation of those studies, and most of the senior officials—such as Nitze, Gilpatric, Hitch, Enthoven, and Rowen—shared assumptions about the necessity for U.S. strategic forces to be invulnerable, a requirement which had gained widespread recognition and acceptance during the defense debate of the late 1950s. Virtually all were at least cognizant of the RAND–Air Staff counterforce studies, and the RAND studies for effective deterrence, and most found them attractive. Curiously, the senior defense officials of the Kennedy Administration—whether they were from RAND or from Boston—shared a frame of mind which found the type of analysis upon which the counterforce study and, in particular, the RAND and WSEG studies, were based, very appealing—and this, of course, applied to McNamara also.

The Gaither Committee. In April 1957 President Eisenhower ordered a study by an ad hoc civilian group, under the chairmanship of H. Rowan Gaither, of a proposal by the Federal Civilian Defense Administration (FCDA) to spend $40 billion over a period of several years to erect blast shelters. Formally titled the Security Resources Panel of the Science Advisory Committee to the FCDA, the committee broadened the scope of its inquiry to cover the whole range of defense problems facing the United States. The committee's report, entitled *Deterrence and Survival in the Nuclear Age*, was finished about a week after the launching of Sputnik I and presented to the president and the National Security Council (NSC) on 7 November 1957.[76]

From the outset, the members of the Gaither Committee realized that the top echelons of the government did not fully appreciate the extent of the Soviet threat as it was described by

76. *Deterrence and Survival in the Nuclear Age*, NSC5724, report to the president by the security resources panel of the science advisory committee (Washington, D.C.: Executive Office of the President, Office of Defense Mobilization, November 1957). The report, commonly referred to as the "Gaither report," was declassified in full on 10 January 1973, subject to the deletion of three lines on p. 29 which continue to be classified Top Secret. For an account of the Gaither committee, see Morton H. Halperin, "The Gaither Committee and the Policy Process," pp. 360–84. Gaither, a West Coast lawyer, was chairman of the RAND Corporation's Board of Trustees.

the Pentagon and the CIA. The report began with an analysis of Soviet and American capabilities. It compared the economic situation in the two countries, and pointed out that on the basis of current growth rates the Soviet Union would soon be devoting much larger sums to defense than the United States.

In its analysis of the current military situation, the report stressed the danger of the vulnerability of the U.S. strategic force. It was pointed out that what must deter the Russians was not the force which the United States had, but the force which was capable of surviving an all-out Russian attack. The vulnerability of SAC was stressed, and the committee warned that by the early 1960s, when Russia had an operational ICBM force, she would be capable of destroying the U.S. retaliatory force. In the period commencing in 1959 or early 1960 and ending in 1961–62, the committee warned,

> 1. A surprise attack by either SAC or SUSAC in a period of lessened world tension might almost completely disarm the other's long-range air atomic strike capability, unless and until either side has successfully implemented an adequate "alert" concept.
> 2. During this period a surprise attack could determine the outcome of a clash between these two major powers.
> 3. As soon as SAC acquires an effective "alert" status, the U.S. will be able to carry out a *decisive* attack even if surprised.[77]

The committee argued that if the United States failed "to act at once, the risk, in our opinion, will be unacceptable," and went on to propose a long list of recommendations. Overriding priority was to be given to the development of an invulnerable second-strike force. It was urged that for the short run everything possible be done to enable SAC to survive an attack. The committee specifically suggested that bomber reaction times be reduced; that tactical warning be improved; that SAC bases be given active defenses against enemy bombers, and in the longer term against ICBMs; that SAC aircraft be dispersed; and that a large proportion of SAC planes be protected by providing shelters capable of withstanding 100–200 pounds per square inch (PSI) of blast overpressure. To increase SAC's offensive power, the committee

77. *Deterrence and Survival in the Nuclear Age*, pp. 15–16.

called for "an earlier and stronger initial operational capability (IOC) with intermediate-range and intercontinental ballistic missiles"; and specifically recommended that the initial number of IRBMs (Thor and/or Jupiter) be increased from 60 to 250; that the initial operational capability (IOC) of the ICBMs (Atlas and Titan) be increased from 80 to 600 missiles, to be deployed by the end of F/Y 1963; and that the IOC of the Polaris submarine system be accelerated, and the planned force of six submarines for 1965 be increased "by approximately a factor of three." The committee reckoned the cost of these recommendations to strengthen U.S. deterrent and offensive capabilities to be approximately $19 billion over the five-year period F/Y 1959–1963.[78]

Although there is some evidence that the Gaither report briefly influenced Eisenhower's thinking,[79] the proposals were not adopted by the administration. The report did, however, provide those favoring increased investment in armaments with ammunition. In particular, it was used by Senator Kennedy in his 1960 campaign indictments of the Eisenhower defense effort.[80]

During the 1960 campaign and the interregnum, Kennedy was assisted and advised by a number of people who had worked on the Gaither report. Jerome Wiesner, for example, who had been staff director on the Gaither Committee, was Kennedy's major science adviser during this period. Paul Nitze, special adviser to the Gaither Committee, was his major defense and national-security policy adviser. Robert C. Sprague, who became co-director of the Gaither Committee when Gaither himself was taken ill, and James A. Perkins also advised Kennedy on defense questions during the campaign and the interregnum.

More than a dozen of those who had participated in the work of the Gaither Committee were later involved in the strategic policy decisions of the Kennedy Administration. These included

78. Ibid., pp. 6–7, 11, 23–26.
79. See Halperin, "Gaither Committee," pp. 369–70.
80. See, for example, Senator Kennedy's principal campaign speech on defense, delivered in Miami on 18 October 1960 (*Aviation Week & Space Technology*, 24 October 1960, p. 21).

Jerome Wiesner, Spurgeon Keeny, and Vincent McRae in the White House's Office of Science and Technology; Paul Nitze, Brockway McMillan and Herbert York in the Pentagon; Richard Bissell in the CIA; James Killian as chairman of the president's Foreign Intelligence Advisory Board; and John J. McCloy and William C. Foster as arms control and disarmament advisers. And the work of the committee prepared much of the ground for McNamara's later reconstruction of U.S. strategic policy.[81]

The Rockefeller Report. In 1956 the Rockefeller Brothers' Fund commissioned a study, under the direction of Henry Kissinger, on *International Security: The Military Aspect.* The study group (which included Roswell Gilpatric) began meeting together in November 1956, and the report was published on 6 January 1958. It began with a grim summary of the U.S. strategic position: "The United States is rapidly losing its lead in the race of military technology." The report contended that developing trends pointed to "the economic superiority of the West becoming less and less significant militarily at our present levels of effort," and that "corrective steps must be taken now."[82]

It argued that the U.S. military establishment must be adequate to discharge two tasks—"one, to discourage an all-out attack through the existence of a powerful, instantly ready retaliatory force, and, two, to react effectively to limited aggression through the ability to make our response fit the challenge." It also recognized the "problem of 'concealed' aggression." And it asserted that civil defense must be considered as part of the overall U.S. strategic posture. Its specific recommendations included the following: that aircraft procurement be modernized; that the development and procurement of operational IRBMs and ICBMs be accelerated; that the SAC base structure be made less vulnerable to surprise attack through dispersion and other protective measures; that accelerated R&D support be provided for key programs such as missiles; that SAC alert time be reduced; and that the development and production of SLBMs be expedited. It estimated that to fulfil these requirements "will

81. See Schlesinger, *A Thousand Days*, p. 190.
82. Rockefeller Panel, *Prospect for America, report no. 2*, pp. 91, 93, 104.

require successive additions [to the defense budget] on the order of $3 billion each year for the next several fiscal years." [83]

During the defense debate of the late 1950s, the Gaither and Rockefeller reports were invariably mentioned together. Their findings and recommendations were very similar, and there were half a dozen members common to both groups.[84] The Rockefeller report was, in fact, often regarded as something like an unclassified version of the Gaither report. Senator Kennedy was impressed with the findings and recommendations of the Rockefeller panel, and during the campaign he mentioned it several times.[85] A large number of people who were associated with the Rockefeller report later assisted Kennedy during the campaign and as president-elect, and some became senior members of his administration. For example, Walt W. Rostow and Roger Hilsman served on Kennedy's "Academic Advisory Committee" from December 1958 until the end of 1960; Adolph A. Berle, James B. Fisk, Rostow, and Hilsman served as advisers to Kennedy during the 1960 campaign and the interregnum; Roswell Gilpatric, a principal author of the report, was a member of two major Kennedy task forces in 1960–61, and later became McNamara's deputy secretary of defense; Dean Rusk, later secretary of state, and Chester Bowles, undersecretary of state, were also associated with the Rockefeller report; Kissinger himself was a sometime consultant to the administration in 1961 and 1962.

The new administration adopted most of the recommendations of the Rockefeller report. The panel's budgetary recommendations, for example, though slightly on the low side, turned out to be remarkably accurate projections. But this was, of course, not pure coincidence.

Counterforce and "No-cities"—the Birth of a Strategy. One of the key influences on the early Kennedy-McNamara strategic pos-

83. Ibid., pp. 101, 113, 139, 150, 152.
84. For example, Col. George A. Lincoln, James B. Fisk, James R. Killian, and Gen. James McCormack. Laurence Rockefeller, president of the Rockefeller Brothers' Fund, had access to the Gaither report.
85. See, for example, the Miami speech of 18 October in which he spoke of both the Rockefeller and Gaither reports (*Aviation Week & Space Technology*, 24 October 1960, p. 21).

ture was a series of studies on counterforce and "no-cities" strategy done in 1959–60.[86] This work was begun at the RAND Corporation by W. W. Kaufmann in late 1959. He worked closely with General Thomas D. White (USAF chief of staff) to convert other Air Force leaders to a posture of controlled response. General White was seeking "a posture which would be so designed and controlled that it could attack enemy bomber and missile sites, retaliate with reserve forces against enemy cities if that should prove necessary, and also exert pressure on the enemy to end the war on terms acceptable to the United States."[87]

Within the Air Staff (Directorate of Plans, Office of the Assistant for Coordination), Brigadier-General Noel F. Parrish and Colonel Donald F. Martin had also begun initial studies in 1959 on "no-cities" strategy. In early 1960 briefings on this work were given to Generals White and Gerhart. White decided that the Air Council should hear of it, and a briefing was given to them. Following the latter briefing, General Curtis Le May decided to set up a task force to investigate this work—and thence to conduct a complete force structure study; and he directed Martin to brief SAC and RAND.

The "new objectives" task force was set up under the direction of General Robert C. Richardson. It included representatives from both SAC and the Tactical Air Command (TAC). But SAC had been depending on a strategy of complete devastation since its creation, and believed that anything less would weaken deterrence; and TAC was opposed to planning for war on the strategic nuclear level, as it was equipped for conventional limited war. The group could not reach any agreement, and the

---

86. This is in no sense an authoritative account of the development of "counterforce" strategy, which has, in fact, a rather longer and more varied history than might perhaps be suggested here. As early as 1956, for example, Andrew Marshall and Herbert Goldhamer at RAND had worked on an Air Force study which showed the advantages of holding attacks on cities and population to a minimum. My concern here is simply to show how the particular version of "counterforce" strategy which was adopted by the Kennedy-McNamara Administration in 1961–62 was developed and introduced into that administration.

In addition to the published sources cited, this account is based on interviews with Richard Fryklund on 20 July 1970 and 2 February 1973; Al Goldberg on 20 July 1970, 12 February 1973 and 26 November 1975; Col. Donald F. Martin, 29 July 1970; Gen. Robert C. Richardson, 25 July 1970; and Dr. Marvin Stern, 21 August 1970.

87. See Harland B. Moulton, "American Strategic Power," p. 132.

report on the "no-cities" strategy, completed in November 1960, said little of importance. The SAC briefing was held at Omaha in April or May of 1960, and the RAND briefing in June. RAND was then formally asked for assistance on the project, and a study group was set up under Kaufmann that same month. Quantitative evidence was prepared by Frank Trinkl and David McGarvey at RAND.

This was the first thorough Pentagon study of the outcome of possible future wars between the United States and the Soviet Union. Numerous war games were played, involving a wide range of variables and assumptions, including the hypothetical year of the nuclear exchange, the warning time received, the level of civil defense, whether the United States or the Soviet Union struck first, and the respective strategic-force levels of each side. By September 1960 it was apparent to the Pentagon analysts that if urban areas were not deliberately targeted and measures were taken to avoid as much collateral damage as possible, some 100–150 million American lives would be saved.[88]

The strategic consequences of these findings were not accepted automatically. As Richard Fryklund, a committed observer, has noted, "Air force jealousies and interservice rivalries almost strangled the epochal new strategy in its cradle." By mid-1961, all work on the strategy within the Air Force had virtually stopped.[89]

But the findings were taken up by civilians in the new admin-

88. Richard Fryklund, *100 Million Lives*, pp. 2, 4, 14 and 15–16. See also series of articles by Richard Fryklund in the *Washington Star*, 18 December 1960 to 26 December 1960.

89. Richard Fryklund, *100 Million Lives*, p. 30. Within the Air Force, the "no-cities" strategy was opposed on a number of grounds. To begin with, SAC, and especially General Power, its commander in chief, did not really understand the new strategy. Part of SAC's opposition was ideological—SAC was suspicious of strategic policies which involved reduction of Soviet casualties, considering them weak and unpatriotic. Others within the Air Force were more concerned with the budgetary implications of the new strategy. With the Air Force being the dominant service in terms of funding, many officers were afraid of "rocking the boat," even though it might have been argued that the new policy would probably have actually favored the Air Force. Part of the opposition was also personal, with many officers regarding Gen. Parrish and Col. Martin as being rather eccentric; and when an unfortunate "leak" occurred in early 1961, the opposition within the Air Force itself became ascendant. The Air Force offices involved in the "no-cities" studies were in fact disbanded in May 1961 (see *Aviation Week & Space Technology*, 15 May 1961, p. 25).

istration. McNamara was introduced to counterforce and "no-cities" in a formal briefing by Kaufmann within a week of his taking office, in the last week of January 1961. Only four people were present—McNamara, Kaufmann, Enthoven and Marvin Stern. The briefing lasted for several hours, and McNamara was immediately impressed. Two of McNamara's key deputies—Hitch and Nitze—were both familiar with the details of the Air Force study before they entered the Pentagon. These in turn chose as some of their top assistants people who had also heard about the study and were impressed by its findings. Hitch's first assignment in Washington was to head a general-war study committee. One of his recommendations was to include the "no-cities" concept among the strategy "options" that McNamara might later adopt. Nitze's staff, meanwhile, saw to it that the contents of the Air Force study were made known to strategists throughout the Pentagon, and in the State Department and White House. And Frank Trinkl pressed the strategy in Dr. Alain Enthoven's office. During 1961 Colonel Martin worked with Colonel George Sylvester and managed to convert him to "no-cities." Sylvester then became Air Force representative to McNamara, and was helpful in pushing the idea. By the end of 1961 "no-cities" had become the official U.S. nuclear war strategy.[90]

WSEG No. 50. About eighteen months before McNamara became secretary of defense, the joint chiefs of staff and the director of defense research and engineering (DDR&E) commissioned the Weapons Systems Evaluation Group (WSEG) to undertake a comprehensive report on the optimal U.S. strategic force structure. The study, begun in September 1959, developed into what was probably WSEG's major report.[91]

The project, WSEG study No. 50, involved about thirty peo-

90. See Richard Fryklund, "U.S. War Plan Shift Would Spare Cities," *Washington Star*, 17 December 1961.

91. WSEG was created in December 1948 by Secretary of Defense James Forrestal, to give the Department of Defense "comprehensive, objective and independent" military opinion on the relative merits of separate service weapons systems as they related to or duplicated each other, and to evaluate the impact of those weapons systems on strategy, organization and tactics. It has been involved in most major questions of defense policy since the early 1950s. WSEG studies

ple working in teams on several subprojects (e.g., the estimation and analysis of the threat; command and control, etc.) with George Contos (deputy director of WSEG) as project director. The report, officially entitled "Evaluation of Strategic Offensive Weapons Systems," was finished in December 1960, but was not briefed to the outgoing Eisenhower Administration.

The analysis of the Soviet threat implicitly rejected the possibility of a missile gap.[92] The conclusion was that the planned Eisenhower strategic-forces posture was inadequate to conduct a successful first strike against the Soviet Union—as was *any* feasible posture—but more than adequate for deterrence. Since policy was not to launch a first strike in any event, the U.S. force was more than adequate for the only strategy seriously being considered.

The main issue which WSEG No. 50 took up was what mix of strategic forces and how much the United States should have.[93] The study made no formal recommendations, but the analysis was clearly indicative. With regard to long-range bombers, it judged that the B-52s provided an adequate force. The B-47 and B-58 bombers were regarded as superfluous, the former being too old, and their operating and maintenance costs too high. The report came down very definitely against the B-70. It argued that on cost and technical (e.g., poor accuracy) grounds, the Skybolt air-launched ballistic missile (ALBM) program should be cancelled. With regard to the Polaris force, the study indicated that a program of about 40 or so submarines would provide *all* the countervalue deterrent that the United States needed. However, because advances in anti-submarine warfare (ASW) or anti-ballistic missile (ABM) systems could not

are always secret. This account of WSEG No. 50 is based on interviews with four members of the project and with several other persons in the Kennedy Administration familiar with that project, and on correspondence with three WSEG No. 50 members, including the project director.

92. During 1960 WSEG in fact briefed Secretary Gates on the question of the "missile gap," and suggested that the growth of the Soviet ICBM force so threatened the U.S. bomber force that greater dispersal or an air alert should be initiated. By about November, however, WSEG had accepted that the Soviets were not deploying their first generation ICBMs, and the threat was regarded to have passed.

93. The numbers were treated parametrically; WSEG had been directed by the joint chiefs not to look at the question of force levels per se.

be ruled out, a mixture of submarines, land-based missiles, and bombers was necessary. The question of deploying Polaris missiles aboard cruisers was also looked at, but the main alleged advantage over submarines, that of cost, was shown to be illusory.

With regard to ICBMs, the study indicated that the early missiles—the Atlas (including the Atlas F) and the Titan I—were too costly, especially as regards operation and maintenance. On the other hand, the Titan II was worth keeping in the U.S. arsenal, because with its capacity for carrying large payloads it might prove useful for some as yet undetermined purpose. In its analysis of the Minuteman force, the study favored the mobile over the silo-based version. In graphing the cost-effectiveness of the two types of Minuteman deployment against various postulated Soviet threats, it was shown that the choice was an either/or one —there was only a very narrow region on the graph where a mix of fixed *and* mobile missiles was optimal. The crossover point was "very close to 900 missiles." If the United States was to procure less than that number, the mobile version was more cost-effective. As the order for missiles increased, the advantage passed to fixed Minuteman ICBMs in silos. In calculating the optimum number of Minuteman missiles needed, it was shown that diminishing returns set in well before the number requested by the Air Force was reached (the Air Force was at this time suggesting to WSEG a force of 2,000 Minuteman missiles), with the "knee" of the curve between 600 and 1,000 missiles. WSEG No. 50 therefore suggested that a force of 800–900 Minuteman missiles was optimal, and that these be mobile missiles.

McNamara was looking for studies on national strategic issues when he inevitably came across WSEG No. 50, and asked for a briefing on it.[94] The briefing took place several days after he took office; it was led by George Contos, with segments being given by various members of the senior staff who had partici-

94. The joint chiefs of staff tried very hard to keep the report away from the White House—officers of the special assistants for both science and technology and national security affairs experienced difficulties in obtaining copies. When the White House staff did manage to get a copy they (especially Wiesner) were very attracted to its conclusions, particularly those relating to the command and control of U.S. strategic forces (interviews with Jerome Wiesner, 20 February 1973; McGeorge Bundy, 18 December 1972; Dr. Marvin Stern, 21 August 1970; and Marcus Raskin, 6 February 1973).

pated in the study. Charles Hitch and Marvin Stern were also present. The session lasted the whole day, and McNamara was apparently very impressed. WSEG No. 50 was also communicated to the new administration in a number of other ways. Briefings on the study were given to other persons and groups within the new administration besides Secretary McNamara. For example, a briefing was given to the office of the director of defense research and engineering (DDR&E) at which about thirty people were present, including representatives of the joint chiefs of staff; the joint chiefs were briefed directly; a briefing was given to a group which included Adam Yarmolinsky (then special assistant to McNamara and Gilpatric) and Eugene G. Fubini (then director of research, DDR&E); and a briefing was given to Jerome Wiesner by Laurence Dean and Hugh Everett of the WSEG No. 50 team. Some members of the new administration, such as Alain Enthoven and his staff (including Frank Trinkl) had been familiar with the development of the project during 1960. In February 1961 Colonel Robert D. Bowers (USAF) prepared "an appreciation of WSEG No. 50" for the joint chiefs of staff. And Daniel Ellsberg prepared a short critique of WSEG No. 50 which was widely circulated within the new administration.[95] A number of WSEG members (in particular Hugh Everett) were consulted by Alain Enthoven during the defense reappraisal undertaken by the new administration in February and March 1961.[96]

It is, of course, always difficult to identify the policy impact of any particular research product. As the director of the WSEG No. 50 project has written, "on issues of such magnitude, complexity, and cost, one could not establish cause and effect rela-

95. Daniel Ellsberg, *Should Primary Command Sites be Hardened? Comments on WSEG No. 50* (Santa Monica: RAND Corp., 17 February 1961), classified Top Secret.

96. In the longer term, most of the principals involved in WSEG No. 50 continued to be attached to the Kennedy-McNamara defense establishment. This included virtually all the military officers attached to WSEG. Some of the civilians stayed in WSEG (e.g., Hugh Everett), and hence assisted in further weapons studies and programming during the Kennedy Administration; others moved to other branches of the administration (e.g., George Pugh, transferred to the Arms Control and Disarmament Agency); still others have continued as consultants (based particularly at the Lambda Corporation, Arlington, Virginia) to the defense establishment.

tionships and one would be hard pressed indeed to establish weights to the various factors which contributed to the [Kennedy-McNamara strategic missile] decisions."[97] But, while it is true that one cannot "prove" the relative weight of WSEG No. 50, the coincidence in time and in the substance of its recommendations with the missile decisions of 1961 (particularly the 28 March special message) is so strong that one has to conclude that WSEG No. 50 was, at least, "very significant."

RAND Corporation Studies on the Requirements for Effective "Deterrence." Throughout most of the 1950s, it was generally believed that nuclear war could take only a single form: a cataclysmic final catastrophe, which was unlikely because of its very enormity. It was also thought that the major nuclear countries would always possess overwhelming offensive strength, regardless of the scale of attack to which they might be exposed. Deterrence, in this general view, was virtually automatic.

Perhaps the most important event in strategic studies in the 1950s was the recognition that there existed a wide range of possible nuclear attacks and that various "thresholds" determined whether a country's nuclear power produced deterrence or constituted an invitation to aggression. In particular, attention was called to the question of the "vulnerability" of one's strategic nuclear forces. This recognition was first achieved systematically at the RAND Corporation, by Albert J. Wohlstetter and several colleagues, in one of RAND's most significant studies: the strategic bases study (RAND Report R-266).[98]

Perhaps the main conceptual contribution of R-266, from which a number of specific policy recommendations were de-

---

97. Letter from Dr. George Contos, 19 March 1971. Of course, this problem applies to any assessment of the policy impacts of the other strategic studies described in this section of the book.

98. A. J. Wohlstetter, F. S. Hoffman, R. J. Lutz and H. S. Rowen, *Selection and Use of Strategic Air Bases*, RAND Corp., R-266, declassified 1962. In January 1958, A. J. Wohlstetter, the principal author of R-266, published a seminal article based upon the general strategic insights of that study (see A. J. Wohlstetter, "The Delicate Balance of Terror," pp. 211–34). See also A. Wohlstetter and F. Hoffman, *Defending a Strategic Force after 1960* (Santa Monica: RAND Corp., D-2270, 1 February 1954); and A. J. Wohlstetter, F. S. Hoffman, and H. S. Rowen, *Protecting U.S. Power to Strike Back in the 1950s and 1960s* (Santa Monica: RAND Corp., R-290, 1 September 1956).

rived, was the distinction between first-strike and second-strike capability. At the time, this was essentially a novel concept. Although increasing thought was being given in various parts of the strategic community to the possible implications for U.S. policy of the acquisition of a substantial nuclear capability by the Soviet Union, the basing study (and follow-up research by Wohlstetter and his colleagues) was the first clear recognition of the importance of a secure deterrent force. It was the first to draw explicit attention to the need for developing a deterrent force capable of surviving an initial enemy nuclear assault and still inflicting unacceptable damage on the enemy.[99]

Wohlstetter showed that the conditions for deterrence were particularly stringent, and that the "balance of terror" between the major nuclear powers was "delicate," depending on a subtle interplay of vulnerability and offensive power. He demonstrated that it was theoretically possible to eliminate a hostile striking force without unacceptable damage to the attacker. Therefore, the existence of powerful delivery capability was not in itself an assurance of security. In addition to its striking power, the effectiveness of a force would depend on its invulnerability, and on the state of opposing active and passive defenses. Wohlstetter also emphasized the inextricable connection between strategic doctrine and the choice of weapons systems.[100] His conclusions, summarized in his insistence on a secure second-strike deterrent force, later emerged as central elements in the McNamara strategic doctrine. Wohlstetter's work was communicated to the administration in three principal ways. First, it was taken directly to the Air Force. In talks and briefings to large numbers of Air Force officers from 1952 on, Wohlstetter and his associates began injecting the findings and insights of their work into the Air Force hierarchy.[101] Second, Wohlstetter's findings were taken up during the strategic debate of the late 1950s by several of the Democratic critics of the defense and national-security policies of the Eisenhower Administration. For example, Kennedy's important speech on the missile gap in the Senate on 14 August

99. See Bruce L. R. Smith, *The RAND Corporation*, p. 232.
100. See Henry Kissinger's introductory note to Wohlstetter's "The Delicate Balance of Terror" in Kissinger, ed., *Problems of National Strategy*, p. 34.
101. See Smith, *RAND Corporation*, pp. 210–29.

1958 was partly based on a draft of Wohlstetter's "Delicate Balance" article. And in 1960 during the presidential campaign Wohlstetter "sent a lengthy explanation to the man [Walt W. Rostow] who was writing John Kennedy's main campaign speech on defense, specifically to suggest why the 'missile gap' was . . . a theoretical and operational misunderstanding of the problem."[102] In addition to their more general, and somewhat misplaced, worry about U.S. missile numbers, Kennedy's 1960 entourage had thus been presented with an articulated concern about the vulnerability of U.S. strategic forces.

Wohlstetter was assisted in the strategic bases study and the follow-up work by, inter alia, F. S. Hoffman, H. S. Rowen, Alain Enthoven, Charles Hitch and W. W. Kaufmann, all of whom later became important officials in, and/or consultants to, the Kennedy-McNamara defense establishment. During the interregnum, Wohlstetter was himself offered a senior position in the new administration, but chose not to accept formal office. Throughout 1961, however, he gave frequent briefings to Gilpatric, and often to McNamara, and was an adviser to International Security Affairs (ISA) and the Office of the Comptroller in the Pentagon. He also remained in very close contact with such RAND alumni as Henry Rowen and Alain Enthoven, who did become important members of McNamara's staff.[103] Henry Kissinger has opined that "more than any other individual, Professor Wohlstetter provided the intellectual impetus for the recasting of American military strategy in the 1960s."[104] Certainly, the evidence clearly suggests that the work of Albert Wohlstetter and his colleagues at the RAND Corporation in the 1950s was a major catalyst in the many changes in U.S. defense posture and national-security policies which were undertaken by the new administration after January 1961.

102. A. J. Wohlstetter, "Vietnam and Bureaucracy," in Morton A. Kaplan, ed., *Great Issues of International Politics*, p. 286, and interviews with Wohlstetter, 16 August 1970 and 18 November 1972.

103. See Bernard Brodie, *A Review of William W. Kaufmann's "The McNamara Strategy,"* p. 11. Also interviews with Albert Wohlstetter 16 August 1970, and Dr. Alain Enthoven, 17 August 1970.

104. Kissinger, ed., *Problems of National Strategy*, p. 34. Wohlstetter's contribution was officially and publicly acknowledged in the glowing citation when McNamara presented him with a Distinguished Service Award in February 1965 (see Brodie, *A Review of "The McNamara Strategy,"* p. 11).

2 The Missile Background

This chapter sets out the missile-hardware background to the strategic missile decisions of the Kennedy-McNamara Administration. It provides "background" to the later description and analysis of the missile decisions in two senses. First, an outline of the strategic missile programs developed by the Eisenhower Administration provides the bench mark from which the Kennedy Administration necessarily proceeded. All of the strategic missile systems which were deployed during the Kennedy-McNamara Administration—the Atlas, Titan and Minuteman ICBMs, the Thor and Jupiter intermediate-range ballistic missiles (IRBMs) and the Polaris submarine-launched ballistic missile—were conceived, and development initiated, before 1961. And, although much of Eisenhower's current and projected missile program did not involve actual commitments to production before 1961, the new administration was at least partly committed, politically and technologically, to a certain finite and characteristic strategic missile force. The outline of the development of the Eisenhower strategic missile program is also "background," in that it introduces into the study the fact of pressure from the Air Force (and to a lesser extent the Navy) and from Congress which forced Eisenhower to make several increases in the projected U.S. strategic missile force.

Second, assessments of the actual numbers of U.S. and Soviet ICBMs operational at any given time between 1959 and the completion of the American strategic missile build-up in 1967 provide the "hardware background" to the U.S. missile program decisions. The quantitative data for 1959–60 and the early years of the Kennedy-McNamara strategic missile build-up are especially important, because it was at this time (and against this "hardware" background) that thinking on eventual force levels was beginning to mature; and this assessment also illustrates the formidable problems associated with bringing a new weapons system into the operational inventory. It is now known that the Russians experienced similar, if not quite the same, problems; hence, from intelligence evidence available at the time, the U.S. administration could, and should, have known that the Soviet ICBM program was proceeding only slowly.

This account of the Soviet missile program is not intended to be a comprehensive description. It is considered only to the extent that it has relevance to those aspects of the U.S. missile program which are the concern of this study—where, for example, it lays the basis for subsequent discussion of such questions as the possibility of a missile gap, deterrence strategies, action-reaction phenomena, uncertainties in U.S. intelligence estimates, etc.

Despite the enormous amount of literature available on the Soviet and American missile programs, precision has proved relatively difficult to achieve. For example, the exact size of the planned Eisenhower missile force is difficult to determine for several reasons. The operational-ICBM environment was still several years off, and the conditions of the 1960s might have forced changes in the plans and programs of the 1950s. Eisenhower himself had no "program" in the sense of the later McNamara programming; rather, force plans depended essentially on prevailing budgetary and political circumstances. Programming was done in terms of dollars rather than numbers of missiles, and until 1961 (87th Congress, 1st session), the Armed Services Committee of Congress did not have to *authorize* U.S. defense spending; there is thus no counterpart to the informative hearings of the post-1960 period. It is possible, however, to give an approximate figure for the strategic missile force commitments which Eisenhower passed on to Kennedy in January 1961.

Assessment of the Soviet missile program is made even more difficult because of the secrecy, even deliberate distortion,[1] which has surrounded it. Even here, however, the declassification in 1975 of the strategic-forces sections of the annual reports of the secretary of defense to Congress from 1961 to 1972, together with material released during the SALT I and II discussions, make it possible to reconstruct the Soviet missile deployment program—and how much of that program was known to U.S. decision makers. But assessment of missile programs and deployments in quantitative terms is, in some ways, a very inadequate procedure, especially since qualitative factors are often of greater strategic significance. Some of the more important qualitative developments in the U.S. strategic missile program are discussed later in this chapter; it is known that the Soviet missiles have had much the same history in terms of operational capability, reliability, effectiveness, etc.

Within these limitations and subject to the qualifications stated, the missile programs and deployments outlined here should approximate sufficiently closely to the actual situations to provide adequate background for subsequent discussion of the Kennedy-McNamara strategic missile build-up.

THE EISENHOWER LEGACY

The original U.S. ballistic missile program intended a force of 20 to 40 missiles.[2] But the progress of the Soviet ICBM program to full-range tests in August 1957, and especially the launching

1. See Arnold L. Horelick and Myron Rush, *Strategic Power and Soviet Foreign Policy*, especially part 2.
2. Robert L. Perry, *The Ballistic Missile Decisions*, p. 14; and Johan J. Holst, in Johan J. Holst and William Schneider, eds., *Why ABM?* p. 169.

of Sputniks I and II, led to fears of a missile gap, during which the Soviet Union would have overwhelming superiority, and pressures from the Air Force and from Congress forced Eisenhower to increase the projected U.S. missile force several times.

From about 1958 on, certain columnists (especially the Alsop brothers), Air Force officers, congressmen and Democratic politicians, etc., began talking in terms of missile forces numbering in the thousands. Eisenhower refused to go along with these larger numbers, but he did head the United States toward a force of something over 1,100 missiles (including both ICBMs and SLBMs).

With regard to ICBMs, at no time before 1958 did the ballistic missile policy group seriously recommend to the Air Force that more than about 200 missiles be sent to operational sites.[3] On 5 October 1957, the day after the launching of Sputnik I, Secretary of Defense Wilson gave final consent to the first IOC program to be fully approved and funded at all levels. He authorized funds to deploy four Atlas squadrons and four Titan squadrons (80 missiles) by December 1962.[4]

During budget hearings in early 1958, 1959, and 1960, on the F/Y 1959, 1960, and 1961 defense budgets respectively, the Air Force testified on each occasion that it considered the administration's ICBM program to be unsatisfactory, and that proposals for larger programs had been submitted to the administration. Congress generally supported the Air Force's position, in some cases providing funds over and above those requested by the administration.

Most reluctantly, the administration succumbed in part to the congressional and Air Force pressures. In April 1958, for example, the programmed missile force was expanded to nine Atlas squadrons. In January 1959 the authorized Titan force was set at eleven squadrons. In January 1960 a further four Atlas and three Titan squadrons were added.[5]

3. See Perry, *Ballistic Missile Decisions*, p. 14; James Baar and William E. Howard, *Combat Missileman*, p. 47; and Ernest G. Schwiebert, *A History of the U.S. Air Force Ballistic Missiles*, pp. 217–20.
4. Schwiebert, *History of the U.S. Air Force Ballistic Missiles*, p. 222.
5. Ibid., p. 223; *New York Times*, 12 January 1959, pp. 1, 16; and *Aviation Week & Space Technology*, 25 January 1960, pp. 27–28.

The F/Y 1962 defense budget, the last prepared by the Eisenhower Administration, contained no new authorizations for the Atlas and Titan force. The 255 of these ICBMs which had now been authorized were in fact approximately twice as many as the administration had originally believed necessary.

With regard to the Minuteman program, the Eisenhower Administration had initially approved a force of eight squadrons of 50 missiles each in October 1958.[6] However, the F/Y 1962 Military Construction Bill, submitted to Congress in January 1961, increased the authorization to nine squadrons, or 450 silo-based missiles. In addition, the F/Y 1962 defense budget also contained funds for three mobile Minuteman squadrons of 30 missiles each, or 90 mobile Minuteman missiles.[7]

With regard to the Polaris SLBM program, the administration suffered the same service and congressional pressures as were applied in the case of the Atlas and Titan programs. These proved particularly difficult to resist because the administration had come to no agreed position on what it itself regarded as a satisfactory Polaris force.[8]

The Navy's requests on any given occasion were typically for more than twice as many submarines as the administration saw fit to authorize. For example, in 1958 the Navy requested funds for twelve Polaris submarines; during the year the administration made several concessions, which brought the authorized program to six submarines.[9] In 1959 the Navy asked for funds for six new submarines and for the long-lead-time items (mainly the nuclear reactors) for a further seven; the administration compromised and authorized full funding for three submarines and the long-lead-time items for three others.[10] In 1960 the Navy asked for nine new submarines and long-lead-time funding for a

6. Testimony of Gen. Schultz, House Appropriations Committee, *Department of Defense Appropriations for 1970*, part 4, pp. 650–51.

7. Senate Armed Services Committee, *Military Construction Authorization Fiscal Year 1962*, pp. 370–71; and House Appropriations Committee, *Department of Defense Appropriations for 1962*, part 3, p. 9.

8. George B. Kistiakowsky, *A Scientist at the White House*, p. 162.

9. *New York Times*, 3 April 1958; and James Baar and William Howard, *Polaris!*, pp. 158, 197.

10. *Missiles & Rockets*, 30 March 1959, p. 15; Baar and Howard, *Polaris!*, p. 199; *New York Times*, 25 January 1959.

further twelve; the administration initially approved only three of these, but following the successful missile tests with the first two Polaris submarines, the *George Washington* and the *Patrick Henry*, approval was given for another two.[11] In its F/Y 1962 budget proposals, the Navy asked for full funding for twelve submarines and long-lead-time funding for a further twelve; the administration agreed to authorize only five of these, though it did approve the long-lead-time funding for five others.[12]

These successive increases in Polaris submarine authorizations conceded by the administration from 1958 to 1960 brought the authorized program as at January 1961, when the Kennedy Administration assumed office, to nineteen submarines (304 missiles); long-lead-time funding had also been approved for five submarines, although there was no commitment to build these. In addition, on January 16, just four days before Eisenhower left office, the administration approved the deployment of eight Polaris missiles aboard the nuclear-powered cruiser *Long Beach*.[13] As illustrated in table 9 (page 116), the strategic-force commitments which Kennedy inherited from the Eisenhower Administration in January 1961 involved approximately 1,100 strategic missiles.

U.S. MISSILE DEPLOYMENT, 1959–1967

Despite the widespread fears of a missile gap, and the fact that the Eisenhower Administration was consistently reluctant to concede to the pressures from Congress and the services for greater missile deployments, there was never a time between the first ICBM deployments in 1959–61 and the final American deployments in 1967 when the United States did not have many more operational ICBMs than the Soviet Union. When the first Soviet ICBMs became operational, with the deployment of four SS-6 Sapwood missiles at Plesetsk in the spring of 1961, the United States had 27 Atlas D missiles operational; when the last

11. *Missiles & Rockets*, 1 January 1960, pp. 19–20, and 25 July 1960, p. 12; and Baar and Howard, *Polaris!*, pp. 208, 240.

12. Testimony of McNamara, House Appropriations Committee, *Department of Defense Appropriations for 1962*, part 3, p. 7.

13. Richard Witkin, "Polaris Adopted for Atom Cruiser," *New York Times*, 17 January 1961, p. 4.

of the 1,054 U.S. ICBMs was declared operational in April 1967, the Soviet Union had only about 550 ICBMs deployed. The disparity in SLBMs during this period was even greater.

The first U.S. ICBMs, three Atlas D missiles at Vandenberg Air Force Base (AFB), California, were officially declared operational in September 1959. During 1960, nine other Atlas D missiles were deployed, making twelve ICBMs operational when the Kennedy Administration took office. In addition, two Polaris submarines, with 32 SLBMs, officially began operational patrol in late 1960. Deployment of the Atlas D force was completed on 30 March 1961, and all the Atlas E missiles had been deployed by the end of the year. Three more Polaris submarines also became operational during 1961.[14]

Nineteen sixty-two was described by Major-General Thomas P. Gerrity, commander of USAF's Ballistic Systems Division in charge of setting up the USAF's missile structure, as the "year of payoff" in gaining operational ICBMs.[15] Over twelve months the number of ICBMs at operational sites increased approximately fourfold, from 50 to 200. This included the deployment of all the Titan I missiles, all of the Atlas F missiles, and the first 20 Minuteman missiles. Nine Polaris submarines with 144 SLBMs had also been deployed.[16]

The 54 Titan II ICBMs were all deployed in the second half of 1963. From December 1962 until the last Minuteman I flight was turned over to SAC on 15 June 1965, Minuteman missiles were brought into service at a rate of about 20 to 25 per month. Minuteman II missiles began to enter the force in the second half of 1965, and the 1,000th Minuteman ICBM was officially declared operational on 21 April 1967. The last of the 41 FBM submarines was deployed on 3 October 1967.[17] The U.S. submarine-launched and intercontinental ballistic missile force has remained at 1,710 missiles to this date. This build-up is set out in

14. *Development of Strategic Air Command 1946–1976* (Office of the Historian, Headquarters, Strategic Air Command, 21 March 1976), pp. 79, 81, 88; *Polaris and Poseidon Chronology* (U.S. Navy, 1970), p. 6; and *Polaris and Poseidon: F.B.M. Facts* (Washington, D.C.: Navy Department, 1970), p. 11.

15. *Air Force & Space Digest*, May 1962, p. 19.

16. *Development of Strategic Air Command 1946–1976*, p. 97; and *F.B.M. Facts*, p. 11.

17. *USAF Fact Sheet* 68–13, August 1968; *F.B.M. Facts*, p. 11.

U.S. ICBM Deployment, 1959–Present
(Air Force Bases)

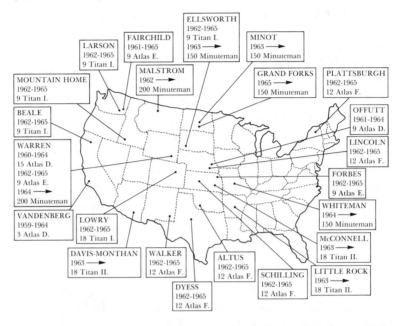

the accompanying map and in tables 1 and 2. These quantitative developments, however, are only part of the story of the U.S. strategic missile build-up. Of at least equal significance were the qualitative developments which took place during the period.

In the first place, operational readiness rates were especially low during 1959–61. Some missiles were often not mated to launchers (pads or silos), crews were often inexperienced, some missiles were used either partly or exclusively for training purposes, and new missile models typically had very short mean times between failures (MTBFs), making them unreliable as operational weapons. In the case of the first Atlas D missiles, these were deliberately declared operational, because of "the need to strengthen our deterrent," even though they could not really be regarded as operational weapons.[18] Alert rates were consequently also very low. During 1959–60, for example, it was accepted that only about one-third of the Atlases at Vandenberg

18. Kistiakowsky, *A Scientist in the White House*, p. 376.

could have been fired in 15 minutes; the others would have taken anywhere from half an hour to ten hours.[19] Herbert York now doubts "that we could have gotten even one in five of the early operational Atlases off in that time [15 minutes] under surprise-attack conditions."[20] This problem recurred, to some extent at least, whenever a new model was deployed. For example, in 1963–64 the operational readiness of the Atlas F was lower than that of the earlier models, a fact directly connected with the Cuban missile crisis. Many of the F missiles were rushed to completion and delivered far ahead of schedule, before shakedown testing had been completed. The indications are that a fairly high percentage of the Atlas F's might not have worked if they had been needed. Several later blew up in practice countdowns; the remainder were phased out of service in 1965, four years earlier than planned.[21] With regard to the Minuteman II, random component failures in the more complex guidance computer caused it also to have lower alert rates initially than the Minuteman I. (At least until 1967, about 40 percent of the Minuteman II force was out of commission at any one time because of guidance problems.)[22] However, given the size and more varied composition of the strategic ballistic-missile force after 1963, this problem had much less impact on the operational viability of the force as a whole.

Second, the vulnerability of both U.S. and Soviet ICBM systems has decreased greatly in the last two decades. The first ICBMs were particularly vulnerable. For example, the first three Atlas D missiles at Vandenberg were emplaced vertically on exposed launching pads, and were capable of withstanding only about 2 PSI blast overpressure. The Atlas Ds in the 576B Complex at Vandenberg and the 564th and 565th squadrons at Warren were emplaced in horizontal concrete "coffins," above-

19. *Newsweek*, 20 February 1961, p. 13.
20. Herbert F. York, *Race to Oblivion*, p. 150; and interview with Eugene M. Zuckert, 21 July 1970.
21. John S. Tompkins, *The Weapons of World War III*, pp. 175–77. See also Preparedness investigating subcommittee, Senate Armed Services Committee, *Hearings on Series of Explosions of Air Force's Atlas F Intercontinental Ballistic Missiles* (1964), p. 136.
22. A. Ernest Fitzgerald, *The High Priests of Waste* (New York: Norton, 1972), pp. 114–16, 127–28. See also *Aviation Week & Space Technology*, 13 November 1967, p. 33.

TABLE 1. *U.S. ICBMs*
(operational as of December of given year)

YEAR	TYPE	NUMBER	TOTAL
1959	Atlas D	6	6
1960	Atlas D	12	12
1961	Atlas D	30	
	Atlas E	32	
	Titan I	1	63
1962	Atlas D	30	
	Atlas E	32	
	Atlas F	80	
	Titan I	62	
	Minuteman I	20	224
1963	Atlas D	28	
	Atlas E	33	
	Atlas F	79	
	Titan I	63	
	Titan II	56	
	Minuteman	372	631
1964	Atlas D	13	
	Atlas E	30	
	Atlas F	75	
	Titan I	56	
	Titan II	59	
	Minuteman 1A	142	
	Minuteman 1B	556	931
1965	Titan II	59	
	Minuteman	821	880
1966	Titan II	60	
	Minuteman	908	968
1967	Titan II	54	
	Minuteman	1,000	1,054

NOTE: These figures are taken from *Development of Strategic Air Command 1946–1976*, produced by the Office of the Historian, Headquarters, Strategic Air Command, 21 March 1976. They are slightly higher than the nominal inventory figures because of the inclusion of ICBMs operational at test and evaluation sites. At December 1976, for example, when the nominal inventory stood at 54 Titan II and 1,000 Minuteman missiles, the SAC historian gives the figures as 58 and 1,046.

ground and capable of withstanding about 5 PSI. These missiles were deployed in clusters of three.[23] Assuming a 10 megaton warhead, even a Soviet missile with a two-mile circular error probability (CEP) would have had a greater than 99 percent chance of "taking out" a whole complex.

The Atlas E missiles, on the other hand, were deployed in dis-

23. See Wohlstetter, Hoffman and Rowen, *Protecting U.S. Power to Strike Back in the 1950s and 1960s* (Santa Monica: RAND Corp., R-290, 1956), pp. 28–29.

TABLE 2. *U.S. Fleet Ballistic Missile (FBM) Submarines*
(operational as of 31 December of given year)

YEAR	LAUNCHED	COMMISSIONED	DEPLOYABLE	SLBMs DEPLOYED
1959	4	1	0	0
1960	6	3	2	32
1961	9	6	5	80
1962	15	9	9	144
1963	27	16	10	160
1964	32	29	20	320
1965	39	33	29	464
1966	41	40	37	592
1967	41	41	41	656

SOURCE: Strategic Systems Project Office, *Polaris and Poseidon FBM Facts* (Washington, D.C.: Navy Department, 1973), pp. 16–17.

NOTES: Not all operational FBM submarines (and accompanying missiles) are on station at any given time. On the average, each operational submarine is on patrol for eight months each year, and in port for overhaul and maintenance for four months. Of the full fleet of 41 FBM submarines, about 27 are normally on station; however, at any given time the actual figure ranges from about 22 to 34.

It should also be noted, with particular regard to the period 1959–62, that a number of submarines not certified as deployable had some IOC and could have been put on station within a few weeks if a real emergency had developed.

persed and semihardened configurations. Each Atlas E, at all three squadrons, was deployed at least 18 to 20 miles away from any other, and emplaced in a concrete "coffin" buried flush with the surface, capable of withstanding 25 PSI blast overpressure. In this configuration, no single thermonuclear explosion would knock out more than one missile.

The Minuteman force was the first to be truly dispersed and hardened. The silo launcher for the Minuteman missile is approximately 80 feet deep and 12 feet in diameter; the silo was originally hardened to withstand some 300 PSI of blast overpressure, but several "silo up-grade" programs have improved this to 2,000 PSI.[24] There are several miles between silos; for example, Wing I at Malstrom AFB in Montana, which contains 200 Minuteman ICBMs, covers a total area of 18,000 square miles.[25]

The question of vulnerability also includes not only silo protection of the missile against blast overpressure, but also the

24. Schwiebert, *A History of the U.S. Air Force Ballistic Missiles*, p. 227; and *Aviation Week & Space Technology*, 24 April 1978, p. 18.

25. John W. R. Taylor, ed., *Jane's All the World's Aircraft, 1970–71* (London: Sampson Low, Marston & Co., 1970), p. 609.

vulnerability of command and control centers, guidance and electronic fusing systems, etc. With regard to guidance systems, the Atlas D was particularly vulnerable, because it relied upon radio command. This vulnerability was greatly reduced with the shift to all-inertial systems in the Atlas E and all subsequent American ICBMs. Since 1965 Minuteman II and III missiles have also been increasingly protected against the electromagnetic pulse (EMP) effects of nuclear blasts.[26]

Lastly, the missiles of the late 1970s are very different weapons systems from the missiles of the late 1950s and early 1960s. Improvements in reliability, in warhead technology, in range, in accuracy, and in targeting flexibility have made them many times more effective. The reliability of the first-generation ICBMs was very low. Throughout 1960, for example, attempts to demonstrate the operational readiness of the Atlas proved most disappointing—in one exercise three attempts to fire Atlases from Vandenberg into the Eniwetok Atoll target area all failed.[27] Herbert F. York has since stated:

> overall reliability from count-down to launch to flight was never very good, especially for operational units. Perhaps only as few as 20 percent of them would have reached their targets in a real war situation during the first year or so of so-called operational readiness.[28]

In April 1968 the chief counsel of the Senate Armed Services Committee noted that the Atlas "went off the board at something like four percent [reliability]."[29]

The accuracy of ballistic missiles has also increased enormously. The CEP of the Atlas D was only about two miles.[30] On the

26. Richard Davis, "Industry Pushes New Radiation Hardened Microcircuits to Skeptical Missile Planners," *Electronic Warfare/Defence Electronics*, March 1978, pp. 45–66.

27. *Aviation Week & Space Technology*, 19 September 1960, p. 25.

28. *Race to Oblivion*, p. 94. York adds that because of this low reliability, the early operational missiles were "rather ineffective as strategic weapons for the first several years after their deployment began" (p. 103).

29. Testimony of Mr. Kendall, Chief Counsel, Preparedness investigating subcommittee, Senate Armed Services Committee, *Status of U.S. Strategic Power* (1968), part 1, p. 144. Reliability here includes missile availability, readiness and launch reliability, as well as in-flight reliability.

30. *Aviation Week & Space Technology*, 11 January 1960, p. 28; and 18 January 1960, p. 25.

basis of tests in 1961, the CEP of the Titan I was estimated at 0.65 miles.[31] This was probably twice as accurate as the all-inertial Atlas E and F missiles at that time.[32] By comparison, the CEP of the Minuteman III is currently as low as 600 to 800 feet.[33]

As with the quantitative situations during the first decade of the missile age, the United States held a clear advantage in virtually all of these qualitative factors. Even in the case of megatonnage, despite the relatively large warheads of the Soviet ICBMs, the American ICBM force was capable of delivering more than its Soviet counterpart until at least 1966.

Qualitative progress in the United States was parallelled in the Soviet Union. In particular, at the time when the U.S. missile decisions were taken, the few Soviet ICBMs that were deployed were extremely vulnerable, had very low reliability, and very poor accuracy (the CEP of the SS-6, for example, was only about 8 km.)[34]

THE SOVIET MISSILE PROGRAM

On 26 August 1957 the official Soviet news agency, TASS, announced that a "super-long-range multi-stage inter continental ballistic missile" had recently been successfully tested, and that the results indicated "it is now possible to send missiles to any part of the world. . . . The problem of the creation of ICBMs [has been solved]."[35] The missile, an SS-6 or "Sapwood" ICBM, was launched on 3 August from Tyuratam, the prime Soviet ICBM test facility, situated in Kazakhstan, about 200 miles northeast of the Aral sea.

Long-range testing of the SS-6 continued until April 1958, by which time about ten ICBM test launchings had been carried out (four abortive and six successful). The irregular intervals be-

31. J. Michael Fogarty, letter to *Aviation Week & Space Technology*, 14 January 1963, p. 126.

32. See chart, "ICBM Guidance Techniques Compared," *Aviation Week & Space Technology*, 2 May 1960, p. 159.

33. The International Institute for Strategic Studies, *Strategic Survey* (London: IISS 1978), p. 114.

34. Doug Richardson, "Soviet Strategic Nuclear Rockets Guide," *Flight International*, 11 December 1976, p. 1731.

35. *Pravda*, 27 August 1957, cited in *Key Khrushchev Missile Statements*, Bureau of Intelligence and Research, Intelligence Report no. 8288, 1 July 1960, p. 1.

tween the missile firings, and the variety of tests conducted, indicated that at this time the Soviet ICBM program was still in the development-test stage, with production and operational capability still two or three years away. In April 1958, ICBM tests ceased completely until March 1959, indicating that the Soviet program had run into very serious troubles.[36]

During the congressional hearings in early 1959, Department of Defense intelligence spokesmen continued to assert in a closed briefing that the Russians as yet had no operational ICBMs,[37] and at a press conference in late January, McElroy stated that he did not think the Soviet Union had an operational ICBM at that time, that there was "no positive evidence" that it would have ICBM initial operational capability before the United States, and that any difference in U.S. and Russian stocks of war-ready ICBMs would be only "one or two missiles" by the year's end.[38] And in September, when the first Atlas missiles were officially declared operational, it was reported that U.S. and allied intelligence had been unable to locate a single site from which Russia could launch operational ICBMs aside from the known missile test ranges.[39]

In March 1959 the Soviet Union resumed testing ICBMs at a fairly regular rate (about four a month);[40] on the basis of these missile tests, the U.S. NIE of Soviet ICBMs was revised in November 1959. The new estimate, prepared for President Eisenhower and the NSC, was the first to credit the Soviet Union with operational ICBMs—a "small number"—at the test sites at Tyuratam and Kapustin Yar.[41] (This NIE also projected that the Soviets would have 350 to 640 ICBMs operational by mid-1963!)[42] In closed testimony before the Senate Aeronautical and Space Sciences Committee on 29 January 1960, CIA Director

36. Joseph Alsop, *International Herald Tribune*, 22 March 1959; *Newsweek*, 13 July 1959, p. 52.
37. *Missiles & Rockets*, 2 February 1959, p. 9.
38. *U.S. News and World Report*, 30 January 1959, p. 16.
39. *Newsweek*, 28 September 1959, p. 10.
40. *Newsweek*, 13 July 1959, p. 52.
41. *Newsweek*, 23 November 1959, p. 11.
42. *Statement of Secretary of Defense Robert S. McNamara before a Joint Session of the Senate Armed Services Committee and the Senate Subcommittee on Department of*

Allen Dulles was reported to have presented figures showing that the Soviet Union had more than a three-to-one lead over the United States in ready-to-launch ICBMs (that is, about ten), and to have stated that Russia would have 35 ICBMs "on launchers" by the end of June (though he is also said to have admitted that this figure was an estimate which could be on either the high or the low side). This was the first actual reported reference to Soviet ICBM bases by an administration official.[43] In other congressional testimony on 9 February, Admiral Burke stated that "Russia in 1960 will have no more than a few dozen" ICBMs.[44]

In fact, in 1960, apart from the two known ICBM test sites, the Soviet Union had no operational ICBM bases. The SS-6 ICBMs undergoing testing and crew training at Tyuratam would have achieved some initial operational capability in late 1959. In July 1960 a new NIE was prepared which reported "the total absence of observed operational sites."[45] Construction of the SS-6 base near Plesetsk, in northwest Russia, was begun in early 1960,[46] but it was not completed until 1961. Only four of the SS-6 ICBMs were actually ever deployed, and these would not have been operational before the spring of 1961.[47]

When the Kennedy Administration took office in January 1961, then, the Soviet Union had no operational ICBMs apart from those at the two test sites. Within the intelligence community, however, the estimates of Soviet ICBMs then operational ranged fairly widely—even though, as late as mid-1961, it was

Defense Appropriations on the Fiscal Year 1965–69 Defense Program and 1965 Defense Budget, 3 February 1964, p. 37 (declassified 1975).

43. *Missiles & Rockets*, 15 February 1960, p. 28; and 29 February 1960, p. 21.

44. *U.S. News and World Report*, 22 February 1960, p. 45.

45. Kistiakowsky, *A Scientist in the White House*, pp. 366–67.

46. David Wise and Thomas B. Ross, *The U-2 Affair*, pp. 10, 178; interview with Roger Hilsman, 12 June 1970, and interview with Dr. Robert A. Kilmarx, 22 July 1970.

47. Interviews with Roger Hilsman, 27 May 1970 and 12 June 1970, and with Daniel Ellsberg, 24 August 1970; see also Lt. Gen. Daniel O. Graham, "The Soviet Military Budget Controversy," p. 35. Even four may be an upper figure for the number of SS-6 ICBMs at Plesetsk. According to a former senior U.S. intelligence officer interviewed in 1973, there were "only one or two missiles, certainly not more than four" deployed at the Plesetsk base (interview with Herbert Scoville, 9 February 1973).

reported that U.S. intelligence was still unable actually to locate many missiles.[48]

In May 1961 the Soviet Union resumed testing from Tyura-tam after an eight-month halt. The missiles were a new model (with a storable liquid propellant), and the regularity and frequency of the tests (two to three a week) indicated that production of operational models was not far off.[49] Construction of sites for this new ICBM, designated the SS-7, began in the second half of 1961, and initial deployment of these missiles began in 1962.[50]

In his classified statement to the Senate Armed Services Committee on 19 January 1962, McNamara reckoned that the Soviets had a capability to launch "about 25 ICBMs,"[51] but it is now apparent that even this was a substantial overestimate. It is now known that by the time of the Cuban missile crisis in October 1962 only about 30 of these ICBMs were operational,[52] and according to the *Penkovsky Papers* most of these were still prototypes or undergoing tests, and they were not in a state of war readiness.[53]

In July 1962 it was revealed that the Soviet Union was beginning to "harden" its ICBMs in "coffin-type" silos, though all operational ICBMs were still "soft" (above ground) and in clusters; some Soviet sites apparently had two missiles for each launcher.[54] The new missiles for these launchers, designated

48. *Missiles & Rockets*, 17 July 1961, p. 11.

49. *Newsweek*, 15 May 1961, p. 8.

50. Interview with Herbert Scoville, 9 February 1973.

51. *Statement by Secretary of Defense Robert S. McNamara before the Senate Committee on Armed Services on the Fiscal Year 1963–67 Defense Program and 1963 Defense Budget, 19 January 1962*, p. 15 (declassified 1975).

52. Joseph Alsop, *Washington Post*, 14 November 1969; George E. Lowe, "The Only Option?", p. 25.

53. Oleg Penkovsky, *The Penkovsky Papers*, pp. 327–28. Penkovsky wrote that "there are altogether not more than a few dozen . . . missiles with nuclear warheads capable of reaching the United States." One NSC study of the Cuban missile crisis reportedly estimated that the Soviets had only about 10 ICBMs in war readiness at this time.

54. *New York Times*, 26 July 1962; *Newsweek*, 31 December 1962. These reports were confirmed in testimony of Secretary McNamara in January 1963. See House Armed Services Committee, *Hearings on Military Posture* (1963), p. 332.

SS-8 "Sasin," entered service in 1963. By mid-1963, the Soviets had "about 100" ICBMs operational.[55] In February 1964 McNamara testified that the Soviets were

> deploying their ICBM's both in a soft configuration with two launchers per site, plus one refire missile per launcher, and in a hard configuration with three launchers (silos) per site, and no refire missiles. Our own experience suggests that the hardness of their silos would fall in the range of 100–300 p.s.i.[56]

In August 1964 he claimed that the Soviet Union had fewer than 200 ICBMs, and fewer still in hardened silos.[57] In fact, the Soviet ICBM force did not reach 200 until about mid-1965.[58] According to recent testimony by Secretary of Defense Harold Brown, the Soviets had deployed only 224 ICBMs in 1966.[59] The rate of Soviet ICBM deployment increased greatly with the entry of the SS-9s and SS-11s into operational service in the latter half of 1966, however, and in August 1968 the Soviets overtook the U.S. figure of 1,054 ICBMs.[60]

As a result of the strategic arms limitation talks, the Soviet ICBM build-up was stopped, in 1972, at 1,618 missiles: 190 SS-7s, 19 SS-8s, 313 SS-9s, 1,036 SS-11s, and 60 SS-13s. The phasing-out of the SS-7s and SS-8s was begun in 1976, and the current Soviet force no longer includes any ICBMs deployed during the period of the U.S. strategic missile decisions. The estimates of Soviet ICBM deployment from 1959 to 1966 are summarized in the accompanying graph.

The picture of the development of the Soviet missile program was not altogether as clear in 1961–62 as it is today. It is known,

55. *Statement of Secretary of Defense Robert S. McNamara before a Joint Session of the Senate Armed Services Committee and the Senate Subcommittee on Department of Defense Appropriations on the Fiscal Year 1965–69 Defense Program and 1965 Defense Budget, 3 February 1964*, p. 37 (declassified 1975).

56. Ibid.

57. *Missiles & Rockets*, 24 August 1964, p. 14.

58. *Statement of Secretary of Defense Melvin R. Laird before the House Subcommittee on Department of Defense Appropriations on the Fiscal Year 1971 Defense Program and Budget, 25 February 1970*, p. 35.

59. Harold Brown, *Department of Defense Annual Report Fiscal Year 1979*, 2 February 1978, p. 45.

60. Laird, *Fiscal Year 1971 Defense Program and Budget*, p. 102.

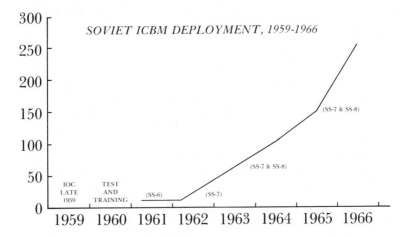

however, that much of the information which has reached the public record in recent years was available to the Kennedy Administration. Certainly by the time the most important of the missile decisions were taken, the missile gap had been proved a myth, and the NIE of operational Soviet ICBMs was much more in line with reality.

3 Quasi-Sovereignties and Alternative Positions in the Defense Establishment

In the United States the principal decision makers in the field of defense and national-security policy are, of course, the president and his secretary of defense, with their military and civilian advisers. But decisions are not made by the president simply giving a command. There are in the U.S. policy-making process a multiplicity of actors, each with various perspectives and interests, many of whom have developed and articulated positions on the subjects and issues at hand, and many of whom have a quasi-autonomous political power base from which to press their respective positions. These actors in the politics of defense policy making have been termed "quasi-sovereignties."[1] In the case of

1. William T. R. Fox, foreword to Michael H. Armacost, *The Politics of Weapons Innovation*, p. vii.

the U.S. strategic missile program, the most important of these were the two military services principally involved in that program—the Navy and the Air Force.

Throughout the late 1950s and early 1960s, to a greater or lesser extent, both of these services developed relatively identifiable positions on the question of the U.S. strategic-forces requirement, including the strategic ballistic-missile requirement. These positions were not necessarily held universally throughout the respective services, nor continuously throughout the period under study. This was particularly the case within the Air Force —but even there various positions were held, if only with respect to relative orders of magnitude rather than to precise force goals, which can be identified with groups within that service, and which were significant for a sufficient length of time to warrant description here. The first two sections of this chapter outline these service positions.

There were also various groups and individuals, both within and without the Kennedy Administration, who developed and articulated arguments for a relatively limited strategic missile force. Although these groups and individuals were not "quasi-sovereign," in that generally they lacked most of the elements of a quasi-autonomous political power base, their views and arguments for an alternative strategic-forces posture were important factors in the defense policy-making process. An outline of the theories, studies and sponsors of this "lesser option" completes this chapter.

THE POSITION OF THE U.S. NAVY

Within the Navy, the Special Projects Office was established in December 1955 to develop the Polaris Fleet Ballistic Missile system, but it was not wholeheartedly welcomed. According to Admiral Arleigh Burke, "many naval officers (perhaps most naval officers) [had] serious and valid doubts about the desirability of making the effort at all."[2] Besides the numerous technical problems involved in the development of the new weapons system (including the development of a small, proven warhead

2. Adm. Arleigh Burke, "Polaris," unpublished paper, no date, pp. 13–15.

of sufficient yield, an accurate guidance system, a fire-control system, an accurate navigation system, a solid propellant fuel, miniaturization, etc.), there were many problems which affected the Navy as a service:

> How can we raise the money? Is it possible to get the funds in addition to our present budget? How can we provide enough men to man the new ships? What will happen to other important projects? Since this new weapon system will be good only for general nuclear war, how can we maintain our conventional and limited war capability at the necessary level? How can this program be organized so as not to disrupt everything else we must do?[3]

To develop the Polaris, Admiral Burke had asked the then secretary of defense, Charles E. Wilson, for $1 billion, and this was allowed by Wilson only on condition that it came out of the Navy budget. Throughout the Eisenhower Administration, the Navy received no extra money for the increasingly expensive Polaris program. Instead, this was financed with money that normally would have been spent on other Navy activities—all Navy projects were cut by about 10 percent, causing much opposition to the program within the service.[4]

Moreover, many in the Navy, including senior officers, looked upon Polaris as "a national program, not a Navy program." By this they meant that the Polaris mission was not a traditional Navy mission, and therefore should not be financed out of the Navy's share of the defense budget. The Navy as a service was more interested in carriers and cruisers, and Polaris funding from F/Y 1958 through F/Y 1962 was therefore consistently below the requests of those involved in the Polaris program, and below what was considered "the very great national need."[5]

The U.S. Navy is a much more composite defense establishment than other services—with the Marine Corps included, it

---

3. Ibid., p. 13.
4. Interview with Adm. Burke, 29 July 1970. For an excellent discussion of the internal Navy opposition to the Polaris program, including opposition of Navy submariners, see Harvey M. Sapolsky, *The Polaris System Development*, pp. 16–21.
5. Alain C. Enthoven and K. Wayne Smith, *How Much is Enough?*, pp. 16–17. The Navy at this time was working under the arbitrarily imposed ceiling of 28 percent of the U.S. defense budget.

has a wide range of land, sea, and air elements. Certainly the independent existence of the Navy has never depended upon the Polaris system. There were therefore very strong bureaucratic interests within the service working against a high-priority Polaris program.

Finally, the Navy had by the mid-1950s accepted the concept of "minimum or finite deterrence" as a nuclear strategy. This strategy involved the deployment of a relatively small, long-range strategic nuclear delivery force, aimed at a finite number of enemy population and industrial centers as well as military targets. And, the strategic argument went on, to deploy a larger force than this would be to enter into a provocative counter-force capability. Many Navy theorists believed that the Polaris fleet ballistic missile (FBM) system would become a provocative counterforce weapon when the number of units exceeded 45. At any rate, the "finite deterrence" theory placed a definite limit on the number of Polaris submarines which the Navy was willing to request.[6]

For these reasons, the Navy has never fought for Polaris as an "open-ended" program (unlike the Air Force, which developed around the strategic bombing mission and has therefore fought for a much more open-ended procurement of strategic-weapons systems). However, it was some years before the Navy finally settled upon what the number of Polaris submarines to be procured should be. During most of the Eisenhower Administration, Navy energy focused on getting a higher annual FBM submarine-procurement authorization, rather than on setting an ultimate force goal.

The first attempt to put a figure on the size of the end program was made by Admiral Burke in January 1957, in response to a congressional request. Ironically, in view of the later McNamara program, Burke estimated that 41 submarines would be required. This calculation was based on an assumption of about 200 targets in the Soviet Union, and the need for about 647 missiles—discounted for reliability, anti-submarine warfare (ASW), numbers of submarines at sea, etc.—to destroy them. Implicit

6. See Arthur I. Waskow, *The Limit of Defense* (Garden City, N.Y.: Doubleday, 1962), p. 35; and George E. Lowe, *The Age of Deterrence*, pp. 170–76.

in this estimate was a deployment schedule of about 4 to 6 submarines per annum. If the rate of deployment were increased, the Navy wanted a higher total program. This calculation of Polaris numbers, like all those done before 1961, was made completely independently of whatever numbers were to be chosen for the Minuteman program: Polaris numbers were based only on Soviet targets.[7]

In early 1958 a number of senators and Navy officers began to talk of a Polaris fleet of as many as 100 submarines.[8] As further details of the Polaris FBM system emerged, however, planning within the Navy reverted to a program of about 40 to 50 submarines.[9] On 6 April 1959 Admiral Raborn first proposed the figure of 45, asserting that "in order to have an orderly program in the number of submarines at sea, 45 is the number that it looks like we could keep where we would have an adequate number at sea constantly and on station."[10]

By the beginning of 1960, in time for the F/Y 1961 congressional hearings, the Navy appears to have settled on a program of 45 Polaris FBM submarines. On 6 February 1960, the *Washington Post* reported testimony by Admiral Burke in which he announced that the Navy was aiming at a 45-submarine program, and in a television interview on 22 February 1960, Admiral Burke repeated his belief in the need for 45 submarines. In the hearings before a Government Operations Committee subcommittee, held on 30 and 31 March 1960, Admiral Raborn inserted a statement which analyzed the cost of the FBM system based on a program of 45 submarines. And on 16 March 1960, Admiral Hayward recommended a 45-submarine program. Throughout the rest of 1960, Admirals Burke and Raborn

7. Interview with Adm. Burke, 29 July 1970. According to Burke, this estimate of 41 submarines was made

in about one hour . . . I figured it out on the back of an envelope. . . . It turned out that the factors weren't correct, but the over-all number was.

8. *Missiles & Rockets*, January 1958, p. 39; February 1958, p. 137; and March 1958, p. 66.

9. *Missiles & Rockets*, May 1958, p. 59; 24 August 1959, p. 36; 7 September 1959, p. 9; and 21 September 1959, p. 22. Forty is the smallest number of submarines ever mentioned publicly by a Navy official.

10. Testimony of Adm. Raborn, House Appropriations Committee, *Department of Defense Appropriations for 1960*, part 4, p. 314.

stated several times that 45 submarines was the accepted Navy program, and this figure became generally accepted among defense commentators and analysts.[11]

There were, however, differences of opinion within the Navy as to the production and deployment schedule which should be adopted in putting the 45 submarines to sea. Those closely concerned with the Polaris development program, such as Vice Admiral J. T. Hayward, deputy chief of naval operations for development, favored a one-per-month schedule for F/Y 1962 and 1963. Those more concerned with operational factors, such as Admiral Burke, supported by Congressman Cannon, chairman of the House Appropriations Committee, advocated a four- to six-per-year schedule. (See schedules A and B in table 3.)[12]

In May 1960 Admiral Burke in fact rejected additional Polaris funds, voted the Navy by Congress as a supplement to the administration's F/Y 1961 request, on the grounds that it would "tend to upset the balance which the Navy Department has striven to achieve in the fiscal 1961 budget."[13]

The emphasis on Polaris in President Kennedy's State of the Union message of 30 January 1961 was welcomed by the Navy —the 45-submarine program never looked more assured. The service opposed the acceleration in delivery schedules, however, and the 30 January 1961 speed-up was forced by McNamara over the Navy's objections. According to Admiral Burke, the Navy opposed a schedule of more than six submarines per year (on the assumption of a 45-submarine program) because: (a) it would result in the submarines becoming obsolete in blocks; (b) it would allow inadequate room for an orderly modification and improvement program; and (c) there was no perceived need vis-à-vis the Soviet threat.[14]

The question of schedules again became an issue within the Navy in May 1961, after McNamara testified that following the

11. See Congressman Gubser, *Congressional Record, House*, 24 May 1961, pp. 8808–10 and 8820–22, for documentation of the development of the 45-submarine position within the Navy by early 1960.

12. These schedules are derived from the *Congressional Record (House)*, 21 June 1960, p. 13626; and 24 May 1961, p. 8809.

13. Adm. Burke, cited in *Missiles & Rockets*, 30 May 1960, p. 38.

14. Interview with Adm. Burke, 29 July 1970.

TABLE 3. *Alternative USN Polaris Development Schedules* (by fiscal year)

	SSBN	LLTI	FUNDING (IN MILLIONS OF DOLLARS)
Schedule A			
Previously authorized	9	18	—
1961	9	12	—
1962	12	12	2,344.5
1963	12	3	2,119.6
1964	3	0	636.2
Total	45		—
Schedule B*			
Previously authorized	9		
1961	6		
1962	6		
1963	6		
1964	6		
1965	4		
1966	4		
1967	4		
Total	45		

*Schedule B applied only to the number of SSBNs and never included LLTIs or national funding. It was simply a slower way than schedule A for getting to the 45-SSBN goal.

28 March defense review the administration would make no decisions on the Polaris program (beyond the 29 submarines already authorized) until the F/Y 1963 budget.[15] What this meant, essentially, given the failure to authorize long-lead-time items for the 30th and subsequent submarines, was that there would be a gap of up to twelve months between the deployment of the 29th and 30th submarines. This would effectively cancel out the January 30 and March 28 accelerations of the program. Such "stop-go" procurement was precisely what the Navy did not want.[16]

In briefings and submissions to McNamara throughout the

15. Testimony of McNamara, House Appropriations Committee, *Department of Defense Appropriations for 1962*, part 3, p. 113.

16. See Congressman Gubser, *Congressional Record (House)*, 24 May 1961, pp. 8820–22. A ten-month gap in new FBM submarine deployment did in fact occur between June 1965 and April 1966. See *Polaris and Poseidon FBM Facts*, p. 11.

spring and summer of 1961, the Navy continued to recommend the 45-submarine program. During the development of the F/Y 1963 defense budget, for example, the service repeatedly requested authorization for an ultimate strength of 45 submarines.[17] The Navy's initial program package, submitted to McNamara on 3 July 1961, contained this magic number, with ten more submarines to be funded in F/Y 1963 and the remaining six in F/Y 1964.[18] When McNamara tentatively set the Polaris program at 41 submarines on 22 September 1961,[19] the Navy raised its goal to 50,[20] presumably to give itself some bargaining leeway. McNamara refused, however, to shift from his earlier 41-submarine decision.

Within the Navy the 41-submarine program was accepted after January 1962 without argument. During testimony on the F/Y 1963 budget, Admiral Griffon stated that although the subject was "under active and continuing review in the Department," the figure of 45 no longer represented the Navy's position. Secretary Korth testified that the cut in the Navy's original request was no longer "a point of active argument." Admiral Anderson, the new CNO, stated that the difference between 41 and 45 represented submarines which would not be available for some years, and that the Navy would have a chance later to request "four or more" if necessary. Referring to the McNamara program of 41 submarines, he added that: "We fully support that program."[21]

In February 1963, during hearings on the F/Y 1964 defense

17. Testimony of Alain C. Enthoven, Senate Committee on Government Operations, subcommittee on national security and international operations, *Planning, Programming, Budgeting* (1970), pp. 248–49; testimony of McNamara, House Armed Services Committee, *Hearings on Military Posture* (1962), p. 3328; testimony of Sec. Korth, Senate Appropriations Committee, *Department of Defense Appropriations for 1963*, p. 210; and testimony of Adm. Anderson, ibid., p. 218.

18. *Aviation Week & Space Technology*, 24 July 1961, p. 34.

19. *Polaris and Poseidon Chronology*, p. 7.

20. *Aviation Week & Space Technology*, 11 December 1961, p. 38; *Missiles & Rockets*, 27 November 1961, p. 13.

21. Testimony of Adm. Griffon, House Armed Services Committee, *Hearings on Military Posture* (1962), p. 3885; testimony of Sec. Korth, Senate Appropriations Committee, *Department of Defense Appropriations for 1963*, p. 210; and testimony of Adm. Anderson, CNO, Senate Armed Services Committee, *Military Procurement Authorization, Fiscal Year 1963*, p. 461.

budget, the House Armed Services Committee was very anxious to know whether or not the Navy was satisfied with the currently approved 41-submarine program, which McNamara saw no need to increase, or whether it still wanted to proceed with the 45-submarine program, which the committee was willing to consider. However, both the CNO, Admiral Anderson, and the secretary of the navy, Mr. Korth, testified that both the Navy and the joint chiefs of staff were satisfied with 41 Polaris submarines, and that "there has been no further request for any increased number beyond 41." [22]

During 1963 the Navy carried out some research into FBM-system improvements which might have called for enlarging the Polaris fleet beyond 41 submarines, [23] but it made no proposals either to the joint chiefs of staff or to McNamara for more Polaris submarines to be included in the F/Y 1965 budget; [24] and no such proposals have subsequently been made by the Navy.

In addition to developing an internal service position on the Polaris FBM submarine requirement, the Navy also at least implicitly held a position on the land-based strategic ballistic-missile requirement. In accordance with its policy of "finite deterrence," and especially during the period before 1961 when the services competed directly for budget funds, the Navy opposed any large-scale strategic missile build-up. The Navy believed that the Polaris FBM submarine system could provide all the countervalue deterrent that the United States needed, and despite the fact that most of the U.S. strategic retaliatory forces were in the Air Force, the Navy's calculations, briefings, and submissions on the number of Polaris submarines required never acknowledged the

22. House Armed Services Committee, *Hearings on Military Posture* (1963), pp. 391, 939–40 and 1081–82. Navy acceptance of the 41-submarine program at this time was confirmed in an interview with Paul H. Nitze, 7 February 1973. (Mr. Nitze succeeded Mr. Korth as secretary of the Navy, 1963–67.) There was, however, one study done for the joint chiefs of staff in 1962 by the chairman's special study group (CSSG) which suggested a Polaris force of 44 submarines, but this included 26 submarines with a Polaris A-3A missile which was never approved.

23. *Missiles & Rockets*, 20 May 1963, p. 9.

24. See testimony of Gen. Taylor, House Appropriations Committee, *Department of Defense Appropriations for 1965*, part 4, p. 51; testimony of McNamara, ibid., p. 52; and remark of Congressman Andres, ibid.

existence of the Air Force.[25] And during the development of
the F/Y 1963 defense budget in 1961, the Navy argued that the
Department of Defense was "recommending far too many Minuteman."[26] But from January 1962, when it accepted the administration's decision to procure only 41 Polaris submarines, the
Navy acquiesced in the 1,200-missile Minuteman program.[27]
However, there is no evidence of any Navy support for Air
Force requests for a larger land-based strategic missile force;
and if anything one would expect the Navy to have supported
the Department of Defense in denying those requests.

THE POSITION OF THE U.S. AIR FORCE

Unlike the Navy, the Air Force never developed a missile force
goal which was accepted either right throughout the service or
over any substantial period of time. The public record is replete
with statements attributing to the Air Force proposals for an
ICBM force ranging from several hundred to many thousand
missiles. But at the authoritative level (that is, statements by
relevant holders of official posts at the time, congressional testimony, etc.), the evidence is both too incomplete and too insub-
stantial to enable one to develop anything like "a history of official Air Force submissions."

Within the Air Force, views on the size of the ICBM force
needed by the United States ranged widely.[28] Those sections of
the Air Force closest to the development of the missiles (for
example, the Ballistic Missile Division), were at the lower end of

25. Interview with Adm. Burke, 29 July 1970. See also Enthoven and Smith,
How Much is Enough?, p. 21, and Stewart Alsop, *The Center*, p. 138.
26. Testimony of McNamara, House Appropriations Committee, *Department of Defense Appropriations for 1963*, part 2, p. 24. Unlike the Air Force in its
opposition to the Polaris program, the Navy was never vocal in its opposition to
the USAF's Minuteman program—the Special Projects Office saw itself as being
too vulnerable in a power-political sense to deprecate the Minuteman. See
Sapolsky, *Polaris System Development*, p. 57.
27. See L. J. Korb, "The Role of the Joint Chiefs of Staff," pp. 166, 198.
28. Many Air Force officers were actually very lukewarm towards the missile
program. A large number, for example, favored continued reliance on long-
range bombers, and regarded the missile effort as an unnecessary diversion;
others, especially in the earlier period, regarded accurate ICBMs as technically
unfeasible—for example, Gen. Le May stated in the early 1950s, at a meeting
of the Von Neumann committee at Omaha, Nebr., that "I can guarantee that
10 years from now there will be no operational long-range ballistic missiles"
(interview with George Kistiakowsky, 20 February 1973).

the range; the user (the Strategic Air Command) at the highest; and the Air Staff in between.[29]

In developing the Minuteman, for example, the Ballistic Missile Division (reorganized into the Ballistic Systems Division in March 1961), as the responsible office within the Air Force, had to make assumptions about missile characteristics, deployment patterns, cost-effectiveness relationships, etc., which necessitated some assumption about production numbers. BMD had assumed from the beginning that the Minuteman missile was to be developed under a "requirement for many missiles at low cost." The weapons system was designed to make maximum use of production capacity, and in fact the concept would not have been cost-effective at a production run of less than about 600 to 800 missiles. It was therefore implicit in the approval of the Minuteman operational development program that a deployment figure for Minuteman of at least that range had been approved; certainly there was no suggestion that *production* should be less than that.[30]

In fact, BMD proposals were for a somewhat higher Minuteman strength. The original BMD working plan called for 1,000 to 1,500 Minuteman missiles, to be deployed in a single geographic location. In October 1959 this plan was refined, after lengthy discussions between BMD and SAC, "to a strength of 1,200." Although the idea of forming squadrons of 50 missiles each soon replaced the plan for a single "missile farm," BMD does not appear to have lowered its estimate of the desirable deployment figure. In mid-1962, when the approved Minuteman force level was 800 missiles, General Phillips expressed his personal belief that "we should have several hundred more."[31]

At the other end of the spectrum, within the Air Force, was the Strategic Air Command, the command responsible for "using" the missiles, fitting them into actual war plans and strategies, and day-to-day operation of the deployed force. For example, Gen-

29. It is interesting to compare this with the Navy, where it was the office responsible for developing the Polaris FBM system (the Special Projects Office) which pressed most strongly for greater submarine production.

30. Interviews with Dr. Robert Kilmarx, 22 July 1970, and Gen. Robert C. Richardson, 25 July 1970.

31. *Missiles & Rockets*, 6 August 1962, p. 16; and Roy Neal, *Ace in the Hole*, p. 132.

eral Thomas S. Power, commander in chief of SAC from 1957 to 1964, spoke of a requirement for 10,000 Minuteman ICBMs, and is known to have personally suggested that figure to President Kennedy.[32]

The "official" USAF position was much nearer to that of BMD than to that of SAC.[33] However, it was never constant, and changed frequently and substantially throughout the early 1960s, depending on various factors. These included:

1. The nature of the missile itself. The Minuteman was originally intended to be a very simple, cheap missile, all to be fired "in one flush," and the weapons system was initially designed to operate as "all or nothing." However, from mid-1961 on the Minuteman system was improved to allow for selective response, and the missile became much more sophisticated and expensive. Improvements such as greater target selectivity, accuracy, and payload, multiple reentry vehicles, etc., changed the meaning of the designation "a Minuteman missile" immensely.[34]

2. The international situation, especially the Air Force's estimate of the Soviet threat.

3. Internal political factors. At every point at which a decision was made, the Air Force consistently argued for more missiles than were actually approved. Its actual requests partly reflected its own assessment of its bargaining position (for example, the Minuteman "requirement" was doubled after the Kennedy inauguration), and usually took into account a consideration of the position of the Office of the Secretary of Defense (OSD).[35] Though it never developed a consistent and finite figure, it always wanted "more," and its positions at any given time were more than anything else adopted for the purpose of bargaining for "more."

Public estimates by former non-Air Force officials and com-

32. See Herbert F. York, *Race to Oblivion*, p. 152; Enthoven and Smith, *How Much is Enough?*, p. 195; and interview with Enthoven, 17 August 1970.

33. By "official" is meant formal proposals, recommendations, or requests under the signature of the Air Force chief of staff or the secretary of the Air Force to OSD or the president which were relevant to decisions on force levels.

34. Interview with Neil A. Harlan, 21 July 1970; and testimony of Gen. Schultz, House Appropriations Committee, *Department of Defense Appropriations for 1970*, part 4, pp. 650–51.

35. Interview with Neil A. Harlan, 21 July 1970.

mentators on the Air Force's position during the early 1960s on the end strength of the Minuteman force range from nearly 2,000 to 3,000 missiles.[36] However, Air Force officers deny that any formal requests for more than about 2,000 missiles were ever made.[37]

Within the Air Force, "wish lists" of unilateral desires, projections to aid in future planning, studies on alternative force requirements and on strategies and related postures, etc., were continually being prepared, and there is no doubt that many of these suggested figures were in the 2,000–3,000 range. But the civilian officials within the Air Force and OSD whose positions required them either to have signed any formal requests or to have acted upon them agree that, at the points in the decision-making process where final decisions were made on force sizes, formal Air Force requests were always above 1,000 but never more than about 2,000 missiles.[38]

When the Kennedy Administration took office in January 1961, the USAF position as contained in the joint strategic objectives plan (JSOP) of 1961, setting out the force requirements for the period F/Y 1963–F/Y 1967, was 1,450 Minuteman ICBMs.[39] Cognizant of the widespread impression that the new administration was prepared to greatly increase U.S. defense expenditure, and believing it to be more receptive to proposals for increases in strategic-forces programs, the Air Force quickly increased its Minuteman programs and funding requests by approximately 100 percent. And McNamara's total disregard in planning for the joint strategic objectives plan of 1961 allowed the services to do this without attracting any critical notice.

During March 1961 the Air Force made several submissions on strategic-force programs to OSD in relation to President Kennedy's revision of the F/Y 1962 defense budget. For fixed Min-

36. See, for example, York, *Race to Oblivion*, p. 152; Richard J. Barnet, *The Economy of Death*, p. 178; and Jerome Wiesner, "Arms Control," p. 6.

37. 1,700 Minuteman missiles is the only figure publicly reported by an Air Force officer. See Gen. Curtis E. Le May, *America is in Danger*, p. 281. That this was an Air Force figure rather than Le May's personal position was confirmed in an interview with Gen. Le May, 16 August 1970.

38. Interviews with Charles J. Hitch, 11 August 1970; Eugene Zuckert, 21 July 1970; and Gen. Robert C. Richardson, 25 July 1970.

39. Interview with Dr. Marvin Stern, 21 August 1970.

uteman ICBMs, the service proposed that the Eisenhower F/Y 1962 program of 450 missiles be doubled to 900 missiles.[40] The administration, however, only agreed to an increase to 600 missiles in this category—and, moreover, deferred any deployment decision on mobile Minuteman missiles, and reduced the Titan II program by two squadrons.[41] Throughout April and May, the Air Force pressed to have these Titan squadrons restored, and to have $62 million added to the mobile Minuteman program to carry on development.[42]

In May and June 1961, the Air Force drew up its package plans for the Central War Offensive Forces, and submitted them to McNamara on 3 July. This package was prepared without any consideration for the strategic-forces programs of the other services, and without any consideration of dollar amounts; it represented the unilateral Air Force position on the U.S. strategic-forces posture over the period F/Y 1963 to F/Y 1967. The package included plans for 3,190 Air Force ICBMs (excluding the already authorized 126-missile Atlas program) at a predicted cost of $18.5 billion over the five years.[43] This was a two-thirds increase over the highest previous Air Force missile submissions, and a fourfold increase over what had been authorized by the administration through F/Y 1962 (table 4). This submission revealed not only that the Air Force wanted a very large fixed Minuteman program, but that it was still committed to the concept of mobility for part of its ICBM force, and that at least sections of the service strongly supported continued Titan deployment, presumably because of the much greater payload capacity of that missile.

The Air Force's funding request for Minuteman procurement in F/Y 1963 was $1,594 million, which the administration reduced to $1,155.1 million, or by 27.5 percent.[44] The Air Force had wanted this additional money to procure a F/Y 1963 pro-

40. Interview with Eugene Zuckert, 21 July 1970.

41. President Kennedy, *Special Message*, 28 March 1961, pp. 6, 10.

42. Testimony of Gen. White, House Appropriations Committee, *Department of Defense Appropriations for 1962*, part 3, p. 467.

43. *Aviation Week & Space Technology*, 24 July 1961, p. 34.

44. House Appropriations Committee, *Department of Defense Appropriations for 1963*, part 4, pp. 422–23.

TABLE 4. *Air Force ICBM Programs*

MISSILE PROGRAM	EISENHOWER AUTHORIZA-TION THROUGH F/Y 1962	KENNEDY 28 MARCH 1961 REVISION OF F/Y 1962 BUDGET	HIGHEST PREVIOUS FORMAL AIR FORCE POSITION	3 JULY 1961 PACKAGE PLAN FOR SRF PROGRAMS
Fixed Minuteman	450	600	1,450	2,500
Mobile Minuteman	90	0	300[a]	415
Titan	126	108	126	275
Total Air Force ICBMs[b]	666	708	1,876	3,190

[a] General Power, *Strategy for Survival*, p. 161.
[b] Excludes Atlas. In late 1959 the Air Force had supported congressional moves to authorize 17 Atlas squadrons (144 missiles); by 1961, however, it had accepted the Eisenhower Administration's position of 13 Atlas squadrons (126 missiles).

gram of 250 Minuteman missiles more than Secretary McNamara had approved. About half of this number were to be fully funded by F/Y 1963, and long-lead-time items (principally silo construction) were to be funded for the other half,[45] making the Minuteman funding commitment through F/Y 1963, on the Air Force's proposed schedule, 1,050 ICBMs.

It is not clear from the public record just what the Air Force's position was in the fall of 1961 on the F/Y 1963 to F/Y 1967 force posture. In the transcripts of the congressional hearings in which the cut in the Air Force's F/Y 1963 request is discussed, all references to its requested end strength are deleted. And despite attempts by Congressman Gerald Ford to clear up the question,[46] there is still doubt as to whether the cut of 250 Minuteman missiles was a reduction in the F/Y 1963 program which also represented a cut in the end program (implicitly, but not necessarily, by only 250), or a cut in the end program of x Min-

45. Testimony of Gen. Le May, Senate Appropriations Committee, *Department of Defense Appropriations for 1963*, pp. 192–94.
46. See the exchange between Congressman Ford and Mr. Meyer of the Air Force, in House Appropriations Committee, *Department of Defense Appropriations for 1963*, part 4, pp. 422–25.

uteman ICBMs, of which 250 were reflected in the F/Y 1963 budget; hence any conclusions drawn from the transcripts are not reliable. Other sources, however, have revealed that at this time the Air Force was asking for an end-program strength of 1,700 to 2,000 Minuteman missiles.[47]

In November 1961 General Le May set up a small group within the service under General Burchinal to study the Air Force's strategic-force requirements for the 1963–67 period. This group recommended that a force of 1,850 Minuteman ICBMs be procured.[48] (In addition, this study suggested that 32 Polaris submarines, or 512 missiles, would be sufficient at least during this time frame, and that by 1967 the force should include 126 Atlas and Titan ICBMs, 1,012 GAM-87 Skybolt missiles, and 20 RS-70 bombers, each with 21 to 28 very accurate strike missiles.) The findings of this study were presented to Secretary McNamara at a meeting in December 1961,[49] where the Air Force's formal position was clarified as being that 1,850 Minuteman ICBMs were needed.

During the development of the F/Y 1964 defense budget in the fall of 1962, the Air Force again requested "a substantially

47. Le May has written that "I had recommended seventeen hundred" (*America is in Danger*, p. 281). However, L. J. Korb has reported that "General Le May asked for a fiscal 1967 force of 2,000 ICBM's" ("The Role of the Joint Chiefs of Staff," p. 164). One former senior civilian official of the Department of the Air Force has stated, privately but quite categorically, that Le May requested 1,950 Minuteman missiles. Whatever the size of the end program requested in late 1961, it was less than one which had previously been presented to Congress. See testimony of Gen. Burchinal, House Appropriations Committee, *Department of Defense Appropriations for 1963*, part 2, p. 538.

48. The numbers recommended by this Air Force study were 150 in 1963, growing to 1,850 by 1967, of which 1,000 were to be the Improved Minuteman and 50 the Advanced Minuteman. (The Improved Minuteman had about a 30 percent improvement in accuracy over the basic Minuteman and two possible yields—one about the same as the basic version and the other twice that. The Advanced Minuteman had a maneuvering re-entry vehicle for increased accuracy, giving about half the CEP of the Improved Minuteman.) In addition, the study recommended that should the Soviet ABM threat develop, an additional 300 Advanced Minuteman ICBMs be procured by 1967, for a total of 2,150 Minuteman missiles.

49. Present at this meeting were McNamara, Air Force Sec. Zuckert, Gen. Frederic Smith (acting chief of staff, USAF), Gen. Burchinal, Brig.-Gen. George Brown (Air Force aide to McNamara), and Lt.-Col. Robert Lukeman. Lukeman represented the working group consisting of himself and Cols. Robert Bowers and David Williams which prepared the study for Le May and Burchinal.

larger Minuteman missile force" than McNamara was willing
to approve, and "several hundred million dollars" of the Air
Force's Minuteman request were rejected.[50] But again, it is not
clear exactly what the Air Force had proposed. General Le May
testified before the Senate Appropriations subcommittee that
he had asked for 700 Minuteman missiles more than the Department of Defense program, though he would not give his total
recommendation in open session.[51] Before the Senate Armed
Services Committee, Le May testified: "I have asked for more
missiles by far than the Secretary of Defense has seen fit to give
me."[52] At that time the administration had authorized a total
force of 950 Minuteman ICBMs, but Le May testified that "the
700 . . . wasn't above that program. I recommended a larger
program—and building up at a faster rate."[53] Perhaps Le May
was asking for 700 above the 1,200 to 1,300 program which OSD
had at that time tentatively projected through F/Y 1967. One
authority has stated that the 1,950 missile figure was again presented in F/Y 1964.[54] However that may be, the JCS recommendation on Minuteman was unanimous.[55]

It is known that in 1962, during the preparation of the F/Y
1964 budget, the JCS chairman's special study group (CSSG)
did recommend a Minuteman force of 1,950 to the JCS. But this
study group, set up as Sec Def Project 47 (1962) was not required to, and did not, develop force "requirements." It looked
only at 1968, and compared the relative merits of two alternative
forces for that year—an "OSD Approved Force" (the Five Year
Defense Program extrapolated by OSD to 1968) and a "Services
Force" (OSD's description of the 1968 force then being proposed by the Air Force and the Navy). Both forces had a number of common elements: B-52s/B-58s, GAM-77 Hound Dog

50. Testimony of McNamara, Senate Appropriations Committee, *Department of Defense Appropriations for 1964*, p. 212.
51. Testimony of Gen. Le May, ibid., pp. 350–51.
52. Testimony of Gen. Le May, Senate Armed Services Committee, *Military
Procurement Authorization, Fiscal Year 1964*, p. 954.
53. Senate Appropriations Committee, *Department of Defense Appropriations
for 1964*, pp. 350–51.
54. Interview with Neil A. Harlan, 21 July 1970.
55. Testimony of Gen. Le May, House Armed Services Committee, *Hearings
on Military Posture* (1963), p. 1216.

TABLE 5. *1962 Projections for 1968*

SYSTEM	OSD APPROVED	SERVICES
Minuteman I	150	0
Minuteman II	650	750
Minuteman Improved	400	1,200
Total	1,200	1,950
Polaris A-2	352 (22 submarines)	288 (18 submarines)
Polaris A-3	304 (19 submarines)	0
Polaris A-3A	0	416 (26 submarines)
Total	656	704
RS-70	0	25

(both 408), GAM-87 Skybolt (both 1,012), and Atlas/Titan (both 219). The differences are illustrated in table 5. The study made a number of judgments on the relative merits of the two forces. Principal among these were that there were critical deficiencies in the ability of the "OSD Approved Force" to achieve national objectives.

In its initial F/Y 1965 budget request, in the fall of 1963, the Air Force proposed a funding of $1,172.2 million for Minuteman, which the OSD cut by about 23 percent, to $881.8 million. Moreover, this cut represented a cut in the size of the end strength of the force, rather than merely a dollar decision on the F/Y 1965 budget. Once more the service had requested "a faster rate of build-up to a higher level."[56] But again it is not clear exactly what the Air Force's Minuteman request for F/Y 1965 was in terms of numbers. It is definite that the number 1,200 figured prominently in the budget discussions, but whether this represented the service's revised end target, or was simply the F/Y 1965 request (requiring authorization for 250 new Minuteman missiles) on the way to the 1,950-missile target is not clear.[57] Finally, there is the complication that the force level which the Air Force had recommended and that finally approved by the OSD had different numbers of Minuteman I and

56. House Appropriations Committee, *Department of Defense Appropriations for 1965*, part 3, pp. 98–101.
57. Interviews with Neil A. Harlan, 21 July 1970, and Eugene M. Zuckert, 21 July 1970.

TABLE 6. *Minuteman Funding, Fiscal Year 1963–Fiscal Year 1966*
(in millions of dollars)

	1963	1964	1965	1966
Air Force program package of 3 July 1961	2,100	2,600	2,800	1,900
Air Force budget requests	1,594	—	1,172.2	1,522
OSD approval	1,155.1	1,458.8	881.8	796

Minuteman II missiles, the OSD program including a faster refit of the improved Minuteman IIs into the Minuteman I force.[58]

In the F/Y 1966 budget, the Air Force request of $1,522 million for Minuteman was cut nearly in half by the OSD, to approximately $796 million. The Air Force position at this stage "was that we still required 1,200,"[59] although it was now clear that McNamara had decided to level the program off at 1,000 missiles. However, the 1965 JSOP, prepared early in 1965, setting out the requirements for F/Y 1967, accepted the figure of 1,000 as the JCS requirement.[60] And, a year later, McNamara testified publicly that both the secretary of the Air Force and the chief of staff of the Air Force had agreed to the 1,000-missile program, and General Wheeler added that the JCS agreement was unanimous.[61] The Air Force funding requests for the Minuteman program and the amounts approved by the OSD, for the period 1961 to 1964, are summarized in table 6.

Like the Navy, the Air Force also developed, at least implicitly, a position on the strategic-forces programs of the other service. From the beginning of the Polaris program, the Air Force looked upon the Polaris as not only competing for "Air Force" funds, but "challenging the future supremacy of SAC as the nation's primary retaliatory force," and throughout the last years of the Eisenhower Administration the Air Force attempted to

58. Testimony of Gen. Merrell, House Appropriations Committee, *Department of Defense Appropriations for 1965*, p. 100.
59. Senate Armed Services Committee and Senate Appropriations subcommittee, *Military Procurement Authorization, Fiscal Year 1966*, pp. 1023, 1059.
60. Interview with F. S. Hoffman, 25 August 1970.
61. Senate Armed Services Committee, *Military Procurement Authorization for Fiscal Year 1967*, pp. 248, 252.

downplay the strategic value of the Polaris FBM system. Some attempts were also made by the Air Force to have the Polaris submarines assigned to the Air Force as a strategic bombardment weapon.[62]

During the development of the F/Y 1963 defense budget in 1961, the Air Force consistently opposed increasing the Polaris program and, for planning purposes, "assumed that no more Navy systems would be deployed than those already approved by Congress"—whatever the existing number happened to be.[63] In late 1961 this meant opposing anything more than a "29-boat program."[64]

The Air Force's argument was that since to destroy any given target (city or hardened site) would cost more with Polaris than by using Minuteman, the only value of the Polaris system lay in making the Soviet Union spend resources on ASW systems. As one former senior Air Force general has explained: "The proper solution was to build just enough [Polaris submarines] to make Russia build a defense against them." The actual number of Polaris submarines necessary for this was impossible to determine—it depended on what was necessary to induce the Soviet Union to spend resources on counterweapons systems, a necessarily subjective judgment—but it "certainly wasn't 40 boats."[65] As Le May later wrote: "Distinctly we went overboard on the Polaris."[66] When the Navy sought 45 FBM submarines, the Air Force thought 15 to 20 would be sufficient.[67] In cutting the Navy's requests for 45 Polaris submarines, the Kennedy Administration certainly had the support of the Air Force.

LESSER OPTIONS: THE THEORIES, STUDIES, AND SPONSORS

Throughout the Kennedy-McNamara missile build-up of the early 1960s, there existed various groups and individuals both

62. See James Baar and William E. Howard, *Polaris!*, pp. 198, 212–17.
63. Enthoven and Smith, *How Much is Enough?*, pp. 21, 171.
64. Testimony of McNamara, House Armed Services Committee, *Hearings on Military Posture* (1962), p. 3328.
65. Interview with Gen. Le May, 16 August 1970.
66. Gen. Curtis E. Le May, with MacKinlay Kantor, *Mission with Le May*, p. 532.
67. See Sapolsky, *The Polaris System Development*, p. 40; and Richard Witkin, *New York Times*, 28 March 1960, p. 22.

within and without the administration who opposed the extent of that build-up. Instead of the 1,710 strategic missiles which were eventually deployed by the United States, these people favored only "a few hundred such missiles."

The "Overkill" Theorists. Throughout 1962–64, several members of the U.S. Congress argued that the United States had developed an "overkill" posture, or a capability of destroying Russia's population and industrial centers many hundreds of times over. The argument is best exemplified in a report entitled *A Strategy for American Security*, prepared by Professor Seymour Melman and others at Columbia University in early 1963, and presented to the Congress during hearings on the F/Y 1964 defense budget. The report argued that the United States was overstocked in nuclear weapons, and reckoned a U.S. overkill capability of a factor of from 231 to 1,250; it recommended that from $16.45 to $25.65 billion be cut from the F/Y 1964 defense budget, including $1 to $2 billion for Air Force missile procurement.[68]

In 1963–64 Melman tried several times to contact members of the Kennedy-McNamara Administration to discuss his report. He was unable to see either the president or any one of his immediate staff; he did meet with the president's Council of Economic Advisers, but their main response was to express complete confidence in McNamara. Apparently the only people who responded affirmatively to Melman's analysis were "a few lower level staff around the National Security Council," including Marcus Raskin.[69] Melman did meet with many members of the Senate and House, and a number of these, including particularly Congressman William Fitz Ryan (Liberal Democrat, New York), questioned McNamara about the Melman Report. Melman himself also appeared before the Senate Appropriations Committee during hearings on the F/Y 1964 defense budget, and the Department of Defense was actually induced to make a

68. Seymour Melman, ed., *A Strategy for American Security*; Senate Appropriations Committee, *Department of Defense Appropriations for 1964*, pp. 1390–1415, 1626–29.
69. Letter from Seymour Melman, 31 May 1972; and interview with Marcus Raskin, 6 February 1973.

"detailed analysis" of the Melman Report for the committee.[70]

Within the Congress, the "overkill" theory and its implications as spelt out in the Melman Report were especially pushed by Senator George McGovern (Democrat, South Dakota). On 2 August 1963, McGovern made a memorable address in the Senate in which he proposed that $4 billion be cut from the strategic-weapons budget. (This represented about half of the F/Y 1964 strategic-forces budget.) McGovern said that U.S. stockpiles already represented a huge overkill capacity. "How many times," he asked the Senate, "is it necessary to kill a man or a nation?"[71] In the Senate on 24 September 1963, McGovern and three Democratic colleagues proposed an amendment to the F/Y 1964 defense budget to make a 10 percent cut in the procurement and research and development portions of the F/Y 1964 defense bill—a reduction of approximately $1.5 billion in the procurement of weapons and approximately $700 million in research and development. In speaking to this amendment, Senator McGovern argued that the cut was justified because the United States "already had sufficient nuclear power to deter or retaliate against any likely enemy action." According to McGovern, the United States had had a full deterrent capability "for at least two years." McGovern's amendment was, however, defeated in a crushing seventy-four-to-two rollcall vote.[72]

During testimony on the F/Y 1964 defense budget in early 1963, McNamara denied that the United States either had or planned to have any "overkill" capability. He testified that he had "examined alternative programs of lesser quantity and a lesser acceleration rate" than the program presented to Congress, but did not say why those lesser alternatives had been rejected.[73]

In his F/Y 1965 posture statement, transmitted to Congress in January 1964, McNamara paid explicit attention to the "over-kill" theory. However, because that theory would, in effect, have

70. See testimony of Deputy Sec. of Defense Roswell Gilpatric, Senate Appropriations Committee, *Department of Defense Appropriations for 1964*, p. 1626.
71. *Congressional Record, Senate*, 2 August 1963, pp. 13986–89.
72. *Congressional Record, Senate*, 24 September 1963, pp. 17882–83.
73. Testimony of McNamara, House Appropriations Committee, *Department of Defense Appropriations for 1964*, p. 235.

restricted U.S. strategic forces to those required for retaliation against cities only (and with the calculation assuming near optimum conditions), McNamara could not accept it. He did point out that the "overkill" theory had been debated within the Defense Department before he came to the Pentagon, but stated that he knew "of no responsible official within the Department who would support it today."[74]

During the 1950s, it is now known, several studies made independently by the U.S. Army and Navy argued that, even in the absence of agreements limiting force sizes, 100 to 200 relatively secure missiles would provide an adequate deterrent.[75] No doubt many in the Army and Navy still accepted this argument, but when the Kennedy Administration brought down its "budget-for-everyone," these services lost interest in their critique of the strategic forces.

As Army chief of staff under Eisenhower, General Maxwell D. Taylor had been an advocate of the "finite deterrence" posture, a position which argued that the purpose of nuclear weapons was to deter rather than to fight nuclear wars, and that the threat of destroying a finite (and relatively small) number of enemy targets (usually cities) would be a sufficient deterrent. In his *The Uncertain Trumpet*, published in 1960 after he had resigned as chief of staff, Taylor argued that "a few hundred reliable and accurate missiles" would be a sufficient deterrent force.[76]

In June 1961 Taylor was recalled to active service by President Kennedy as "Presidential Military Advisor for foreign and military policy and intelligence operations," and in July 1962 Kennedy appointed him chairman of the joint chiefs of staff. However, there is no direct evidence that General Taylor opposed the Kennedy-McNamara missile build-up. At least in his public pronouncements, General Taylor in fact argued against the position which he had held before 1961. During the nuclear test

74. Senate Armed Services Committee and Committee on Appropriations, *Department of Defense Appropriations for 1965*, p. 30.

75. Arthur T. Hadley, *The Nation's Safety and Arms Control*, p. 112; and Jerome Wiesner in *Arms Control, Disarmament, and National Security*, ed. Donald G. Brennan, pp. 217–18, 220.

76. Gen. Maxwell D. Taylor, *The Uncertain Trumpet*, p. 158.

ban treaty hearings in August 1963, for example, he stated that the president should have "the maximum number of options" made available to him, and that the "overkill" theory was far too constraining in its implications for targeting options.[77] However, Taylor's principal interests lay elsewhere—particularly, in 1961, with Berlin, and later with the building up of U.S. conventional and limited-war forces (including tactical nuclear weapons) and the development of the strategy of "flexible response." There is no doubt that Taylor, who was the military's chief representative, was not an advocate of relatively large strategic forces.[78]

Arms Control Studies. During the period of the Kennedy-McNamara strategic missile decision making, there were at least two official arms-control studies which concluded that the programmed missile build-up was excessive. The first was in early 1961, when William Foster (then about to become director of the U.S. Arms Control and Disarmament Agency) appointed a group, which included Jerome Wiesner, Paul Doty, Hans Bethe, and Henry Kissinger, to work on a plan for submission to the president for a comprehensive arms-control agreement with the Soviet Union and perhaps other nations. In constructing this plan, the group gave primary emphasis to reducing as well as to freezing the level of strategic nuclear delivery vehicles on the part of both the United States and the Soviet Union. The work of this group was directed mainly to determining what sort of disarmament policy to adopt for negotiations with the Soviet Union, rather than recommending policies that the United States should pursue to develop its own military strength in the absence of any disarmament agreement.

Nevertheless, it did address the question of what size the U.S. strategic nuclear force should be. In doing this, the group was given a framework of three choices with regard to numbers of delivery vehicles: 500, 1,000 or 1,500 missiles and/or bombers.

77. *Congressional Record, Senate*, 24 September 1963, pp. 17886–88.
78. General Taylor has said, in an interview on 27 July 1970, that he believed a force of 1,000 ICBMs was "excessive"; and he has since written in his memoirs that, "I favored only a few hundred strategic weapons" (see Gen. Maxwell D. Taylor, *Swords and Plowshares*, p. 172).

The group believed that even 500 seemed rather high; some members, such as Wiesner, argued for many fewer than 500 and even for as few as 100 or, at one meeting, 20. But it was forced by its terms of reference to formally decide on 500 delivery vehicles. It did, however, recognize that the administration was already committed to a larger program than this, and suggested that 1,000 be the cut-off point.[79]

Second, there was a series of studies made within the Department of Defense in 1963. At least by the middle of that year, DoD had accepted that it was legitimate to consider whether or not the United States could reduce its nuclear stockpiles and its warhead procurement. The existence of these studies was apparently first revealed in the press in a front-page story in the Sunday *New York Times* of 30 June 1963, which disclosed that:

> The administration is giving serious consideration to ordering the first substantial cutback in the production of atomic weapons since the United States began building up its nuclear arsenal after World War II. Behind the current study is a belief that the United States with an arsenal of tens of thousands of atomic weapons has a sufficient and perhaps an excessive number of nuclear arms to meet its military needs.

The *Times* reported a growing fear by the members of the Joint Committee on Atomic Energy that the production of atomic weapons is "coming to be based more on the capabilities of the Atomic Energy Commission to manufacture them than on the actual requirements of the military." It reported that at a recent Pentagon press briefing, "a highly placed Defense Department official" estimated that it might be desirable to make a $1 billion cut in this expenditure. Another policy-making official said, "We have tens or hundreds of times more weapons than we would ever drop even in an all-out war, and we have had more than we needed for at least two years."[80]

79. Betty Goetz Lall, "Mutual Deterrence: The Need for a New Definition," *Bulletin of the Atomic Scientists*, December 1977, p. 11. Further details of this study were obtained from correspondence with Lall, 20 May 1971, and in interviews with Paul Doty, 20 February 1973, and Marcus Raskin, 6 February 1973.

80. John W. Finney, "U.S. Considering Cut in its Output of Atomic Arms," *New York Times*, 30 June 1963.

On 13 August 1963, during hearings on the limited nuclear test ban treaty before the Senate Foreign Relations Committee, Senator Stuart Symington pointed out that none of the sections of this important news article had been challenged by any administration spokesman, and asked Secretary McNamara whether it would be safe to assume that the *New York Times* report was well grounded. In response to this question, McNamara had a reply inserted into the transcript of the hearings in which he argued that the United States did not have an excessive nuclear stockpile if one considered that it had to be ready for various kinds of limited and tactical wars as well as all-out nuclear war. But McNamara went on to say:

> the fact that we do not agree that our present warhead procurement level is excessive should not be taken to imply that our needs are unlimited. We are currently conducting detailed studies on this issue to see whether any cutback in weapons procurement is justified and if so, how much. The results of these studies, should they indicate that reductions in warhead procurement would be advisable, will be reflected in the fiscal 1965 budget now in preparation.[81]

Unfortunately, the results of these studies have never been disclosed. However, they definitely figured in the F/Y 1965 defense budget deliberations,[82] and may have aided McNamara in imposing the 1,000-missile ceiling on the Minuteman force.

The White House Staff. Various members of the Kennedy Administration have since disclosed publicly that the White House staff at the time thought the Minuteman build-up to be greater than national security required, and recommended holding down the force level to "a few hundred" missiles. According to Jerome Wiesner, for example, "some persons within the government" believed that a force of 200 to 400, including Polaris, Titan II, and "a few" Minuteman missiles, would be sufficient.[83]

81. Testimony of McNamara, Senate Foreign Relations Committee, *Nuclear Test Ban Treaty* (1963), p. 150.
82. Ibid.
83. See Jerome B. Wiesner, "Arms Control," p. 6; see also Arthur M. Schlesinger, Jr., *A Thousand Days*, p. 438; Richard J. Barnet, *The Economy of Death*,

Within the White House staff, opposition to the missile build-up centered on four groups—Jerome Wiesner, Spurgeon Keeny, and Vincent McRae in the President's Office of Science and Technology, and other scientists in the President's Science Advisory Committee (PSAC), such as James Killian, George Kistiakowsky, Paul Doty, and Harvey Brooks; McGeorge Bundy, Carl Kaysen and a number of lower-level staff such as Marcus Raskin in the Office of Special Assistant for National Security Affairs; members of the Bureau of the Budget (including BoB's Director David E. Bell, Deputy Director Willis H. Shapley, and Ellis H. Veatch in the National Security Division of the BoB); and several White House advisers, including Arthur Schlesinger and Theodore Sorensen. The three most active individuals were Kaysen, Keeny and Wiesner.[84]

In 1960 Wiesner had argued that a deterrent force "in the range of from 100 to 400 large nuclear weapons and accompanying delivery vehicles, either aircraft or missiles," would be adequate, and expressed his confidence in a force of 200 missiles.[85] In March 1961 Wiesner, now President Kennedy's special assistant for science and technology, argued that an adequate deterrent force would be "two hundred relatively secure missiles . . . even in the absence of an agreement limiting force size and permission for inspection."[86]

During the development of the F/Y 1963 defense budget in 1961, White House personnel worked closely with the Department of Defense. From the beginning of their involvement in the development of that budget, the White House staff argued, for a variety of reasons, for minimal missile levels. Strategically,

p. 178; Theodore C. Sorensen, *Kennedy*, p. 460. In this section, the term "White House staff" is used loosely, to cover not only the staff of the White House Office, but also the members of other offices of the Executive Office of the President.

84. Letter from Betty Goetz Lall, 20 May 1971; letter from Jerome B. Wiesner, 21 March 1972; letter from Marcus G. Raskin, 9 June 1971; Marcus G. Raskin in *The Pentagon Watchers*, ed. Leonard S. Rodberg and Derek Shearer, p. 77; Sorensen, *Kennedy*, p. 460; some thirteen of these former White House staff officers have been interviewed on their opposition to the build-up.

85. Jerome Wiesner in *Arms Control, Disarmament, and National Security*, ed. Brennan, pp. 217–20.

86. Donald W. Cox, *America's New Policy Makers*, p. 104.

most held an elementary minimum-deterrence position; some, such as Willis Shapley, believed that as few as 12 or 15 invulnerable missiles were a sufficient force; many saw this as the only position compatible with halting the strategic arms race with the Soviet Union. In the BoB in particular, the principal motivation was economic and budgetary; a strategic build-up was an unnecessary diversion of limited budgetary resources. Still others believed that as they had no vested interests in the missile program, their role was "to keep the process honest."[87]

The White House staff position on the U.S. missile program was formally put to the president and the secretary of defense in December 1961. In October Dr. Vincent McRae of Wiesner's office obtained from OSD the assumptions and parameters upon which McNamara's (then) planning figures of 950 and 1,050 Minuteman ICBMs were based. Working with others from the Office of Science and Technology (OST), NSC and BoB staffs, McRae was able to graph missile numbers against "strategic effectiveness" and show that the knee of the curve occurred at about 450 missiles. The extra 500–600 added virtually nothing to "effectiveness," regardless of the strategy followed (the projected 1966 Soviet force being relatively low in the fall 1961 NIEs).

There was much discussion of this graph within the White House staff, and Wiesner and Kaysen prepared a memorandum for the president on the basis of it. This memorandum actually recommended a Minuteman force of 600 missiles, going further around the curve than 450 for both security (insurance) and political reasons. The McRae graph and the Wiesner-Kaysen memorandum were discussed with Henry Rowen, Alain Enthoven, Adam Yarmolinsky, and Charles Hitch in DoD, and Theodore Sorensen. Two meetings were then held with McNamara and Kennedy. McNamara apparently accepted the logic of the White House staff's argument, but for bureaucratic political reasons he refused to compromise on his planning figures. Nine hundred and fifty Minuteman missiles, he said, was the smallest

87. Interviews with Willis H. Shapley, 8 February 1973; and Spurgeon M. Keeny, 7 February 1973.

number he could imagine asking Congress for and, in his words, "not get murdered."[88]

Wiesner, like the other members of the White House staff who opposed the missile build-up, had, of course, no authority to take his views out of the White House. And within the White House the staff members had no constituency in the sense of a quasi-autonomous political power base. The White House staff had only argument to back up its position, and this was apparently not sufficient. By 1962, with a larger strategic-force program an accomplished fact, the White House staff, and particularly Wiesner, were more interested in "holding the line" than in cutting that program back.[89]

The White House staff do see themselves as having had some success as forces of restraint. This was effected in two ways. First, they forced the Defense Department to explicate and justify its assumptions. In the words of one former White House staff member, "we were of some use to McNamara in questioning his own military advisors. . . . In a very small way, I think we helped McNamara keep his own organization honest." David Bell believes that at the budgetary meetings during 1961, the White House staff "had a very real impact on the judgments that were reached." McNamara's own "smallest number" might not have been as low as 950 or 1,050 without the pressure from the White House staff for lower numbers.[90] Secondly, the position of the White House staff, and particularly that of the BoB, was important after 1961, because the president was able to counterpose it to the higher requests of the Air Force at the budget meetings where the ceiling of 1,000 was finally imposed upon the Minuteman missile force.

88. McNamara reportedly made this statement to Wiesner on 9 December 1961 at the first and the smaller of the two meetings, but the sentiment was also made obvious to those at the second and larger meeting. Present at these meetings besides the president and McNamara, were Roswell Gilpatric, Charles Hitch, Theodore Sorensen, McGeorge Bundy, Jerome Wiesner, Carl Kaysen and David Bell (with some present at both). This discussion of those meetings and of the McRae graph and Wiesner/Kaysen memorandum is based on interviews with the participants.

89. Cox, *America's New Policy Makers*, p. 104.

90. Interviews with Spurgeon M. Keeny, 7 February 1973; and David E. Bell, 20 December 1972.

4 The Kennedy Administration and the Demise of the "Missile Gap"

When John F. Kennedy assumed office as president of the United States in January 1961, opinion on the missile gap remained divided. This was reflected in the political-military differences between the president-elect and the out-going president. In his farewell address of 12 January, President Eisenhower attempted officially for the last time to dispel what he believed was the myth of the missile gap, saying, "The bomber gap of several years ago was always a fiction and the 'missile gap' shows every sign of being the same."[1] President Eisenhower's confidence flowed directly from a December 1960 national intel-

1. *New York Times*, 13 January 1961.

ligence estimate which indicated that U.S. intelligence had failed
to identify positively any Soviet ICBM bases other than the two
Soviet missile test sites at Kapustin Yar and Tyuratam.[2]

However, when the Kennedy Administration took office, the
NIE still showed a "gap" favoring the Soviet Union in numbers
of ballistic missiles. The NIE actually contained several estimates, coinciding in the case of the military intelligence representatives with the strategic views and roles of their respective
services. The intelligence estimates of Soviet missiles then operational reportedly ranged from about 35 to 150, depending on
what and whose criteria were used.[3] The projections for mid-
1961 contained similar discrepancies; on 28 February General
Lemnitzer reportedly testified that the Army and Navy had estimated that the Russians would have 50 ICBMs on launching
pads by the middle of the year, whereas the Air Force estimate
was 200.[4] And in the projections for mid-1963, the Air Force
argued that the Russians would have 600 to 800 ICBMs, while
the Navy estimated only 200; the CIA took an intermediate position with 450.[5] A composite listing of the Soviet and U.S. strategic forces in being in early 1961, constructed from published
estimates at the time,[6] is presented in table 7.

Just two weeks after the inauguration of the new administration, an event occurred which presaged the end of the missile
gap myth. On the evening of 6 February 1961, McNamara,
along with Gilpatric and the assistant secretary of defense for
public affairs, Arthur Sylvester, held a "not-for-quotation-or-
attribution" "backgrounder" press conference, "to acquaint . . .
correspondents with the studies underway in the Department
[of Defense] relating to the review of the defense program and
the possible recommendations relating to the fiscal year 1962
budget."[7]

2. *New York Times*, 11 December 1960; and *Washington Star*, 15 January 1961.
3. *Missiles & Rockets*, 20 February 1961, p. 9.
4. *New York Times*, 1 March 1961.
5. Cf. Arthur M. Schlesinger, Jr., *A Thousand Days*, p. 438.
6. See Edgar M. Bottome, *The Missile Gap*, pp. 229–31, for a collection of
some of these estimates.
7. Testimony of McNamara, House Armed Services Committee, *Military
Posture Briefings* (1961), p. 646.

TABLE 7. *Soviet and U.S. Strategic Nuclear Delivery Forces,
January–February 1961*

UNITED STATES	USSR
12–15 Atlas ICBMs	30–65 SS-6 ICBMs
32 Polaris SLBMs	none comparable
30 Snark intercontinental cruise missiles	none comparable
60 Thor IRBMs based in United Kingdom 45 Jupiter IRBMs based in Italy and Turkey	500–800 MRBMs not capable of reaching the United States
600 B-52 long-range bombers	150–200 long-range bombers
1,100 B-47 medium-range bombers based in Europe	1,000–1,500 medium-range bombers not capable of reaching the United States
400 carrier-based bombers	none
2,000 Air Force fighter-bombers	none capable of reaching the United States

The emphasis at the meeting was not on the current U.S.
defense posture, "but rather on the process that we are now going through in the Department to provide for the defense needs
of the Nation over the months and years to come."[8] McNamara acquainted the reporters with the progress of the new
administration's defense reappraisal and disclosed his planning-
programming-budgeting system and his five-year package system at that meeting. During the meeting, however, reporters
asked for an early impression as to whether the Soviet Union
had more combat-ready missiles than the United States. McNamara replied that officials had not yet been fully briefed on the
situation, and that during the February defense reappraisal they
hoped to look into this point more closely. Reporters pressed for
at least some preliminary appraisal. McNamara then reportedly
stated that there were "no signs of a Soviet crash effort to build
ICBMs,"[9] and that Russia and the United States had "about the

8. Letter from McNamara to Dirksen, *Congressional Record, Senate*, 16 February 1961, p. 2177.
9. *Wall Street Journal*, 9 February 1961. McNamara later stated that this sen-
tence "is directly from our national intelligence estimates" (see House Armed
Services Committee, *Military Posture Briefings* [1961], p. 647).

same number of ICBMs at present—not a very large number," though he stressed that these "were early and concededly incomplete impressions" and that the question as stated distorted the real issues.[10]

Several reporters at the meeting had notes according to which McNamara said: "There is no missile gap today." This judgment was made on the basis of the December 1960 intelligence estimate, which indicated that the United States had experienced difficulties in finding Soviet missiles—nowhere near the 50 or so missiles supposed to be operational by January 1961 had been found.[11] However, the thrust of McNamara's remarks was that he was still looking for them. In other words, McNamara was not ready to reject the possibility of a missile gap that evening, and he apparently still thinks he did not do so.[12]

The next morning, 7 February, the front pages of almost every major U.S. newspaper came out with headlines that President Kennedy's advisers had reported that there was no missile gap. That afternoon, after meeting on his own initiative with other defense information officials (including Arthur Sylvester from the Department of Defense and Roger Jubly from the State Department), Pierre Salinger, White House press secretary, issued a statement, with President Kennedy's approval, that the reports were "absolutely wrong." Studies on the subject had still not been completed and "the stories, therefore, are inaccurate," he said.[13]

At a news conference the following morning, President Kennedy was asked directly whether or not he believed a missile gap

10. *Washington Post*, 7 February 1961; and *Wall Street Journal*, 9 February 1961.

11. Letter from Richard Fryklund, 16 February 1961. In addition to accepting the favorable conclusions of the December 1960 NIE, McNamara independently studied the satellite photographs on which the December estimates were based, and those which had been received subsequent to the December NIE, and agreed that there was little evidence of a crash Soviet ICBM program. During the transition, Secretary Gates had also impressed upon McNamara his sincere belief that there was no missile gap (interviews with Daniel Ellsberg, 8 October 1972; Roswell Gilpatric, 30 January 1973; Carl Kaysen, 19 December 1972; and Paul Nitze, 7 February 1973).

12. Letter from Richard Fryklund, 16 February 1971.

13. *New York Times*, 8 February 1961.

existed. He replied that he had spoken with McNamara the previous afternoon and,

> Mr. McNamara stated that . . . no study had been concluded in the Defense Department which could lead to any conclusion at this time as to whether there is a missile gap or not. In addition I talked this morning with Mr. Hitch, who . . . informed me that no study had been completed on this matter . . . [and] therefore it would be premature to reach a judgment as to whether there is a gap or not a gap.[14]

However, the president's comments did little to clear up the confusion over the news stories and the White House statement of 7 February, and the issue became the first major political flap of the new administration. In Congress, the Republicans expressed indignation at the reports and demanded that Kennedy apologize to Eisenhower for what they called "slander" by those Democrats who had charged there was a "missile gap." Congressman Thomas M. Pelly (Republican, Washington) sarcastically praised the Kennedy Administration for closing the missile gap in "just 18 days."[15] In the Senate, Symington responded for the Democrats with his charge that during 1960 the previous administration had prevented Kennedy from obtaining adequate information about U.S. defenses.[16] To add to this confusion it appears that there was an intelligence estimate still extant, which was leaked during this controversy, to the effect that the Soviets had a three-to-one advantage in ICBMs over the United States.[17]

Despite the confusion and contradictions, many people date the demise of the missile gap within the Kennedy Administration from the McNamara "backgrounder" of 6 February. This includes members of that administration—Arthur Schlesinger,

14. President Kennedy, news conference of 8 February 1961, in Harold W. Chase and Allen H. Lerman, *Kennedy and the Press*, pp. 19–20. In fact, while Hitch did say that the strategic weapons study was still incomplete, he did tell Kennedy that sufficient evidence was in hand to reject the possibility of a "missile gap" developing, but the president could not, politically, accept this finding (interview with Charles J. Hitch, 11 August 1970).

15. Cited in *Missiles & Rockets*, 13 February 1961, p. 14.

16. Senator Stuart Symington, *Congressional Record, Senate*, 9 February 1961, pp. 1955, 1958.

17. *Missiles & Rockets*, 13 February 1961, p. 14.

for example, states that McNamara dismissed the missile gap as "an illusion" at the February meeting.[18] It is certain that many people in the Pentagon (such as Deputy Secretary Gilpatric, Assistant Secretary Hitch, and Deputy Assistant Secretary Nitze) and many of Kennedy's White House staff (for example Jerome Wiesner, McGeorge Bundy, and David Bell) were convinced that there would be no missile gap.[19] But while McNamara was skeptical of the gap claims,[20] it appears he was still prepared to admit the possibility that it existed. In order to clear up some of the uncertainty, he in fact directed Adam Yarmolinsky, his special assistant, to determine the exact position of the United States vis-à-vis the Soviet Union at that time.[21]

President Kennedy's position was that regardless of his own current beliefs he could not afford to dismiss the missile gap. To admit so early that some of his severest criticisms of the Eisenhower Administration had been unfounded would no doubt have been too politically embarrassing. Had he publicly accepted the optimistic reports, it would have been politically more difficult for him to make the broad changes in U.S. defense posture that he felt were necessary.

Throughout February and March 1961, the interested media continued to press Kennedy for a definitive answer on the missile gap question, and each time the president replied that he was waiting for the completion of the defense study he had ordered the department to undertake. On 1 March 1961 Kennedy said that the study would be completed in several weeks and at that time he would make his recommendations to Congress.[22] On 8 March the president stated that the study would

18. Schlesinger, *A Thousand Days*, pp. 288, 438.
19. Interviews with Roswell Gilpatric, 30 January 1973; Charles Hitch, 11 August 1970; Paul Nitze, 7 February 1973; Jerome Wiesner, 20 February 1973; McGeorge Bundy, 18 December 1972; and David Bell, 20 December 1972.
20. See Roger Hilsman, *To Move a Nation*, p. 163.
21. At the same time McGeorge Bundy asked his deputy, Carl Kaysen, to also look at the question. With Henry Rowen from ISA (DoD) and Spurgeon Keeny from OST, Yarmolinsky and Kaysen continued their inquiry into the summer of 1961, by which time they were thoroughly convinced that the CIA evaluation of the Soviet missile program was more likely to be correct than that of the Air Force (interviews with Adam Yarmolinsky, 10 July 1970, and Carl Kaysen, 19 December 1972).
22. Chase and Lerman, *Kennedy and the Press*, p. 33.

be completed in several days, and that he would then indicate "what I believe to be the relative defense position of the United States."[23] But for various reasons the Washington press corps discontinued its questions on the missile gap from 8 March till early October 1961, and the issue was ignored in presidential news conferences.

One major reason for the disappearance of the issue from public view was that the agendas for the congressional hearings, which in the past had been the major source of information (and misinformation), and which provided the major access to the mass media for critics, were now under the control of the president's own party. The Democratic-run Congress made no effort to hurry up any public measuring of the missile gap, and plans for all hearings that might have become conspicuous were delayed until Kennedy pointed the way.[24]

When McNamara eventually did face the inevitable inquiry, before the House Committee on Appropriations on 7 April 1961, the issue was no longer news. Under intense questioning from the chairman of the committee, Mr. Mahon, McNamara reversed his reported stand of 6 February, and claimed that there was "evidence to indicate that a missile gap may exist up to and through 1964." But he immediately qualified his statement and indicated that the U.S. missile inventory "at the end of fiscal 1963, or at the end of calendar 1963," could exceed that of the Soviet Union and that the missile gap was "small."[25] However, the media showed no interest, and the ramifications of McNamara's testimony were not examined.

Perhaps another reason for the disappearance of the issue in the spring of 1961 was the tighter control which McNamara exercised over the intelligence estimates of the services. Very soon after he entered the Pentagon, McNamara experienced the self-serving use of intelligence estimates by the military,[26] and

23. Ibid., p. 41.
24. *Missiles & Rockets*, 13 March 1961, p. 11.
25. House Appropriations Committee, *Department of Defense Appropriations for 1962*, part 3, pp. 60–61.
26. For example, a visit to SAC Headquarters on 4 February 1961, in which Air Force estimates were used instead of J-2; and a briefing by Robert Kilmarx about a week after McNamara assumed office, in which Kilmarx had exagger-

determined to set up the Defense Intelligence Agency (DIA) to centralize intelligence throughout the Defense Department. President Kennedy was also understood to have asked McNamara in March 1961 to standardize all intelligence reports to lessen the range of estimates which had faced him when he assumed office.[27]

Within the intelligence community, however, the evidence on the Soviet missile program was still regarded as contradictory, and the intelligence community remained split as late as mid-1961. The June NIE was, in fact, the last of the missile gap NIEs.[28] Because it was not possible to get all the elements of the intelligence community to agree on a single June estimate, the text of the June NIE was prepared by the CIA and the other members of the United States Intelligence Board (USIB) were allowed to submit addenda. In the NIE proper, the CIA argued that the Soviet Union had some 125 to 150 ICBMs deployed. Of the services, only the Army accepted this estimate. The Air Force estimate was still as high as 300 Soviet missiles deployed, while the Navy reckoned only ten. The State Department's Bureau of Intelligence and Research (INR) gave an estimate which was slightly higher than the NIE proper, estimating that about 160 Soviet ICBMs were operational.[29] At this time the United States had only 27 Atlas D missiles operational, though three Polaris submarines (48 missiles) had been deployed. This gave the Soviet Union an estimated two-to-one advantage in missiles, though the American "mix" still ensured U.S. "strategic superiority."

---

ated the intelligence to support the position and policies of the Air Force (interview with Robert Kilmarx, 22 July 1970).

27. See *Newsweek*, 3 April 1961, p. 21. The DIA was established on 1 August 1961, and became operational in October. Separate service intelligence elements were not eliminated, but they lost representation in the highest councils of the intelligence community and many of their functions were taken over by the DIA.

28. Hilsman, *To Move a Nation*, p. 163; interviews with Hilsman, 27 May and 12 June 1970, and interview with Daniel Ellsberg, 24 August 1970. According to Andrew Marshall, it was realized by many people as soon as the June NIE was produced that its estimates were too high (interview, 13 February 1973).

29. Interview with Roger Hilsman, who prepared the INR addendum, 12 June 1970; and interviews with Daniel Ellsberg, 24 August 1970 and 8 October 1972.

In late August or early September 1961, the United States received "positive" intelligence that the Soviet Union had elected to deploy relatively few of its SS-6 ICBMs, and the September 1961 NIE of Soviet missile deployment was correspondingly downgraded.[30] Joseph Alsop, one of the earliest and most prominent of the columnists who had perpetuated the missile gap thesis, reported on 25 September 1961 that intelligence estimates had been recalculated, and the estimate of Soviet ICBMs "drastically reduced" to well under 50 missiles.[31] Of only slightly less importance than this drastic downgrading of the U.S. NIE is the fact that for the first time in many years the Air Force subscribed to the lower estimates of Soviet missile strength that had been accepted before the USIB by the Army and Navy. (Only SAC remained adamant and would not accept the more optimistic interpretations placed on the recent intelligence information.[32] SAC has, however, no separate representation on the USIB.)

At a press conference on 11 October 1961, Kennedy was asked for the first time since 15 March about the adequacy and credibility of U.S. nuclear strength. In his response, the president did not deal with the question of comparative United States–Soviet strategic power, but emphasized the growing nuclear power of the United States brought about by the acceleration of the U.S. missile program since he came to office.[33]

The first public, unequivocal administration statement on comparative United States–Soviet nuclear strength was made

30. Interviews with Roger Hilsman, 27 May and 12 June 1970, and interview with Daniel Ellsberg, 24 August 1970.

31. Joseph Alsop, "Matter of Fact: Facts about the Missile Balance," *Washington Post*, 25 September 1961. Just what the September NIE figure was remains unclear. Philip Klass, in *Secret Sentries in Space*, p. 107, has reported that "the figure was a mere 14 missiles." Daniel Ellsberg has stated, however, that the September NIE contained no definite figure. Rather, according to Ellsberg, it said either the Soviets had "a few missiles," or "less than an IOC," or "an IOC at most," with IOC defined as "10 to 12" missiles (interviews with Daniel Ellsberg, 24 August 1970 and 8 October 1972).

32. Joseph Alsop, *Washington Post*, 25 October 1961; Jack Raymond, *New York Times*, 19 November 1961; editorial, *New York Times*, 20 November 1961; Klass, *Secret Sentries in Space*, pp. 66–67; and interviews with Roger Hilsman, 12 June 1970 and Herbert Scoville, 9 February 1973.

33. Chase and Lerman, *Kennedy and the Press*, p. 119.

several days later by a high official in the Defense Department. Deputy Secretary of Defense Roswell Gilpatric, in an address before the Business Council at Hot Springs, Va., stated on 21 October that the United States had "a second strike capability which is at least as extensive as what the Soviets can deliver by striking first."[34] In other words, the United States would have a larger nuclear delivery system left after a surprise attack than the nuclear force which the Soviet Union could employ in its first strike.

Gilpatric's speech was deliberately prepared by the administration as a message to the Soviet Union (with Berlin in the background) that the United States knew that the Soviets had very few ICBMs deployed. According to Roger Hilsman,

> The American decision to let the Soviets know that we knew was deliberate. But it was made only after much agonizing, since everyone involved recognized that telling the Soviets what we knew entailed considerable risk. Forewarned, the Soviets would undoubtedly speed up their ICBM program. . . .
> On the other hand, Khrushchev's several ultimatums on Berlin indicated that, if he were allowed to continue to assume that we still believed in the missile gap, he would probably bring the world dangerously close to war. Thus the decision was reached to go ahead with telling the Soviets that we now knew.[35]

The deliberation preceding this decision had included the very highest levels of the administration—McNamara, Rusk, McGeorge Bundy, Hilsman, Allen Dulles, and President Kennedy himself. Gilpatric was chosen as the instrument because a speech by the deputy secretary of defense was high enough to be convincing to the Soviets but not so high as to be threatening, which a speech by the president, the secretary of state, or the secretary of defense might well have been.[36] According to Hilsman,

> Among other ways of informing the Soviets, the Gilpatric speech was followed by a round of briefings for our allies—deliberately

34. Cited in Robert M. Slusser, *The Berlin Crisis of 1961* (Baltimore: Johns Hopkins University Press, 1973), pp. 370–76.
35. Hilsman, *To Move a Nation*, p. 163.
36. Interview with Roswell Gilpatric, 30 January 1973.

including some whom we knew were penetrated, so as to reinforce and confirm through Soviet intelligence channels the message carried openly through the Gilpatric speech.[37]

In late September Paul Nitze, assistant secretary of defense for international security affairs, had had lunch with the Soviet ambassador, Mikhail Menshikov, during which Nitze made it clear that the United States was aware that the Soviets had concentrated on their IRBM and medium-range ballistic missile (MRBM) programs while foregoing any extensive ICBM deployment.[38] And on 6 October President Kennedy had met with Soviet Foreign Minister Andrei Gromyko, and is alleged to have shown him American satellite photographs indicating exactly how few ICBMs the Soviets really had.[39] As of October 1961 the U.S. administration had officially dismissed the current existence or future possibility of a missile gap favoring the Soviet Union.

At a press conference on 8 November 1961, Kennedy discussed his 1960 campaign charges of American military inadequacy. He stated that many members of the Eisenhower Administration, including President Eisenhower, had admitted that the United States lagged behind the Soviet Union in missile development, and that "statements that I made represented the best of my information based on public statements by those in a position to know in the late years of the 1950's." He went on to claim that "based on our present assessments and our intelligence, we . . . would not trade places with anyone in the world," and concluded that the military power of the United States was "second to none."[40] Several days later McNamara certified Russia's strategic military inferiority, stating, "I believe we have nuclear power several times that of the Soviet Union."[41] By the time President Kennedy and Secretary of Defense McNamara made their statements in November, the majority of the popular press

37. Hilsman, *To Move a Nation*, pp. 163–64.
38. Interviews with Marvin Stern, 21 August 1970, and Paul Nitze, 7 February 1973.
39. Klass, *Secret Sentries in Space*, pp. 107–8.
40. Chase and Lerman, *Kennedy and the Press*, p. 125.
41. "Was There Ever a 'Missile Gap'—or Just an Intelligence Gap?" *Newsweek*, 13 November 1961, p. 23, quoting the secretary of defense in an interview.

already reflected the repudiation of the missile gap. For example, the *New York Times* printed the following figures from "a recent intelligence study" on the comparative operational missiles of the United States and the Soviet Union capable of reaching the enemy's territory:[42]

United States	Soviet Union
48 Atlas	50 SS-6 ICBMs
80 Polaris	
60 Thor	
45 Jupiter	

On 27 November the *New York Times* asserted in its final editorial on the subject that, "The 'missile gap' like the 'bomber gap' before it is now being consigned to the limbo of synthetic issues, where it has always belonged."[43] As an issue in the continuing debates over U.S. defense policy, the missile gap was now passé. Later developments simply established the superiority of the United States in ICBMs beyond all doubt.

It is impossible to determine the exact date in 1961 when the missile-gap myth was destroyed. Aside from the unwillingness of the Kennedy Administration to admit the fact that President Kennedy had helped to create the myth, there was a natural inertia within the United States operating against the change of an accepted belief.[44] And there remains genuine disagreement among ex-officials of the Kennedy Administration and among defense experts and commentators. On the one hand, many believe that the missile gap was dismissed very soon after the administration assumed office, and McNamara's 6 February "missile gaffe" is often taken as evincing this.[45] On the other

42. *New York Times*, 19 November 1961.
43. *New York Times*, "The Missile Gap" (editorial), 27 November 1961.
44. Bottome, *The Missile Gap*, p. 164.
45. Among ex-officials who take this view, see Schlesinger, *A Thousand Days*, p. 438; McGeorge Bundy, "The Presidency and the Peace," p. 354; Jerome B. Wiesner, "Arms Control," p. 6; and Herbert F. York, *Race to Oblivion*, pp. 57, 147.

Administration personnel who stated in interviews that the missile gap was dismissed in early 1961 were Charles Hitch, Paul Nitze, and Norman Paul from DoD, David Bell and McGeorge Bundy from the White House staff, and James Killian, who was appointed chairman of President Kennedy's Foreign Intelligence Advisory Committee in April 1961. Many members of the administration

hand, many argue that it was not until the summer and fall of 1961 that the Americans discovered the true situation, and the June 1961 NIE is used to support this.[46] Two extremely significant developments occurred during 1960–61 which may help to illumine this question—the successful launching by the United States of photographic reconnaissance satellites, and the "defection" to the West of Oleg Penkovsky.

Although the United States officially refused until 1977 even to acknowledge publicly the existence of an American reconnaissance satellite program,[47] many ex-officials have nevertheless asserted in private that photographs taken by spy-in-the-sky satellites provided the information on the basis of which the missile gap question was dismissed. And, of course, among the "informed public," the assertion that SAMOS satellites were responsible for this is widespread.

The first successful launch of a SAMOS vehicle, SAMOS II, took place from Pt. Arguello, California, on 31 January 1961. The camera-carrying satellite was placed into a near-circular polar orbit allowing it to pass over the Soviet Union seven times a day; the photographs were then radioed down to several ground stations.[48]

Although the SAMOS II satellite remained in orbit for over a year, the transmitters aboard the vehicle were capable of operating for only about 20 days. Another limiting factor in its useful

---

were at this time persuaded by the December 1960 NIE, the satellite reconnaissance photographs of the Soviet Union, and the arguments of former Secretary Gates, which had so persuaded McNamara. Others became convinced on the basis of their own independent evaluations. Those officials who had come from the RAND Corporation, or who had close contacts with RAND, were apparently particularly skeptical of the "missile gap" because of the work on the politics of the Soviet strategic weapons procurement done at RAND by Andrew Marshall and Joseph Loftus, the intelligence input of which came from colleagues in the CIA. Marshall discussed this work with Charles Hitch, Henry Rowen, and Alain Enthoven in the Pentagon, who "over time tended to agree with the arguments" (interviews with Daniel Ellsberg, 8 October 1972, and Andrew Marshall, 13 February 1973).

46. Former officials who place the demise of the "missile gap" issue at much later in 1961 include Theodore C. Sorensen, *Kennedy*, p. 677; Hilsman, *To Move a Nation*, p. 163; and Daniel Ellsberg, *Papers on the War* (New York: Simon & Schuster, 1972), p. 286, *n.* 12.

47. *Aviation Week & Space Technology*, 4 July 1977, p. 13.

48. *New York Times*, 1 February 1961.

life was the exhaustion of the gas supply for the jets which maintained the vehicle in its nose-down attitude. And, finally, the extremely sensitive photographic equipment used in the SAMOS vehicles has an effective life span of only about 30 days. SAMOS II could not, therefore, have been operational beyond the end of February 1961.[49] By this time, however, more than enough photographs had been transmitted to ground stations "to inventory Soviet ICBM strength." Several months were then needed to analyze these photographs.[50]

The next two attempts at a SAMOS launch, those of SAMOS III and SAMOS IV on 9 September and 22 November 1961 respectively, both failed, and it was not until 22 December that the United States successfully placed another SAMOS into orbit.[51] Hence, if it was photographs from SAMOS spy vehicles which convinced the Kennedy Administration during 1961 that Soviet missile deployment would not lead to a missile gap, then that conviction must have been reached during the spring of that year.

Apparently of more importance than SAMOS satellites in the demise of the missile gap issue, however, were a series of super-secret satellites developed by the CIA, and launched under cover of the Air Force's "Discoverer biosatellite program."[52] It is these CIA satellites which former members of the Kennedy Administration are referring to when they speak, with reference to the demise of the missile-gap question, of "new technology introduced at the end of 1960."[53]

The first of these satellites containing reconnaissance cameras,

49. *Missiles & Rockets*, 6 February 1961, p. 15, and 24 July 1961, p. 15; and *Space/Aeronautics*, January 1965, p. 98.

50. Klass, *Secret Sentries in Space*, p. 105.

51. Ibid., pp. 111–12.

52. Ibid., pp. 96–107. In an interview on 9 February 1973, Herbert Scoville (former assistant director of the CIA for science and technology) went so far as to say: "Forget about the early SAMOS satellites—they never produced anything useful at all."

53. Interviews with Robert Kilmarx, 22 July 1970; George Rathjens, 11 July 1970; Paul Nitze, 7 February 1973; David Bell, 20 December 1972; and Karl Kaysen, 19 December 1972. Unlike the Air Force SAMOS satellites, which used radio transmission, these CIA satellites used recoverable capsules for retrieving the photographic information (see George B. Kistiakowsky, *A Scientist in the White House*, pp. 245–46).

Discoverer 14, was launched on 19 August 1960, and recovered the next day. Two more successful recoveries of film capsules were made before January 1961, that is before the Kennedy Administration took office.[54] These fall 1960 launches were followed by a gap of some six months (apart from the SAMOS II launch of 31 January 1961). Then, from mid-June to mid-September 1961, four capsules containing reconnaissance photographs were recovered from Discoverer satellites.[55] These were followed by the drastic downgrading of the NIE of operational Soviet ICBMs in mid-September 1961.

By this time, complete satellite photographic coverage of the Soviet Union was in hand. This included detailed photographs of Plesetsk, obtained "in late August or early September" 1961[56] (presumably from the August 30 launch).

However, the very limited number of satellites which were involved, the almost constant summer cloud coverage over Plesetsk, where the SS-6s were being emplaced, the questionable reliability of the new technology (such as photographic interpretation, faulty telemetry, etc.) and the fact that satellite photographs could provide, at best, only negative intelligence—that few missiles had been found—make it unlikely that spy satellites, by themselves, could have been wholly responsible for the demise of the missile-gap issue.

It has been widely alleged that President Kennedy was finally convinced of the unlikelihood of a missile gap through intelligence received from Oleg Penkovsky. From the spring of 1961 to the fall of 1962, when he was arrested, Penkovsky passed along to Britain and the United States some 5,000 separate items of top-secret military, political, and economic intelligence pho-

54. Discoverer 17 and Discoverer 18, launched on 12 November 1960, and 7 December 1960 respectively (see Klass, *Secret Sentries in Space*, pp. 98–104). According to Herbert Scoville, Discoverers 17 and 18 were "the key ones" before the Kennedy period (interview, 9 February 1973).

55. These successful recoveries were of Discoverer 25, launched on 16 June 1961; Discoverer 26, 7 July; Discoverer 29, 30 August; and Discoverer 30, launched on 12 September 1961 (see Klass, *Secret Sentries in Space*, pp. 71, 106). The next successful recovery was that of Discoverer 32, launched on 13 October 1961.

56. Interviews with Roger Hilsman, 27 May and 12 June 1970.

tographed on microfilm, as well as a great number of reports written by himself on individual subjects.[57]

In April 1961 Penkovsky is reported to have been asked by the United States to deliver a comprehensive, expert, and detailed analysis of the Russian missile program—particularly numbers and schedules. In May 1961 he is said to have delivered three installments of microfilm which contained the number of Soviet missiles deployed, highly technical information on the diffi- culties the Russians had encountered with the giant SS-6 ICBM, excerpts from the minutes of the top-level meetings at which it was decided to scrap the SS-6, and, finally, the admission from official records that the program was nearly a year behind schedule.[58]

Penkovsky's actual significance in the demise of the missile gap is difficult to assess. It is hard to believe he would have been the prime source for the administration's reevaluation—U.S. policy being based on the word of a Soviet officer—but he undoubtedly added to the administration's confidence in that reevaluation. Whatever Penkovsky's contribution was, it would have been felt by the end of the summer of 1961.

The really important question is when the missile gap ceased to be a significant issue for policy, programming, and budgetary purposes. In looking at this question, two major considerations must be kept in mind. First, the demise of the missile gap must have been a *process*, regardless of when it was finally dismissed. Thorough study of the Eisenhower intelligence information and

57. Penkovsky was an officer in Soviet military intelligence (GRU) with the rank of colonel, whose operational cover was a deputy division chief in the State Committee for the Coordination of Scientific Research Work (see Oleg Pen- kovsky, *The Penkovsky Papers*). Although there is considerable doubt about the complete authenticity of the *Papers*, there is no doubt that Penkovsky was an agent of the first importance (see Victor Marchetti and John D. Marks, *The CIA and the Cult of Intelligence* [New York: Dell, 1975], pp. 183–84, 294). Then CIA Director Richard Helms stated in 1971 that it was photographs of Soviet missiles provided by Penkovsky which enabled the United States to identify those em- placed in Cuba in October, 1962 (see the New York *Herald Tribune*, 15 April 1971, p. 1). Another former high-level member of the CIA stated in a private interview in 1973 that "there is no question but that we got some information on Soviet missiles from Penkovsky."
58. Andrew Tully, *The Super Spies*, p. 35.

acquaintance with the source(s) of his confidence undoubtedly convinced many Kennedy officials soon after the inauguration; others would have had their own confidence in the certainty of a missile gap shaken. Those initially more skeptical of the higher estimates of Soviet ICBMs and those closest to the intelligence reevaluations as they were being made by the Kennedy Administration would have dismissed the missile gap earlier, while those whose defense policies and positions were being enhanced by the missile gap and those farthest from the incoming intelligence would have held out longest.

Secondly, since new intelligence must be received, interpreted, digested, accepted, and then passed on to the relevant policy-making office, the second-level policy makers would have been operating under an "intelligence lag." Those who, say, in June 1961 drew up the Air Force's 3 July submission for 3,190 ICBMs would undoubtedly not have known of Penkovsky's revelations of May. It would probably have taken at least two months for revised NIEs to be fully absorbed throughout the top planning levels of the Pentagon.[59]

Given these two considerations, whether the missile gap was actually dismissed in February or September 1961 loses much of its importance. The January and March missile decisions were taken too early for any February reevaluation to have been more than superficially relevant; and the whole administration was apparently convinced of the disappearance of the missile gap by the fall of 1961, when the F/Y 1963 decisions were made.

59. One very rough measure of this is the time it takes for such NIEs to be leaked to the press. In 1961, this was about two months. Bottome (*The Missile Gap*, p. 279) found it was generally four months during 1958–60. For intelligence material which might by its nature compromise the integrity of the source, the lag would be longer.

part two

The Strategic Missile Decisions
of the Kennedy-McNamara Administration,
1961–1964

5 Revising the Eisenhower Strategic Missile Program

Within the first ten weeks of taking office on 20 January 1961, the Kennedy Administration made two major changes in the strategic missile program which it had inherited from Eisenhower. These were, obviously, very hastily prepared. They were amendments to the F/Y 1961 defense budget, then current, and to the F/Y 1962 defense budget, to take effect from 1 July 1961, and given the long lead-times involved in deploying either submarines at sea or missiles on pads or in silos, they could do little to increase the programmed deployment of strategic missiles over the relevant planning period (to 30 June 1962). They were significant, however, because they accelerated Polaris submarine construction and Minuteman production to the maximum that was feasible within the period before F/Y 1963 funds would come into use, i.e., the maximum that could have been incorporated into the F/Y 1961 and F/Y 1962 defense budgets at that time. Since the Soviet Union, at least, knew that it was not favored by a missile gap, this must have caused serious apprehension in Moscow.

More especially, these decisions of January–March 1961 were responsible for changing the qualitative character of the U.S. strategic missile posture. Essentially the effect of these decisions was to determine that, for the next decade, U.S. strategic missile forces would be overwhelmingly composed of small-payload missiles, deployed aboard submarines or in hardened silos, rather than the large-payload Atlas and Titan ICBMs. The strategic consequences of such a change were enormous, and have lasted to the present day.

THE STATE OF THE UNION MESSAGE, 30 JANUARY 1961: "MAKING HASTE SLOWLY"

On 30 January 1961, only ten days after his inauguration, President Kennedy delivered his first State of the Union message to the U.S. Congress.[1] The speech consisted of a stark assessment of the national situation, a call for action and support, and a partial specification of steps to be taken by the new administration to remedy this bleak situation, including, inter alia, several changes in the F/Y 1961 defense program. Kennedy stated that, "in the past, lack of a consistent, coherent military strategy, the absence of basic assumptions about our national requirements and the faulty estimates and duplication arising from inter-service rivalries" had led to widespread doubts in the United States about the adequacy of American defenses. In order to resolve these doubts, he announced, he had instructed Secretary McNamara to undertake a wholesale reappraisal of "our entire defense strategy" and to present his preliminary conclusions by the end of February. However, "three new steps most clearly needed now" were to be initiated immediately: first, an increase in American air-lift capacity; second, "prompt action to step up

1. Department of State *Bulletin* 44 (13 February 1961): 207–14.

our Polaris submarine program"; and third, the acceleration of "our entire missile program."

In his first press conference, on 2 February 1961, McNamara detailed the actual measures involved. To accelerate the Polaris program, the number of FBM submarine keels approved by the administration for F/Y 1961 had been increased from five to ten. The final Eisenhower budget, submitted to Congress two weeks before for F/Y 1962, had authorized five new submarines and long-lead-time items for five more. What Kennedy did was simply to take these submarines out of the F/Y 1962 budget and put them in the budget for F/Y 1961. In effect, he doubled the F/Y 1961 order, and left the F/Y 1962 order to be filled in later. No new money was required for this acceleration—$128 million in unallocated funds already held by the Navy was to be used, as well as some $600 to $800 million which could be extracted from the F/Y 1962 budget then before Congress. The Kennedy order meant that 9 to 12 months could be saved in building the additional five submarines. Starting in October 1963, the Navy would begin to launch a Polaris submarine each month, so that instead of having 19 submarines operational sometime in 1965, the United States would have that number (instead of 14) by about March 1964. McNamara reported that any further action on Kennedy's promise to speed up "our entire missile program" was being held over until the current defense reappraisal had been concluded.[2]

It seems that Kennedy had decided on the need for writing his own State of the Union message soon after his election, if only to dramatize the new urgency he had said he would infuse into the defense effort. He appears to have decided firmly upon some action to improve the U.S. strategic posture considerably before the new administration took office on 20 January—certainly before most of his top-level civilian Pentagon officials (such as Enthoven and Hitch) had either been appointed or had arrived in Washington.[3] It was apparent from Kennedy's inaugural

2. See *New York Times*, 31 January and 1 February 1961; *Missiles & Rockets*, 6 February 1961, p. 39; and *Newsweek*, 13 February 1961, p. 18.
3. Interview with Enthoven, 17 August 1970.

address on 20 January, in which he never mentioned domestic problems, that defense and foreign affairs would occupy his first weeks as president. The day after this address, in fact, Kennedy not only began meeting with Secretary of State Rusk, Secretary of Defense McNamara, and other foreign-policy aides to formulate his State of the Union message,[4] but the BoB also began working on a plan to accelerate the Polaris program.[5]

Support for Polaris in this context came from a variety of sources, and for several disparate reasons. Kennedy himself seems at that time to have had a personal predilection for Polaris over other strategic missile systems, and an acceleration of the Polaris program would have satisfied those in his 1960 entourage who had been worrying about U.S. missile numbers as well as those who were more concerned with vulnerability.[6]

Kennedy's White House staff looked upon Polaris with particular favor. Jerome Wiesner, the president's science adviser and an ardent arms controller, and John J. McCloy, then Kennedy's special disarmament adviser, both participated in the decision making and supported an acceleration of the Polaris program on arms-control grounds. Within the president's Science Advisory Committee (PSAC) there was also a general feeling in favor of Polaris rather than land-based missiles, both because of the relative invulnerability of Polaris and because of the acceptance within PSAC of the minimum-deterrence doctrine. Members of PSAC conveyed this feeling to the president both directly and through Wiesner and McCloy.[7]

Prior to the inauguration, the BoB had prepared a series of "Transition Papers" which included alternative weapons programs to those programmed by the Eisenhower Administration; one alternative included was the acceleration of the Polaris program. These "Transition Papers" were discussed with David Bell and Secretary-designate McNamara in early January before they

4. *Business Week*, 28 January 1961, pp. 32–33.

5. Interview with Ellis H. Veatch, Director of National Security Division, BoB, 6 February 1973.

6. See Theodore C. Sorensen, *Kennedy*, p. 667.

7. *Business Week*, 28 January 1961, p. 33; and interviews with former PSAC members, Harvey Brooks, 15 January 1973, and George Kistiakowsky, 20 February 1973.

had officially taken office. According to Bell, the BoB analysis showed that the Polaris program was progressing well, that the system was relatively invulnerable, and that the program was such that it could be stepped up immediately. These points were made clear to McNamara. Bell himself decided the program should be accelerated, and when he found that "McNamara was arriving at the same conclusion he urged him to take the matter to the President immediately." [8]

McNamara also received support for a Polaris acceleration from the Pentagon. Very early in January, he and his deputy, Roswell Gilpatric, received a letter from Theodore Sorensen in which the president-elect asked that a wide range of defense questions and military programs be examined; one question was directed to the status of the Polaris program. McNamara and Gilpatric established a number of task forces, mainly consisting of hold-over officials from the Eisenhower Administration, to consider these questions and programs, and they "found almost complete unanimity, even from the Air Force, in support of Polaris . . . nobody questioned it." According to Gilpatric, the Polaris program was "the easiest to get hold of." The program was well organized and it was managed from Washington, whereas neither McNamara nor Gilpatric had yet visited the Air Force's systems command. [9]

The final decision on the precise details of the action on strategic weapons was made soon after the inauguration, by McNamara and Gilpatric, principally on the advice of Dr. Marvin Stern, then assistant director of DDR&E. [10] From a development point of view, Polaris was considered more sure than Minuteman. Six FBM submarines had already been launched (two were actually on station) and the seventh was launched on 2 February 1961, whereas the Minuteman had yet to undergo a full-scale test. The next official step was a formal recommendation from Secretary McNamara to the president that the Polaris program be accelerated.

8. See Lester Tanzer, ed., *The Kennedy Circle* (New York: Luce, 1961), pp. 85–86; and interview with David Bell, 20 December 1972.

9. Interview with Roswell Gilpatric, 30 January 1973.

10. Interview with Dr. Marvin Stern, 21 August 1970.

There can be no question that the general decision to accelerate at least part of the U.S. strategic missile program at this stage
was a personal decision by Kennedy, and that any genuine dangers faced by the United States at that time were only one consideration. His decision was supported, even welcomed, by his
leading defense advisers and the Pentagon (again, for several
disparate reasons), who converted the general decision into concrete action—although the specific move, a speed-up of Polaris,
was actually opposed by the relevant service.[11]

As a basis for the decision, the new administration had only
the Nitze and Wiesner task force reports prepared during the
interregnum, and WSEG No. 50, and these were of little actual
value. The task force reports were hastily prepared and superficial, and their authors did not have access to classified information;[12] and the WSEG study was not immediately made available
to the new administration.[13] It was not until late December 1960
that Kennedy asked McNamara to examine the question of
whether additional funds should be requested for the missile
programs, and the secretary had still been unable to answer this
definitively by the end of January 1961.[14]

The decision had, then, been preceded by no thorough study,
but was rather based on the conjunction of Kennedy's belief in
the need for action in the strategic field with a "gut feeling"
among his civilian advisers that Polaris was the only program
that they could recommend with assurance. In contrast to the
urgency which Kennedy sought to convey with the State of the
Union message, and the stress the message placed on positive
moves to improve the U.S. strategic posture, the 30 January
decision was actually, both from a military and a monetary

11. Interview with Adm. Arleigh Burke, 29 July 1970. Navy opposition to an
acceleration of the Polaris program at this time was due to the fear of a lack of
follow-on orders in the mid-1960s, and of block obsolescence of the FBM submarine fleet in the future.

12. The admittedly "hasty" Wiesner report, for example, has been described
as "a melange of observations based on superficial study." Roscoe Drummond,
cited in Lloyd S. Swenson, James M. Grimwood and Charles C. Alexander,
This New Ocean: A History of Project Mercury (Washington, D.C.: National Aeronautics and Space Administration, 1966), p. 306.

13. Interview with Dr. Marvin Stern, 21 August 1970; and George W. Rathjens, 11 July 1970.

14. Sorensen, *Kennedy*, pp. 666–67.

standpoint, extremely cautious. No new missiles were authorized, and no new funds were requested for missiles. None of the concrete steps outlined in the message added much to overall U.S. military power. It was, in the apt words of *Newsweek*, merely a reflection of the Kennedy decision "to make haste slowly." [15]

THE SPECIAL MESSAGE TO CONGRESS, 28 MARCH 1961: "A QUICK AND DIRTY LOOK"

By March 1961 the defense reappraisal which President Kennedy had ordered in January had proceeded sufficiently far for the administration "to present the most urgent and obvious recommendations for inclusion in the fiscal 1962 budget." These recommendations were announced by Kennedy in a special message to Congress on 28 March 1961.[16]

This message was far more reasoned in its account of the U.S. defense situation and far less alarmist than his message of 30 January. It stands out, in fact, as a basic document of U.S. defense policy, "the first full statement of a coherent national defense doctrine for the age of mutual nuclear capabilities," [17] applying decision and positive direction to what had been an increasingly shapeless and directionless situation. The tone of the message was one of confidence ("Our military position today is strong"); its purpose was to rationalize this position and ensure that the same could be said in the future. The basic strategic policy, as outlined by Kennedy, was that American strength

> must be adequate to deter any deliberate nuclear attack on the United States or our allies—by making clear to any potential aggressor that sufficient retaliatory forces will be able to survive a first strike and penetrate his defenses in order to inflict unacceptable losses upon him.

Moreover, in addition to this basic deterrent capability, U.S. strategy should be flexible and controlled.[18]

15. *Newsweek*, 13 February 1961, p. 18.
16. *Message from the President of the United States Relative to Recommendations Relating to our Defense Effort*, 28 March 1961, House of Representatives, 87th Cong., 1st sess., document no. 123. [Hereafter referred to as *Special Message*.]
17. Sorensen, *Kennedy*, p. 667.
18. *Special Message*, pp. 2–5.

In order to implement these basic defense policies, Kennedy recommended action in four areas to strengthen and protect the United States' strategic deterrent and defenses. The first area involved improvement of the missile deterrent. Specifically, Kennedy strongly recommended that the Polaris program "be greatly expanded and accelerated." Second, the bomber deterrent was to be protected by an increased ground alert and the development of a capacity to implement an airborne alert at short notice. Third, the continental defense and warning systems were to be improved. And, fourth, the command and control of the strategic deterrent was to be improved.[19]

Because of these improvements, the message continued, the administration had been able to make a number of savings in other strategic programs. Specifically, the last two squadrons of Titan II ICBMs originally contemplated were eliminated; the three mobile Minuteman squadrons funded in the F/Y 1962 budget were deferred and replaced by three fixed-base squadrons; the phaseout of a number of B-47 bombers was accelerated; the Snark long-range cruise missiles were to be immediately phased out; development of the B-70 supersonic bomber was limited to a small number of prototypes; and the plan to install Polaris missiles on the cruiser *Long Beach* was cancelled.[20]

The adjustments recommended by Kennedy added up to a net addition in the F/Y 1962 defense budget of $1,194.1 million in new obligational authority for the strategic-force programs. The recommended adjustments to the F/Y 1962 strategic missile and bomber programs are detailed in table 8.[21] These changes were to give the United States a total of 1,298 long-range strategic ballistic missiles by 1965 (table 9). The Kennedy Administration's amendments to the Polaris program are illustrated in table 10; and the new schedule for Polaris FBM submarine commissionings, as outlined to Congress by Secretary McNamara in early April,[22] is set out in table 11. Under this new schedule, FBM submarines 19 to 29 would be on station some two to three years earlier than they would have been under the previous schedule (if in fact the previous administration had ever autho-

19. Ibid., pp. 5–8.   20. Ibid., pp. 10–12.
21. Derived from ibid., p. 13.
22. See *Missiles & Rockets*, 10 April 1961, p. 15.

TABLE 8. *Kennedy Administration Adjustment to Fiscal Year 1962 Strategic Force Programs, 28 March 1961* (in millions of dollars)

MISSILES	
Cost of improvement and protection of U.S. missile deterrent	
Polaris [a]	$1,340.8
Minuteman [b]	96.0
Skybolt	50.0
Total cost	$1,486.8
Less savings	
Cancellation of 2 squadrons, Titan II	$ 100.0
Phaseout of Snark	6.9
Cancellation of Polaris installation on *Long Beach*	57.7
Total savings	$ 164.6
Adjusted cost of missiles	$1,322.2
BOMBERS	
Cost of protection of U.S. bomber deterrent	
(increased ground alert)	$ 44.6
Less savings	
Phasedown of B-47 medium bomber wings	$ 34.7
B-70	138.0
Total savings	$ 172.7
Adjusted savings on bombers	$ 128.1
Net addition for strategic-forces program	$1,194.1

[a] Cost includes acceleration of production schedule, acceleration of A-3 development, and increase in personnel.
[b] Cost includes substitution of three fixed for three mobile squadrons, expansion of production capacity, and improvement of missile.

rized them). Together with the 30 January acceleration, this meant that the United States now had 464 Polaris missiles programmed and that these would all be commissioned before the end of calendar year 1964 and all operational by June 1965 (or about the same time as the 19 submarines—304 Polaris missiles —as programmed by Eisenhower).

Although many of the recommendations outlined in the message had in one form or another been under consideration at one time or another during the previous couple of years—as exemplified in WSEG No. 50—most of them were a direct consequence of the defense reappraisal McNamara and his task forces had been undertaking since 20 January.[23]

23. Kennedy announced this reappraisal in his 30 January message; however, the task forces had begun working immediately after the inauguration. Interview with Dr. Marvin Stern, 21 August 1970.

TABLE 9. *U.S. Strategic Missile Programs*

	EISENHOWER PROGRAM	KENNEDY PROGRAM, 28 MARCH 1961	KENNEDY ADJUST-MENT
ATLAS			
Squadron sites			
Soft and semi-hard sites	7	7	
Hard sites	6	6	
Total squadrons	13	13	
Launchers per squadron			
First two	6	6	
Next five	9	9	
Last six	12	12	
Total missiles on launchers[a]	126	126	0
POLARIS			
Total submarines	19	29	
Missiles per submarine	16	16	
Total missiles on launchers	304	464	+160[b]
TITAN			
Squadron sites (hard)			
Elevator-launch Titan I	6	6	
In-silo-launch Titan II	8	6	
Total squadrons	14	12	
Launchers per squadron	9	9	
Total missiles on launchers	126	108	−18
MINUTEMAN			
Squadron sites			
Hard sites	9	12	
Train sites	3	0	
Total squadrons	12	12	
Launchers per squadron			
Fixed silo	50	50	
Train	30	0	
Total missiles on launchers	540	600	+60
Total missiles programmed	1,096	1,298	+202[c]

[a] Excludes three test and training Atlas ICBMs at Vandenberg Air Force Base, apparently withdrawn by McNamara from operational status in February or March 1961. Three Atlas D's at Vandenberg were, however, still considered operational and are included here.

[b] Excludes 8 Polaris aboard the *Long Beach*.

[c] Excludes 15 to 30 Snark air-breathing subsonic long-range missiles phased out by the Kennedy Administration.

TABLE 10. *Polaris Submarine Programs, 28 March 1961*
Submarines 10–29 (by fiscal year)

	1960	1961	1962
Eisenhower Budget			
SSBN	0	10–14	15–19
LLT	10–14	15–19	20–24
Kennedy Acceleration, 29 January 1961			
SSBN	0	10–19	0
LLT	10–14	20–24	0
Kennedy F/Y 1962 Budget Amendment, 28 March 1961			
SSBN	0	10–19	20–29
LLT	10–14	20–24	0

TABLE 11. *Polaris Submarine Commissionings*
Submarines 2–29 (by calendar year)

	1960	1961	1962	1963	1964	1965	1966	1967
Eisenhower Schedule	2–3	4–6	7–9	10–13	14–18	19–23	24–28	29
Kennedy Schedule	2–3	4–6	7–9	10–18	19–29			

To conduct this reappraisal, four major task forces were set up in the Pentagon:[24] Strategic Weapons System Requirements, headed by Charles J. Hitch, Pentagon comptroller;[25] Limited War Requirements, under Paul H. Nitze, assistant defense secretary for ISA; Weapons Research and Development under Herbert York, DDR&E; and Bases and Installations, headed by Thomas D. Morris, assistant defense secretary for logistics. Each of the task forces included civilian and military personnel of the

24. *New York Times*, 13 February 1961, p. 17.
25. Hitch went into hospital a few days after the reappraisal began, and the task force was taken over by Enthoven and Stern (interviews with Charles P. Hitch, 11 August 1970, and Dr. Marvin Stern, 21 August 1970).

Department of Defense and representatives of the Bureau of the Budget.

The underlying problems of the defense reappraisal concerned what relative weights to give conflicting Air Force, Army, and Navy strategies, what mix of weapons to procure, and the preparation of new, comprehensive, integrated war-contingency plans. A decision was made within the first two weeks of the reappraisal to increase the emphasis on limited-war forces— non-nuclear weapons, armored cars, electronics equipment, transport planes, etc. According to one source, the first round of estimates involved a total of $8 billion in additional expenditure for new equipment over a period of a few years, though it was understood that Nitze was busy paring this figure.[26]

The Hitch task force on strategic weapons systems included about ten RAND experts, officers of the Navy, Army, and Air Force, OSD personnel, and representatives of the Bureau of the Budget.[27] The task force concluded very early that no missile gap favoring the Soviet Union existed. It did not consider this to be the main issue however. Its major concern was to reduce the vulnerability of U.S. strategic forces (this concern was shared by Hitch, Rowen, Wohlstetter, Enthoven, Nitze, and McNamara), and to see that more order was introduced into the strategic programs. (Enthoven was particularly concerned with the elimination of wasteful duplication.) The members of the task force shared very optimistic assumptions on the invulnerability of large numbers of relatively compact missiles in hardened silos. The group recommended the rejection of Air Force proposals for a slower rate of phaseout of the B-47s, for an additional wing (No. 15) of fifty-two B-52 long-range bombers, and for production of the B-70 bomber. To reduce the vulnerability of the U.S. bomber force, however, it did recommend increasing SAC's 24-hour airborne alert from 12 to 30 long-range bombers and the 15-minute ground alert from some 530 bombers to a full half of

26. *New York Times*, 7 and 11 February 1961.
27. *New York Times*, 7 February 1961, p. 21, and 13 February 1961, p. 17. The principal DoD personnel on the Hitch task force were Drs. Marvin Stern and Alain Enthoven. The Army representative was Gen. Overbeck; Gen. Ellis, assisted by Lt. Cols. Glenn Kent and Robert Lukeman represented the Air Force.

SAC's 1,600-bomber strength. With regard to strategic missiles, the task force recommended the cancellation of the 13th and 14th squadrons of the large-payload Titan II ICBM; the replacement of the programmed mobile Minuteman force by additional fixed Minuteman missiles and a doubling of Minuteman production capacity; an increase in the building of Polaris FBM submarines towards an interim total of 29; the phaseout of the Snark long-range missile; and the cancellation of plans to deploy Polaris missiles aboard the *Long Beach*.[28]

As part of the strategic reappraisal, McNamara and four of his chief aides (Gilpatric, Stern, Lemnitzer, and York) made a two-day visit (4 and 5 February 1961) to SAC headquarters and the Joint Strategic Targeting Center at Offutt AFB, Omaha. The initial concerns of the visit were U.S. policies regarding the number of possible enemy targets for which the United States must prepare, and whether some of the funds going into strategic weapons might be used for other purposes. The visit started with a briefing on the Single Integrated Operational Plan (SIOP), with the intelligence part of it—the estimate of the Soviet threat—given by Admiral Parker, deputy director of the Joint Strategic Targeting Planning Staff (JSTPS). The NIE at this time had four curves: CIA–State Department; J-2 (the JCS estimate); Air Force; and Army-Navy. McNamara was extremely irritated because the Air Force curve (the highest estimate of the threat) was used instead of J-2, and determined to reform the intelligence establishment. Later on McNamara was given a demonstration of SAC's command and control network, but one commander failed to respond, and McNamara determined to improve the strategic command and control system. Finally, McNamara was visibly taken aback by the inflexibility of the SIOP after General Power made a "stupid statement" about SAC's capacity for indiscriminate destruction, and was persuaded of the necessity for options in the targeting system.[29]

28. *Newsweek*, 27 February 1961, p. 22; and interviews with Charles J. Hitch, 11 August 1970, and Dr. Alain Enthoven, 17 August 1970.

29. Interview with Dr. Marvin Stern, 21 August 1971. See also Stewart Alsop, *The Center*, p. 152, and *New York Times*, 7 February 1961. Dr. Stern described this visit as providing, more than any other single event in this early period, "the most crucial formative impression" on McNamara.

As part of the strategic-weapons review, General Lemnitzer also made a tour of U.S. military bases, beginning on 10 February, accompanied by his colleagues in the joint chiefs of staff. Some ICBM sites were at that time up to six months behind schedule, and the JCS were to recommend ways of introducing reforms in management practices with a view to achieving acceleration.[30]

The preliminary reports of the task forces were completed on 20 February. Financially the proposals added up to an estimated $2.1 billion in addition to the Eisenhower F/Y 1962 defense budget.[31] McNamara then consolidated the reports of the task forces, and submitted his report and recommendations to President Kennedy a week later.[32]

Secretary of State Dean Rusk and members of his department had also been consulted in the defense reappraisal. According to published reports, Rusk proposed in a memorandum submitted to McNamara early in February that even massive attacks on Europe should be countered with conventional rather than nuclear weapons. It was also reported that Rusk had indicated that U.S. strategic forces should be employed only to deter direct attacks on the United States, and that the standby airborne alert be discontinued. In a statement cleared for release by the White House on 28 February, Rusk denied that he had proposed such a policy shift, though he stated he favored "the strengthening of the non-nuclear aspects of . . . [Western] . . . defense as well as the maintenance of its nuclear aspects." His hedged position was, apparently, that the United States should not necessarily commit itself in advance to the use of nuclear weapons.[33]

Kennedy spent the first two weeks of March studying the reports and recommendations personally and in a succession of meetings with his White House (Bundy, Wiesner, Sorensen), defense (McNamara, Gilpatric, Hitch), and budget bureau teams the recommendations were hammered out into a $1.9 billion

30. *New York Times*, 11 February 1961; *Missiles & Rockets*, 6 March 1961, pp. 14–15.

31. *Newsweek*, 27 February 1961, p. 22. This was some $6.9 billion less than the three services had said they needed in additional funds.

32. The actual consolidation of the reports was done by Adam Yarmolinsky, McNamara's special assistant (see *Business Week*, 11 February 1961, p. 104).

33. *New York Times*, 28 and 29 February 1961.

adjustment to the defense budget. Right up until the day before the message was transmitted to Congress, "words and paragraphs were still being changed, dollars juggled. . . . Some decisions still hung in the balance."[34] Most of the decisions had, however, been made before the middle of March.

The decisions of March 1961 determined to a very large extent the character of the U.S. strategic-force posture for the next decade. Essentially, the effect of these decisions was to determine that U.S. strategic forces, now numerically expanded, would be overwhelmingly composed of small-payload missiles, deployed aboard submarines and in hardened silos. Because of the importance of the March decisions it is worthwhile looking at some of them more closely, and noting some background aspects.

In the first place, they were made before the new intelligence then becoming available had been fully absorbed. While fears of a missile gap were being dissipated, the new administration was still unaware of how great U.S. strategic superiority was. Consequently, substantial emphasis remained on quick build-up of second-strike capability. Moreover, there existed certain political pressures for changes (particularly in the light of the preceding campaign) that would dramatize and highlight the shift away from the policies of the preceding administration. The atmosphere was one calling for decisiveness in a period of presumed crisis, as is perhaps suggested by James Schlesinger's phrase "a quick and dirty look."[35] The U.S. economy was at that time in the depths of a recession—by February unemployment had reached the extraordinary figure of 8.1 percent of the labor force—and the administration was searching for possible anti-recession measures. Kennedy had made the recession a central issue in the 1960 campaign; he had discussed it in his State of the Union message and had called for action to stimulate the economy. An interregnal task force on the economy had made increased defense spending its primary recommendation, and this became the administration's main resort.[36]

The decision to double Minuteman production capacity from

34. *Newsweek*, 27 March 1961, p. 15; Sorensen, *Kennedy*, p. 667.
35. James R. Schlesinger, in *Defense Management*, ed. Stephen Enke, p. 105.
36. Arthur M. Schlesinger, Jr., *A Thousand Days*, pp. 151, 544–47.

30 to 60 missiles per month was made partly for antirecession reasons. The idea of setting up two production lines was first proposed in early 1959,[37] but no action was taken throughout the missile-gap years. Immediately after the Minuteman test success of 1 February, it was proposed by Zuckert,[38] and McNamara indicated his approval of the proposal on the flight back from Omaha on 5 February.[39] On the face of it, the avowed reason for approving the proposal—to "hedge our risks by buying options on alternative courses of action"—appears quite sensible. However, the major bottleneck to accelerated missile deployment at this time was in base-building[40] and the possibility of ever being able to support a production and deployment rate of more than one missile per day was incredibly remote. (In fact, production never did reach more than 30 Minuteman ICBMs per month.) Certainly, the attraction of the proposal as an antirecession measure figured in the Pentagon deliberations.[41]

For the first time, cost-effectiveness analysis was now explicitly applied in strategic missile decision making. Such analysis was directly responsible for the cancellation of the plan to deploy eight Polaris missiles aboard the *Long Beach*. This plan, first suggested by the Navy in 1959, had been approved by the Eisenhower Administration only four days before Kennedy assumed office.[42] In terms of cost-effectiveness, the $58 million program would purchase only half of a far less vulnerable submarine (16 missiles, $116.2 million). Also, in a limited war, the cruiser's utility would be reduced by the presence of the missiles.[43]

Cost-effectiveness analysis was also important in the decision

37. Roy Neal, *Ace in the Hole*, pp. 118–19.

38. Joseph Alsop, *Herald Tribune*, 6 February 1961.

39. Interview with Dr. Marvin Stern, 21 August 1970.

40. In early 1962 Gen. Le May stated that, "We can produce the missiles all right but we cannot deploy them because of the long leadtime in getting them out on the sites and in the holes in the ground. This is what takes the time" (Senate Appropriations Committee, *Department of Defense Appropriations for 1963*, p. 193).

41. *Missiles & Rockets*, 20 March 1961, p. 9.

42. *New York Times*, 17 January 1961, p. 4.

43. Interview with Dr. Alain Enthoven, 17 August 1970. The figure of $58 million for installing the Polaris missiles on the *Long Beach* is given in the *Special Message*, p. 12. The figure of $116.2 million for a fully equipped Polaris FBM submarine is from *Missiles & Rockets*, 24 July 1961, p. 9.

to cancel the last two Titan II squadrons. The administration argued that the $270 million saved by this cancellation would buy many more Minuteman missiles than the 18 Titan IIs thereby eliminated.[44] However, because of the deficiencies in information (both strategic and technical) the analysis was strongly biased against the Titan II and in favor of the Minuteman; and the analysts were too impatient to wait until these deficiencies were resolved.[45]

The decision to defer production of the mobile Minuteman was made partly on the basis of cost-effectiveness analysis, and partly for political reasons. The first comprehensive analysis of mobile Minuteman deployment, WSEG No. 50, recommended in favor of the mobile version for relatively low force levels; for larger force levels on limited railroad trackage, however, vulnerability increased more than proportionately. Costs were at this stage estimated at $2.4 million and $4.8 million per fixed and mobile Minuteman missile respectively.[46] The Hitch task force, much more impressed by the vulnerability of the mobile version, recommended against it.[47] In the larger field of systems reference, the mobile scheme was incompatible with any strategy which attempted to separate weapons systems and population centers—to avoid populations, the Minuteman trains would have to have been concentrated in a reasonably well-defined area in the western United States. George Kistiakowsky, Herbert York, and Harold Brown also presented technical arguments against the mobile system. But, finally, McNamara was against anything which might have seemed to be turning the United States into a "garrison state."[48] However, the decision to defer production of the mobile system appears to have been made at the last moment, and quite suddenly,[49] which indicates

44. *Special Message*, p. 10. The final decision to delete these two squadrons of Titan II missiles from the strategic forces program was made at a meeting between the president, McNamara, and David Bell in mid-March, primarily on the basis of arguments from Bell (interview with David Bell, 20 December 1972).
45. See James R. Schlesinger in *Defense Management*, ed. Enke, pp. 104–8.
46. *Missiles & Rockets*, 6 January 1960, p. 10.
47. Interview with Charles J. Hitch, 11 August 1970.
48. Interviews with Roswell Gilpatric, 30 January 1973, and Dr. George Pugh, 24 July 1970.
49. For example, the two principal contractors were taken completely by

much anguish on someone's part, a snap decision, or much opposition. Certainly, the grounds for the decision were not self-evident.

The final background aspect to be mentioned here is that, as Pierre Salinger has written,

> The President had just come into office, and he was surrounded by men, none of whom he had ever met before at that time, and they were advising while he had no experience of them on which to base an assessment of their relative merit, intelligence and insight.[50]

The administration was new and relatively inexperienced; not even the president himself had heretofore held any high executive office.

Although in terms of missile numbers the change in the F/Y 1962 defense program was relatively slight (an increase of less than 20 percent), there were important consequences. First, with regard to the composition of the force, the decisions of March 1961 were made, in effect, against large-payload missiles and for small-payload missiles. This had important and direct implications for strategy, for future missile deployment, and for arms control. Future strategic options were undoubtedly foreclosed prematurely.

The expansion and acceleration of the missile program was equally consequential. Although the increase was relatively small, it did represent the maximum that could have been incorporated in the F/Y 1962 budget at that time. The F/Y 1962 Minuteman program, for example, was set at 600 missiles solely on the basis of lead-time funding. Six hundred was all the production that was feasible within the period before F/Y 1963

---

surprise. Both were tooled up and waiting for the order to begin production and deployment (see *Missiles & Rockets*, 3 April 1961, p. 9). Neither was apparently consulted on the system during the defense reappraisal. The media, including the trade press, had expressed no inkling that the mobile system was even under review.

50. See *The Australian*, 23 October 1971, p. 16. A similar point has also been made by both McNamara and Gen. Maxwell Taylor with reference to the Bay of Pigs decision of March 1961 (see Alsop, *The Center*, p. 159; and Maxwell D. Taylor, *Responsibility and Response*, p. 68).

funds would come into use.[51] Total missile procurement for Minuteman beyond this number was kept secret.[52] And the doubling of Minuteman production capability was advertised as providing the option of further acceleration in the future.[53] The atmosphere in which the budget revision was undertaken, the impression of haste, of much action, and the taking-out of options for future action must—at a time when the missile gap was known to be receding—have unnecessarily engendered worried reaction within the Soviet Union.

The message smacked of haste.[54] McNamara was aware that he was attempting an unprecedented feat—as he remarked when the reappraisal was begun, it required "compressing fifteen years of postwar history into four weeks"[55]—and several commentators criticized the attempt. Hanson Baldwin perhaps put it most succinctly when he wrote that, "No man, or no group of men, new to the Pentagon, no matter how brilliant, could possibly provide thoroughly studied, carefully factual judgments on matters of such tremendous scope and complexity within the time frame laid down."[56]

But the most important criticism is not that the administration attempted a task which it was not possible to do thoroughly, but that the haste was not necessary. From a funding point of view, revisions to the F/Y 1962 budget could have been made up to three months later, by which time much more information on the character and rate of build-up of the Soviet missile force would have been on hand; and supplements to the budget could

51. Interview with Dr. Alain Enthoven, 17 August 1970.
52. David Bell believes that the total force number, beyond the 600 Minuteman ICBMs then authorized, was actually left open because of the difficulty of reaching any consensus (interview with Bell, 20 December 1972). However, there is some evidence that a program of 800 Minuteman missiles had tentatively been decided upon at this time (see testimony of Gen. Schultz, House Appropriations Committee, *Department of Defense Appropriations for 1970*, part 4, pp. 650–51; and Herbert F. York, *Race to Oblivion*, pp. 152–53).
53. *Special Message*, p. 6.
54. According to Willis Shapley, then deputy director of the National Security Division of the BoB, the spring review was "superficial and hasty" (interview with Shapley, 8 February 1973).
55. Henry L. Trewhitt, *McNamara*, p. 20.
56. *New York Times*, 1 February 1961, p. 16.

have been made after this. Moreover, decisions on force size and composition need not have been, and, indeed, should not have been made, until forced by long-lead-time items, which would have been much later in 1961.

But the new administration felt compelled to make a decision for other reasons. McNamara himself hinted at the character of these reasons early in the reappraisal. After stating that he was "telescoping a lifetime's work," he added, "but we must take a position because indecision itself results, in effect, in endorsing previous policy decisions."[57] And the new administration needed, for domestic political reasons, and in the light of the 1960 presidential campaign, to contrast itself with the previous administration. The new administration was too impetuous, making haste when haste was unnecessary, forging unnecessary constraints on future strategic options (including, of course, a small ultimate missile force); too absolutist, seeking "certainty beyond doubt" when there would not be any such certainty, or any such thing as absolute security; too self-assured in dismissing the views and policies of the previous administration; and, mainly for domestic political reasons, altogether too cavalier in its treatment of major issues of national security and international relations.

57. *Newsweek*, 27 March 1961, p. 16.

6 The Fiscal Year 1963 Defense Budget: The McNamara Strategic Missile Posture

The F/Y 1963 defense budget and F/Y 1963–F/Y 1967 defense program were transmitted to Congress by President Kennedy on 18 January 1962. Prepared during April–December 1961, this was the first defense program and budget which had been prepared wholly by Kennedy's administration. Despite the fact that the preparation of the F/Y 1963 budget had involved so much more groundwork and basic reexamination of military programs than previous budgets, and was developed in such a short period,[1] by a new and relatively inexperienced administration, there was no doubt within Congress that this was the

1. For example, the work done during the period from 22 September to 23 October 1961 had in previous years usually taken five months (*Aviation Week & Space Technology*, 25 December 1961, p. 16).

most impressive defense budget document it had ever received. Furthermore, despite the testimony of General Lemnitzer that there had been "no past budget in which more attention, or more time, was devoted by the joint chiefs of staff as a corporate body, than was the case in the development of the F/Y 1963 budget,"[2] there was also no doubt in Congress that this was essentially "a McNamara budget." The F/Y 1963 budget was the fiscal representation of the McNamara military posture and strategy. Succeeding budgets really made only marginal force changes to that posture.

The first part of this chapter describes the development of the F/Y 1963 defense budget in great detail. This is done not only because of the intrinsic importance of that particular budget, but also because, since its development was contemporaneous with the public demise of the missile gap within the United States, it is necessary to document when particular submissions were presented and particular decisions made.

The second part of this chapter describes and discusses the F/Y 1963 defense budget as related to strategic nuclear forces. It was primarily this budget which contained the appropriation and authorization requests for the Kennedy-McNamara strategic ballistic-missile build-up. Nearly 400 submarine-launched and intercontinental ballistic missiles were added to the previously authorized (28 March 1961) program, an increase of about 23 percent, and 400 more Minuteman ICBMs were tentatively programmed—a further increase of 20 percent.

THE DEVELOPMENT OF THE F/Y 1963 DEFENSE BUDGET,
APRIL–DECEMBER 1961

The F/Y 1963 defense budget was the first to be developed under the new programming and budgeting procedure which Secretary McNamara introduced into the Pentagon in 1961. Preparation of the budget began in the early spring of 1961, within the framework of two instructions given to McNamara by President Kennedy in January:

2. Senate Appropriations Committee, *Department of Defense Appropriations for 1963*, p. 95.

1. Develop the force structure necessary to our military requirements without regard to arbitrary or predetermined budget ceilings.

2. Having determined that force structure . . . procure and operate it at the lowest possible cost.[3]

The first step in the formulation of the budget was the initiation of a series of studies dealing with what were judged to be the most critical requirements in the Department of Defense, including the question of a basic national strategy. At the same time, DoD began a "detailed review and analysis of the Communist threat now and in the future, based on the latest and best intelligence information available."[4] Revision of the Basic National Security Policy (BNSP) began in late March, to provide general policy guidance for those working on the budget. The revision particularly stressed the importance of non-nuclear forces.[5]

In May, while this work was under way, the military departments were requested to submit their program proposals for the period 1963 through 1967. According to McNamara,

No dollar ceilings were assigned or indicated to the military departments. Instead, the military departments were instructed to submit proposals for such forces and such new programs as, in their judgment, were required to support our basic national security objectives. . . . The service proposals were received during July and August. Including civil defense and the military assistance program, they aggregated over $63 billion in obligational authority for fiscal year 1963 and more than $67 billion for fiscal year 1966, which was one of the program years.[6]

The Air Force and Navy submissions for the Central War Offensive Forces package were received by McNamara on 3 July 1961. As detailed in table 12, these submissions proposed that the United States should have about 3,910 strategic ballistic

3. Testimony of McNamara, House Armed Services Committee, *Hearings on Military Posture* (1962), p. 3162.
4. Ibid.
5. Interview with Henry S. Rowen, 25 August 1970.
6. House Armed Services Committee, *Hearings on Military Posture* (1962), p. 3162.

TABLE 12. *Package Plans for Strategic Retaliatory Force Programs, 3 July 1961*

PROGRAM	NUMBER OF MISSILES	COST OF EACH MISSILE (IN MILLIONS OF DOLLARS)	ANNUAL COST (IN MILLIONS OF DOLLARS)						TOTAL FUNDING (IN MILLIONS OF DOLLARS)
			1962	1963	1964	1965	1966	1967	
U.S. Air Force									
ICBMs									
Minuteman (fixed)	2,500	5	1,300	2,100	2,600	2,800	1,900	1,500	12,500
Minuteman (mobile)	415	7	200	270	585	945	645	264	2,900
Titan	275	11	1,300	600	—	—	—	260	3,100
Total ICBMs	3,190								18,500
Other USAF SRFs									
B-52 (15 wings)			—	1,500	—	—	—	1,300	8,900
B-47			58	—	—	—	—	15	1,820
B-58			170	200	200	200	200	200	1,200
Skybolt			89	325	480	—	—	260	—
U.S. Navy									
Polaris SLBMs (45 submarines)	720	12	2,074	2,000	1,800	—	—	600	8,600
Total USAF and Navy SRF funding			9,800	9,000	8,800	—	—	5,600	50,300

NOTE: Because of the incompleteness of available information and because of rounding, some inconsistencies appear in this table's cost totals.

missiles deployed by 1967 (in addition to the 129 Atlas ICBMs already programmed).[7]

The 3 July Central War Offensive Forces submissions had been separately prepared by the Air Force and Navy. McNamara then distributed them to the JCS for study and comment. Over the next month, the program proposed by the USAF was studied by the Navy, and vice versa, and both programs were studied by the Army. The final proposals of the services were then presented to McNamara and Gilpatric at a two-and-a-half-hour session on 4 August 1961. The presentations were made by the secretaries and chiefs of staff of each of the three services.[8]

The last of the other submissions was received from the services by the end of August. The service proposals were then consolidated and subjected to a systematic analysis by the OSD staff. McNamara later testified,

> With the assistance of our principal military and civilian advisers, Mr. Gilpatric and I then reviewed in great detail each of the programs in the light of—
> First. The mission to be accomplished.
> Second. The cost-effectiveness relationships among the various alternative means of performing the mission; and
> Third. The latest intelligence data on the capabilities of the Soviet Union and its satellites. This took the majority of the summer.[9]

While the services were preparing their final program proposals, a "third review" of U.S. military posture was taking place, beginning on 8 July 1961, within the administration. It was prompted by an announcement by Premier Khrushchev that the Soviet Union was planning to increase its military spending by three billion rubles, and by the crisis developing over Berlin in the summer of 1961. At a press conference on 11 July, Deputy Defense Secretary Gilpatric stated that the review would primarily involve a strengthening of conventional forces. It was made apparent that the administration regarded existing U.S.

7. Larry Booda, "Package Plans Call for 3,900 Missiles," *Aviation Week & Space Technology*, 24 July 1961, p. 34.

8. Testimony of McNamara before Senate subcommittee on national policy machinery, quoted in *Aviation Week & Space Technology*, 14 August 1961, p. 34.

9. House Armed Services Committee, *Hearings on Military Posture* (1962), p. 3162.

strategic striking forces, and the planned build-up of them, as sufficient.[10] As McNamara said in a statement issued by the Pentagon on 10 July: "Currently we are [as] strong—if not stronger—than any potential aggressor." No need was seen for new increases in the F/Y 1962 defense budget for missiles and bombers.[11]

In a special message to Congress on 26 July 1961, President Kennedy asked for $3.45 billion for additional programs. Although this was mainly for general-purpose forces, changes were required in all the program packages to some extent. The message included, for example, requests for funds to increase the number of B-47 and B-52 bombers on ground alert, and to retain B-47s which in March had been scheduled to be phased out in 1961. It also included $206.7 million for civil defense.[12]

McNamara completed his review of the service program package submissions in mid-September, and on 22 September forwarded his tentative program decisions to the military departments and the chairman of the JCS, to serve as the basis for preparing the detailed budget requests for F/Y 1963. "Guideline" decisions were made on more than 300 weapons systems, forces and programs, with projections through F/Y 1967 in most cases. If these tentative program decisions had been costed out, they would have provided a total defense expenditure of $54 billion in F/Y 1963, in contrast to the original $63 billion (the sum of the unilateral service submissions of July and August).[13]

Under McNamara's 22 September SRF program, the Navy goal of 45 submarines was cut to 41, six to be constructed in F/Y 1963, and the final six in F/Y 1964. The most drastic cut in a program goal was in the fixed Minuteman ICBM request—the original Air Force proposal for 2,500 of these missiles through 1967 was cut to 900 missiles; F/Y 1963 funding was, however, increased to $1.8 billion. The previously scheduled 12 Titan squadrons were to be retained, and no further Atlas ICBMs

10. *Aviation Week & Space Technology*, 17 July 1961, pp. 34, 37.
11. *Missiles & Rockets*, 17 July 1961, p. 53.
12. *Aviation Week & Space Technology*, 31 July 1961, pp. 22–23, and 7 August 1961, p. 28.
13. Testimony of McNamara, House Armed Services Committee, *Hearings on Military Posture* (1962), pp. 3162, 3194.

were to be ordered. No funds were included for additional purchases of the B-52 and B-58 heavy bombers, and the B-70 bomber was programmed for airframe development only.[14]

In a memorandum forwarding the 22 September "guidance" to the services, McNamara stated that, "The Services should feel free, in preparing their fiscal year 1963 budget requests, to change details of the guidance wherever they felt such changes essential to meet military requirements."[15]

The services were asked to have their revised requests submitted to OSD by 8 A.M. on 23 October. Each service thus had to act rapidly. Within the month, their policy-setting groups had to settle internal conflicts, and then the working levels had to prepare the submissions for transmission to the secretary. McNamara has testified that, "in total, these Service requests amounted to something of the order of $54.5 billion, something in that range." These service submissions were in the traditional category form—such as personnel, operations and maintenance, procurement, etc. The Department of Defense then undertook to reconvert them to the program-package form by 15 November.[16]

McNamara and Gilpatric, with the assistance of their OSD staff, and "with full consultation with the Chiefs and the Service Secretaries," spent roughly the whole of November going over the service submissions "in great detail." About 620 changes were initially made, either raising or lowering the service requests. Of these, "well in excess of 200" were Air Force considerations. The individual items changed ranged in value "from several hundred thousand dollars of cuts to several hundred million dollars of cuts or increases."[17]

The services were then asked to make one- or two-page comments on these changes—so many, that the reports were quickly

14. *Polaris and Poseidon Chronology*, p. 7; *Newsweek*, 9 October 1961, p. 11; and *Aviation Week & Space Technology*, 16 October 1961, p. 34.
15. Testimony of McNamara, House Armed Services Committee, *Hearings on Military Posture* (1962), p. 3163.
16. Ibid., p. 3194; and *Aviation Week & Space Technology*, 16 October 1961, p. 34.
17. Testimony of McNamara, House Armed Services Committee, *Hearings on Military Posture* (1962), p. 3194; and testimony of Air Force Sec. Zuckert, Senate Appropriations Committee, *Department of Defense Appropriations for 1963*, p. 165.

christened "snowflakes."[18] Decisions that were felt by the services "to be in error or contrary to their interests" were resub-
mitted to McNamara. And,

> of the roughly, say, 620 decisions that I made, I reversed myself
> on about 60, and ended up therefore with about 560 separate
> decisions that cut the service budget from something on the order
> of 54 billion dollars down to the present new obligational author-
> ity of about 51.6 billion dollars. Roughly 2.4 billion dollars was cut
> out at that time.[19]

While this review was taking place, President Kennedy con-
vened his defense experts for a meeting at Hyannis Port, over
the Thanksgiving weekend, to discuss the size of the total F/Y
1963 budget. The main discussion took place at a two-hour
meeting on the morning of 24 November.[20] A Defense Department request for F/Y 1963 of about $51 billion was agreed upon.
Kennedy then returned to Washington on 27 November for a
further budget talk with Budget Bureau Director David Bell.[21]

This tentative defense budget was then sent to the BoB in
early December for inclusion in the overall executive budget
request. Bell had originally recommended that $48.5 billion be
the target for the F/Y 1963 Defense Budget, and through December the BoB continued to insist that cuts be made.[22]

On 13 December funds for the mobile Minuteman were eliminated from the budget and the program cancelled completely.[23]
Fixed Minuteman procurement for F/Y 1963 was left at 300,

18. *Aviation Week & Space Technology*, 11 December 1961, p. 25.
19. Testimony of McNamara, House Armed Services Committee, *Hearings on Military Posture* (1962), p. 3194.
20. Present at the meeting were: President Kennedy; Secretary of Defense McNamara; Gen. Lyman L. Lemnitzer, chairman of the joint chiefs of staff; Ros-well L. Gilpatric, deputy secretary of defense; Gen. Maxwell D. Taylor, military representative of the president; David E. Bell, director of the Budget Bureau; Elmer B. Staats, deputy director of the BoB; Harold Brown, director of de-fense research and engineering; McGeorge Bundy, special assistant to the presi-dent; Dr. Jerome B. Wiesner, science adviser to the president; Dr. Carl Kaysen of the National Security Council; and Theodore C. Sorensen, special counsel to the president (see *New York Times*, 25 November 1961, p. 1; and *Newsweek*, 4 December 1961, p. 17).
21. *Aviation Week & Space Technology*, 11 December 1961, p. 26; and *New York Times*, 27 November 1961.
22. *Aviation Week & Space Technology*, 11 December 1961, p. 27; and 25 De-cember 1961, pp. 13, 16; and interview with David Bell, 20 December 1972.
23. *New York Times*, 14 December 1961, p. 20.

however, for a total proposed program of 900.[24] The bulk of the budget document was then sent to the government printer, but some sections were still being held open for last-minute changes.[25] Among these, in late December, was a reconsideration of Minuteman numbers. Although higher figures of 950, 990 and 1,050 received some support,[26] it was finally decided to cut the F/Y 1963 program from 300 to 200 silo-based missiles, putting the total number of Minuteman ICBMs authorized at 800.

As presented to Congress on 18 January 1962, the administration's defense request for F/Y 1963 was $51.6 billion; of this, a record $9.361 million (or 18 percent) was budgeted for strategic retaliatory forces. This was $2 billion over Eisenhower's F/Y 1962 level and, together with the $2 billion added in Kennedy's three budget supplements during 1961, meant that about $4 billion had been added to SRF programs within 12 months.[27]

THE F/Y 1963 DEFENSE BUDGET AND F/Y
1963–1967 DEFENSE PROGRAM

As the foregoing survey of its development shows, work on the F/Y 1963 defense budget had begun almost as soon as the new administration took office. It was undertaken during a period of extraordinary uncertainty and extraordinary change in U.S. national intelligence estimates of the size and character of the Soviet threat; throughout the formulation of the budget the services had adopted various positions on desired force levels and had bargained and maneuvered in attempts to achieve their respective aims; the defense program as presented to Congress in January was the result of a large amount of groundwork and basic reexamination of U.S. military posture, developed in a very short period, by a new and relatively inexperienced administra-

24. *Aviation Week & Space Technology*, 18 December 1961, pp. 25–26.

25. *Aviation Week & Space Technology*, 25 December 1961, p. 13. Most of these changes were finalized in a meeting between the joint chiefs of staff and President Kennedy and Secretary McNamara at Palm Beach at the end of December (see L. J. Korb, "The Role of the Joint Chiefs of Staff," p. 168).

26. Interviews with Carl Kaysen, 19 December 1972, and Jerome Wiesner, 20 February 1973.

27. Testimony of McNamara, House Armed Services Committee, *Hearings on Military Posture* (1962), p. 3163; and Senate Armed Services Committee, *Military Procurement Authorization, Fiscal Year 1963*, p. 14.

tion; and in the last weeks of its formulation, it had to be re-shaped to fit into the overall executive budget request.

However, the strategic forces requirement recommended to Congress in McNamara's prepared statement showed no evidence of any of this. McNamara gave the impression that the program the administration had chosen was the result of nothing other than a systematic assessment, utilizing analytical procedures, of a number of alternatives, each based on a limited number of parameters, the values of which could be estimated with some certainty and the precision of the calculations accepted with great confidence.

In his prepared statement, McNamara explained to Congress how the specifics of the program proposed for F/Y 1963 and planned through F/Y 1967 had been calculated. He argued that "the requirement for strategic retaliatory forces lends itself rather well to reasonably precise calculation." The number, types and locations of the targets could be determined fairly easily, as could the numbers and explosive yields of the weapons required to destroy them. The next step, he stated, was to determine "the size and character of the forces best suited to deliver these weapons." Since U.S. strategic forces would have to survive a Soviet first strike, the vulnerability of these forces was an essential consideration in this determination.[28] "With these considerations in mind and utilizing analytical procedures, we studied a large number of alternative combinations of weapon systems and finally arrived at the force structure proposed for the next few years," he added.[29] For F/Y 1963, the administration had requested $9.361 billion for strategic retaliatory forces. McNamara particularly emphasized that "this structure would continue a mixed force of missiles and manned bombers throughout the entire planning period." And within the missile force, as he saw it, each particular missile had peculiar characteristics

28. Testimony of McNamara, House Appropriations Committee, *Department of Defense Appropriations for 1963*, part 2, pp. 13–14. McNamara later outlined some of the assumptions about the size and character of the Soviet strategic offensive and defensive forces under which the adequacy of American forces was tested (see House Armed Services Committee, *Hearings on Military Posture* [1962], p. 3219).

29. House Appropriations Committee, *Department of Defense Appropriations for 1963*, part 2, p. 14.

which justified its procurement: Minuteman was valuable for destroying enemy air defenses and hence assisting bomber penetration; Atlas and Titan missiles could attack hard targets; and the Polaris FBM system had the greatest capacity for survival.[30]

McNamara detailed the specifics of the F/Y 1963 strategic-forces programs, as recommended to Congress by the administration. With regard to strategic bombers, he said that the build-up of the B-52 force to 14 wings (some 600 aircraft) would be completed, but a 15th wing, proposed by the Air Force and supported by Congress, would not be procured. Problems had been encountered in the development of the Skybolt missile, to be carried by some B-52s, but it was "unlikely that the project would be cancelled." In the case of the B-58, two wings were still programmed, both to be in service by the end of the year. The B-47 force, which had reached some 900 aircraft, was to be gradually phased out as the missile forces were built up. Fifty percent of these long-range bombers (some 800 aircraft) were to be kept on a 15-minute ground alert, and up to 75 B-52s (one-eighth of the force) on air alert. Finally, McNamara rejected Air Force proposals, supported by Congress, for production of the B-70.[31]

With regard to strategic missiles, the F/Y 1963 program provided for the completion of the 13-squadron (129 missiles) Atlas and 12-squadron (108 missiles) Titan programs. As the Minuteman and Polaris forces were built up, the Department of Defense would consider phasing out some of the soft Atlases. In the case of the Minuteman program, 16 squadrons totalling 800 Minuteman missiles in hardened and dispersed underground silos were funded through F/Y 1963, "and additional squadrons will be procured in later years." (The tentative Minuteman projection through the late 1960s was at this time 1,200 missiles.) Development of the rail-mobile Minuteman system was cancelled. Study of the system had convinced McNamara that "the benefits to be gained are not worth the cost." Finally, the Polaris FBM submarine program was set at 41 submarines. Six (numbers 30–35) were to be procured in F/Y 1963, and long-lead-time items for these would be provided in the F/Y 1962 program; long-lead-time items for the final six submarines (numbers 36–

30. Ibid., pp. 14–15.   31. Ibid., pp. 15–16, 256.

41) would be procured in F/Y 1963, and the submarines completed in the following fiscal year. Polaris submarines numbers
12–29 were scheduled to be delivered at the rate of one a month;
numbers 30–41 at one every two months.[32] "There is no question but that, today, our strategic retaliatory forces are fully
capable of destroying the Soviet target system, even after absorbing an initial surprise attack," McNamara declared.[33] In fact, he
later testified elsewhere, "with the forces which we are proposing
. . . we will have power in excess of our requirements."[34] And as
to the future, he believed that, "the strategic retaliatory forces
programmed for the next few years are fully adequate to the task
of deterring war through their ability to destroy the attacker,
even after absorbing the first strike."[35]

However, apart from explicating the analytical process and
outlining the factors involved in the calculations, McNamara
really said very little about how the administration had reached
the posture it recommended to Congress: why delivery system A
was preferred to B; why x missiles had been chosen instead of y
missiles, etc. Nevertheless, his prepared statement and, in particular, his often exceptionally candid answers to questions in
the hearings do cast some light on the subject.

From the outset, it is clear that certain aspects of strategic
policy and certain nuclear-war-fighting scenarios figured very
prominently in the calculations. In the first place, U.S. strategic
forces, in accordance with the policy of not initiating a nuclear
exchange, were strategic *retaliatory* forces, designed to destroy
the Soviet target system "even after absorbing an initial nuclear
surprise attack," and, obviously, this would "have to be a larger
force than if you could count on a first strike capability."[36]

At the time when the F/Y 1963 defense budget was drawn up,
McNamara had embraced a particular war-fighting strategy

32. Ibid., pp. 16–17.   33. Ibid., p. 14.
34. House Armed Services Committee, *Hearings on Military Posture* (1962),
p. 3185.
35. House Appropriations Committee, *Department of Defense Appropriations for
1963*, part 2, p. 19. This assessment of the current and future adequacy of
U.S. strategic forces was generally accepted by the service chiefs and civilian
secretaries.
36. Testimony of Air Force Secretary Zuckert, House Appropriations Committee, *Department of Defense Appropriations for 1963*, part 2, p. 495.

which soon became known as the "no-cities" version of counter-force strategy. This meant: (a) that the primary targets in any nuclear exchange were to be military bases and missile sites, "to destroy the enemy's war-making capabilities"; and (b) that every incentive was to be given the enemy to avoid the targeting of population centers in any nuclear exchange. The required posture was to allow a variety of options, with responses to enemy actions to be flexible and controlled. Such a strategy, as least as interpreted by McNamara, required a larger force than any other strategy which the United States had considered. On the other hand, McNamara considered it very unlikely that a nuclear war could be fought in that way. He was, in other words, basing U.S. "weapons system design, development and procurement . . . upon this higher requirement," even though he did not think it very probable that the relevant circumstances would in fact ever occur.[37]

Having decided on the design of the U.S. strategic-forces posture, McNamara then had to estimate the size of the force required. However, the practical implementation of the new strategy had not yet proceeded very far—the revised SIOP, containing the new targeting options and specifying the targets themselves, had not even been completed.[38] It was accepted that this strategy required larger strategic forces than others, but only very rough estimates could as yet be given.

In estimating the size of the U.S. strategic-forces requirement, McNamara relied on the technique of "worst case analysis," in which the requirement was for a force able to cope with the "worst plausible case." It was this approach to planning, more than anything else, which allowed (but which should not be held responsible for) the large build-up of strategic nuclear forces by the United States in the early 1960s.[39] At first sight, to ensure that one's forces are adequate "under a wide range of possible

37. Testimony of McNamara, House Appropriations Committee, *Department of Defense Appropriations for 1963*, part 2, pp. 13, 249–50, 529; and House Armed Services Committee, *Hearings on Military Posture* (1963), pp. 571–72.

38. The revised SIOP was officially adopted by the joint chiefs of staff in January 1962, but specific target designation was not completed until June 1962.

39. Robert S. McNamara, speech given at San Francisco, 18 September 1967, in the Department of State *Bulletin*, 9 October 1967, pp. 443–51.

contingencies, ranging from the most optimistic to the most pessimistic"[40] appears to be quite sensible and responsible. However, McNamara's approach was in fact absolutist rather than probabilistic and, since absolute security is not possible, he made a personal estimate of what was. As Herbert York has explained, "worst case analysis" as actually practiced within the Department of Defense served less as a planning device than as a justification for high force levels and accelerated arms development and deployment.[41]

This approach to planning allows relatively little scope for intelligence estimates of the Soviet threat to play a part in deciding the size of the U.S. strategic force. The intelligence used by the Department of Defense in its calculations came from several sources, but primarily from the U.S. Intelligence Board. The wide range of estimates used, and the fact that USIB estimates did not cover the entire period under consideration, must have allowed wide scope for personal interpolation and subjective decisions. Apparently the only criterion was that the U.S. program must be such as to "take account of any reasonable probable change" in the NIE.[42] Or, at least, any upward change, for McNamara testified that the drastic reduction in the NIE through 1960–61 (some 96.5 percent over 19 months, according to Symington) had not had a very important effect on U.S. strategic-force requirements. According to McNamara, "the [downward] modifications in the Intelligence estimates relating to the Soviet missile strength" were "but one of a series of factors, and not the most important by any manner of means," in the determination of U.S. missile and bomber requirements.[43] In regard to the Soviet threat, McNamara's approach to planning allowed him to virtually ignore the 1961 NIE and substitute his personal assumption, which was "that the Soviet Union will

40. Testimony of McNamara, House Appropriations Committee, *Department of Defense Appropriations for 1963*, part 2, p. 19.

41. See Herbert F. York, "A Personal View of the Arms Race," pp. 27–31.

42. Testimony of McNamara, House Appropriations Committee, *Department of Defense Appropriations for 1963*, part 2, pp. 34, 202.

43. See exchange between Sen. Symington and McNamara, Senate Armed Services Committee, *Military Procurement Authorization, Fiscal Year 1963*, pp. 49–50.

eventually build a large ICBM force,"[44] an assumption which he made no public attempt to justify.

On the question of the missile mix which would make up the U.S. strategic requirement, McNamara stressed in his testimony the determining role of cost-effectiveness analysis. He did state that both the Navy and the Air Force disagreed with his recommendations as to the appropriate "mix," but implied that the service positions had in no way affected his decision. According to McNamara,

> The factors determining the mix of Polaris and Minuteman were: (a) the requirements for an invulnerable force and the quantity of such a force required to achieve certain units of target destruction; and (b) the relative costs of achieving that force.
>
> Now, the Polaris is quite a bit more expensive than the Minuteman. . . . If there were no cost differential then I think we would probably select more Polaris because it is probably at least in the short run more invulnerable than Minuteman. But there is a cost difference and therefore it seems wise to select as many Minuteman as possible in relation to the requirement for invulnerability and for a force of a given size, and that was the sequence of logic through which we went and it eventually resulted in these conclusions.[45]

And in discussing the reasons for the cancellation of the Mobile Minuteman system, he explained the decision in similar terms.[46] In fact, all the evidence suggests that the "mix" was determined on a much less systematic basis.[47] And neither the final F/Y 1963 Minuteman number nor the cancellation of the Mobile Minuteman was decided on until the middle of December 1961, when

44. Testimony of McNamara, House Appropriations Committee, *Department of Defense Appropriations for 1963*, part 2, p. 14.

45. Ibid., pp. 24–25.   46. Ibid., p. 16.

47. Professor Robert Kuenne has examined this question systematically and has argued cogently that not only is the major mix (that between Polaris and Minuteman) wrong, but that the intra-submarine mix (that between FBM and attack submarines) is also wrong (see Robert E. Kuenne, *The Polaris Missile Strike*). The Navy's unilateral position on the U.S. strategic-forces requirement, which completely ignored the existence of the Minuteman force, was 45 Polaris FBM submarines. Notwithstanding the different positions on strategic policy and nuclear-war-fighting strategy held by the Navy and Secretary McNamara, it is difficult to believe that McNamara's taking of the Minuteman force into account required only a four-submarine reduction in the Navy's request.

desperate attempts were being made to trim the defense budget to fit it into the overall executive F/Y 1963 request.

McNamara's F/Y 1963 posture statement and his performance in testimony throughout the hearings were admittedly very impressive, and his explanations very attractive. However, the avowed logic of the decisions and the superficial precision of the calculations are belied by the history of the development of the F/Y 1963 defense budget, and by some of McNamara's more candid comments during his testimony. He seems to have avoided the uncertainty regarding the Soviet threat and ignored the 1960–61 downward revisions of the national intelligence estimates of Soviet missiles by basing the U.S. strategic requirement on some much more subjective assessment of the "worst plausible case," whatever that could be; and all this was tailored to the admittedly improbable "no-cities" counterforce strategy. The actual means by which the F/Y 1963 strategic-forces program was decided upon were undoubtedly far less reasoned and finely calculated than McNamara's prepared statement sought to imply. That statement was, rather, a rationalization of substantially grosser calculations, of a posture which attempted to outline a particular strategy when that strategy could not in fact have been the criterion for the force decisions, and of the outcome of a process which was decidedly more political than the administration saw fit to admit.

7 Completing the Kennedy-McNamara Strategic Missile Build-up

Following the extensive strategic missile build-up programmed in the Kennedy Administration's F/Y 1963 defense budget, only two further budgets have sought authorization for the programming of additional strategic missiles—those of F/Y 1964 and F/Y 1965, examined in this chapter. Between them, these two budgets completed the authorization of the programmed fleet of 41 Polaris FBM submarines, and added a further 200 Minuteman ICBMs to the previously programmed force, to bring the total to 1,000 missiles. In fact, except for the final 50 Minuteman missiles, which were authorized for F/Y 1965, the F/Y 1964 defense budget contained all the authorization necessary to complete the build-up.

On 5 November 1964, the DoD officially decided to place a

1,000-missile ceiling on the Minuteman force. This decision was explained and justified in the F/Y 1966 defense budget, presented to Congress in January 1965, which is examined in the last section of this chapter.

The F/Y 1964 defense budget, and to a lesser extent those of F/Y 1965 and F/Y 1966, were based on the approved 5-year defense program presented to Congress in January 1962 for the F/Y 1963 defense budget, and projected through F/Y 1967, as discussed in the previous chapter. But changes in military technology and in the international strategic environment were responsible for fairly extensive modifications to that program, including important amendments to the U.S. strategic missile program.

In December 1962 the Department of Defense officially cancelled the Skybolt air-launched ballistic missile program. In explaining this decision before Congress in early 1963, during hearings on the F/Y 1964 defense budget, administration spokesmen stated that additional Minuteman missiles had been programmed as a functional replacement of the Skybolt. This action to some extent obscured the fact that the strategic missile build-up was already being slowed down by the administration. However, this became considerably clearer when the F/Y 1965 defense budget was transmitted to Congress—not only was new Minuteman authorization limited to 50 missiles, but a definite timetable was set down for the phasing out of the first-generation Atlas and Titan I missiles.

With the cutting back of the tentative Minuteman force projection of 1,200 to 1,000 previously authorized missiles, explained by the administration in the F/Y 1966 defense budget, the imposition of the 1,000-missile ceiling on the Minuteman force was an accomplished fact. The programming of the Kennedy-McNamara strategic missile build-up had been completed.

THE F/Y 1964 DEFENSE BUDGET AND
STRATEGIC-FORCES DECISIONS

Formal development of the F/Y 1964 defense budget began in April 1962, with the institution of the program-change control system. The program-change procedure was established "to provide an orderly method for proposing, reviewing and approving program changes." In this way, account could be taken of, "first . . . the action of the Congress on our fiscal year 1963 budget, and then . . . of all the numerous changes which are bound to occur in the international situation in our requirements for military forces, in technology and in costs." [1]

The first program-change proposals were submitted in July 1962, and by 1 October, when the service budget estimates were submitted to OSD, about 625 program-change proposals had been received. Of these, the Air Force submitted only about 150. These program changes would have added about $40 billion to the previously approved fiscal 1964–67 program base. [2]

All elements of the Defense Department were given full opportunity to present their views on the program-change requests of the other services and defense agencies. Then,

> When all of these views have been assembled, Mr. Gilpatric or I review each proposal, and render a decision or, in some cases, ask for further study. Where major issues are involved we discuss the matter in greater detail with our principal military and civilian advisors. [3]

Supplementing the program-change procedure was a system instituted by McNamara in the spring of 1962, designed to bring the chiefs of staff more directly into the budget-making process. General Lemnitzer was asked by McNamara to establish a series of special studies relating to controversial issues, and was requested to "have these studies prepared under the direction of either himself or the Chiefs, and subsequently reviewed by the Chiefs, after which I asked that they send me their recommendations on the issues." [4] (The most important of these special studies was that done by the strategic forces panel of the chairman's special study group. Instead of the 1,200 Minuteman ICBMs which McNamara had tentatively programmed for the five-year period to 1968, the CSSG suggested a force of 1,950.)

1. Senate Appropriations Committee, *Department of Defense Appropriations for 1964*, p. 26.
2. Ibid., pp. 26, 321.   3. Ibid.
4. Testimony of McNamara, House Armed Services Committee, *Hearings on Military Posture* (1963), pp. 334–35.

McNamara then studied these himself, and often discussed matters orally with the chiefs. Having arrived at his own conclusion, he then prepared a written report—"frequently in the form of a memorandum to the President"—and, after the chiefs had had an opportunity to comment on this, a final decision was made by either McNamara or Kennedy.[5]

The service submissions for F/Y 1964, received by the Office of the Secretary of Defense on 1 October 1962, added up to $67 billion. The formal Air Force request consisted of "a basic submission, which was based on the DoD approved program, and an addendum submission which was based on any of our program change proposals not fully resolved at that time." The service budgets were then,

> carefully reviewed jointly by the budget examiners of my office and the Bureau of the Budget, as has been the custom in the past. The analyses resulting from this review were forwarded to me for decision. In consultation with our principal advisors, Mr. Gilpatric and I then thoroughly reviewed all of the outstanding issues. Our decisions were transmitted to the respective services and, in the final step of our review, outstanding differences were resolved. As a result of this review, we were able to reduce the approximately $67 billion requested by the services to the total of $53.7 billion in new obligational authority recommended in the President's budget.[6]

The reduction from $67 to $53.7 billion involved some 600 items. These items were individually examined through the subject/issue ("snowflake") mechanism that had been used the previous year. For the Air Force, some 220 subject/issue decisions were made.[7]

Of the $53.7 billion recommended to Congress by McNamara, some $7.3 billion in total obligation authority was for strategic nuclear retaliatory forces (SNRF), the smallest authorization request for SNRF for several years. This included new funding for 150 additional Minuteman missiles, and final authorization

5. Ibid.

6. Testimony of McNamara, Senate Appropriations Committee, *Department of Defense Appropriations for 1964*, p. 26.

7. Ibid., pp. 321, 344.

for the six FBM submarines (numbers 35–41) whose long-lead-time components had been authorized in the F/Y 1963 budget.[8]

The U.S. strategic nuclear forces programmed at this time were detailed by McNamara in his F/Y 1964 posture statement. With regard to the strategic bomber force, he confirmed that the B-52 fleet would be limited to 14 wings (630 aircraft), and that the Skybolt ALBM, previously programmed for use on later-model B-52s, was cancelled. The B-58 fleet was still limited to two wings, or 80 aircraft. Some 700 B-47s were still in the operational force, but these were to be phased out by mid-1966. Fifty percent of these B-52, B-58, and B-47 bombers (about 650 aircraft) were maintained on 15-minute ground alert. Production of the B-70/RS-70 was again rejected by the administration.[9]

With regard to strategic missiles, McNamara pointed out that as of the beginning of 1963 the United States had over 200 Atlas, Titan and Minuteman missiles operational, and 9 FBM submarines (144 Polaris missiles) in service. All 13 squadrons of Atlas ICBMs, some 126 missiles, were now emplaced, as were all six squadrons (54 missiles) of Titan I ICBMs. The six squadrons of Titan IIs were scheduled to be emplaced by the end of 1963. The Atlas and Titan I missiles were scheduled to be phased out, but the actual schedule was not made public.[10]

In the particular case of Minuteman, the 1964 budget added a further 150 missiles to the approved program, raising the total authorized force to 950. These missiles were of an "improved type," later to be designated Minuteman II. According to Jack Raymond of the *New York Times*, the decision to add 150 Minuteman missiles to the previously authorized force of 800 was one of the last decisions taken in relation to the F/Y 1964 budget; Secretary McNamara was reported to have recommended the 150-missile addition to President Kennedy on 19 December 1962.[11]

8. Ibid., pp. 45–47.

9. Ibid.; and House Armed Services Committee, *Hearings on Military Posture* (1963), p. 308.

10. House Armed Services Committee, *Hearings on Military Posture* (1963), pp. 316, 1281.

11. *New York Times*, 20 December 1962.

The F/Y 1964 budget also included final funding for the last six of the 41-submarine fleet, comprising 656 SLBMs. In his prepared congressional statement for F/Y 1964, McNamara testified that the programmed SRF authorized and funded through F/Y 1964 provided "for a three-fold increase in the number of alert nuclear weapons in the force, compared with fiscal year 1961." And, moreover, "with ample capacity for manufacturing MINUTEMAN and POLARIS assured for some years to come, more can be added, if they should be needed." [12] However, McNamara argued that, "in adding to a Defense budget as large as the one we now have, we begin to encounter the law of diminishing returns, where each additional increment of resources applied produces a smaller increment of overall defense capability." The programmed SRF were, in his judgment, "fully adequate.... Further increases in the large forces already programmed would provide only marginal increases in capabilities in relation to their additional cost." [13]

In calculating the actual size of the strategic nuclear forces programmed by the administration, McNamara stated, repeating his January 1962 testimony, that a variety of systematic analyses, including cost-effectiveness analysis, had been used. These, he said, took into account

> the character of the target systems: the number and yields of weapons required to destroy that system: the kinds of forces best suited to deliver these weapons, i.e. their payloads, penetration abilities, CEP's, reliability and vulnerability and cost effectiveness, as well as the size and character of the enemy's strategic offensive forces. [14]

The principal consideration governing the size of the U.S. strategic nuclear forces was that of superiority over the Soviet Union. During testimony on his F/Y 1964 budget statement, McNamara referred several times to "our current strategic nuclear superiority over the USSR," and he argued that policy and budgetary actions could only be interpreted as "a series of ac-

12. Senate Appropriations Committee, *Department of Defense Appropriations for 1964*, p. 9.
13. Ibid.   14. Ibid., p. 40.

tions designed to maintain the military strength and superiority of this Nation." [15]

In terms of concrete guiding principles, the foremost was the decision to design a strategic-forces posture which would provide the United States with a variety of options. In particular the U.S. force:

> should have sufficient flexibility to permit a choice of strategies, particularly an ability to (1) strike back decisively at the entire Soviet target system simultaneously, or (2), strike back first at the Soviet bomber bases, missiles sites and other military installations associated with their long-range nuclear forces to reduce the power of any follow-on-attack—and then if necessary, strike back at the Soviet urban and industrial complex in a controlled and deliberate way. [16]

Every incentive was to be provided for the Soviet Union to withhold any attack on U.S. cities in a first strike. In order to allow this, the U.S. missile force "must be larger than would otherwise be the case," permitting the United States to attack in "waves," if it so wanted. Whether the Soviets would accept this strategy was an open question; McNamara himself believed that any nuclear attack by the Soviet Union on the United States would include an attack on major urban areas. [17] However, "considering what is at stake, we believe it is worth the additional effort on our part to have this option." [18]

McNamara rejected the option of building "a full counterforce" capability, however. The recommended posture would provide:

> throughout the period under consideration, a capability to destroy virtually all of the "soft" and "semi-hard" military targets in the Soviet Union and a large number of their fully hardened missile sites, with an additional capability in the form of a protected force

15. Senate Armed Services Committee, *Military Procurement Authorization, Fiscal Year 1964*, pp. 90, 108.
16. Senate Appropriations Committee, *Department of Defense Appropriations for 1964*, p. 41.
17. House Armed Services Committee, *Hearings on Military Posture* (1963), p. 332.
18. Senate Appropriations Committee, *Department of Defense Appropriations for 1964*, p. 41.

to be employed or held in reserve for use against urban and industrial areas.[19]

But McNamara believed that to destroy "any very large portion of the fully hard ICBM sites" would be unfeasible; and he judged this to be so "regardless of how large or what kind of strategic forces we build."[20] Even a force "two, three or several times larger than the force we recommend" would not destroy all Soviet nuclear capability.[21] And even with "an extensive missile defense system and a much more elaborate civil defense program than has thus far been contemplated . . . we could not preclude casualties counted in the tens of millions."[22]

One specific reason was given for part of the addition to the Minuteman program—because of the cancellation of the Skybolt ALBM program, 100 Minuteman missiles had been added to the previously approved program for the purpose of destroying Soviet air-defense installations.[23] (This decision is discussed separately in a later section of this study.)

THE F/Y 1965 DEFENSE BUDGET DECISIONS

With the presentation to Congress in January 1964 of the administration's F/Y 1965 defense budget request, it became obvious that the U.S. strategic missile build-up was being considerably slowed down. Only $3.5 billion in total obligational authority (TOA) was proposed for strategic nuclear retaliatory forces, by far the lowest SRF allocation since the Democrats had taken office in January 1961. In terms of new authorization and funding for strategic weapons, only 50 new Minuteman silos were proposed by McNamara, bringing the authorized force to 1,000 missiles.[24]

19. Ibid.
20. Senate Armed Services Committee, *Military Procurement Authorization, Fiscal Year 1964*, p. 40.
21. House Appropriations Committee, *Department of Defense Appropriations for 1964*, p. 234.
22. Senate Armed Services Committee, *Military Procurement Authorization, Fiscal Year 1964*, p. 40.
23. Testimony of McNamara, House Appropriations Committee, *Department of Defense Appropriations for 1964*, part 1, p. 319.
24. It should be noted that the F/Y 1965 budget was actually presented to Congress over the signature of President Lyndon B. Johnson. However, most of the decisions were made before President Kennedy's assassination on 22

In deciding on the F/Y 1965 Minuteman program, McNamara explained that he had been faced with two alternatives:

> Essentially, the choice is between (1) a faster buildup with a slower rate of retrofit of the earlier model with the Minuteman II; and (2) a slower rate of buildup with a faster rate of retrofit.[25]

McNamara chose the second alternative, which involved a somewhat lower procurement of additional missiles for F/Y 1965 than had previously been planned, but a much faster rate of retrofit of Minuteman II missiles into Minuteman I silos. Additional Minuteman missiles were, however, tentatively programmed for funding in F/Y 1966 and F/Y 1967, though "the actual number to be started will depend upon the situation prevailing a year to two years from now."[26]

McNamara believed that this decision "will greatly affect combat effectiveness." This was based on the fact that, as compared to Minuteman I, the Minuteman II would,

> provide increased range or payload; a smaller CEP; a much greater flexibility in the choice of preassigned targets; the capability of being launched by radio from an airborne command post; and a hardened power supply permitting a much greater postattack sustainability.[27]

Because Minuteman II was such an improvement over Minuteman I, it was felt that "we got more destructive power by retro-

November 1963. The F/Y 1965 defense budget itself had been largely finalized, with most of the staff work completed, and, indeed, the White House staff were having a meeting on it on the day of the assassination (interviews with Ellis Veatch, 6 February 1973; and McGeorge Bundy, 18 December 1972). McNamara's F/Y 1965 posture statement was certainly no less McNamara because of Johnson's accession.

25. House Armed Services Committee, *Hearings on Military Posture* (1964), p. 6923.

26. Ibid. On 27 January 1964 McNamara reportedly told the House Armed Services Committee that current plans called for 1,200 Minuteman ICBMs (see Congressional Quarterly Service, *Congress and the Nation, 1945–1964: A Review of Government and Politics in the Postwar Years* [Washington, D.C.: Congressional Quarterly, 1965], p. 328). And during the F/Y 1966 hearings in January 1965 McNamara disclosed that the tentative program for F/Y 1966 and F/Y 1967 had been, at this time (January 1964), 100 Minuteman missiles each fiscal year, for a total program of 1,200 missiles (see Senate Armed Services Committee, *Military Procurement Authorization, Fiscal Year 1966*, p. 59).

27. Testimony of McNamara, House Armed Services Committee, *Hearings on Military Posture* (1964), pp. 6922–23.

fitting more rapidly than we would by substantially increasing total force size."[28] And further, by integrating Minuteman II and Minuteman I squadrons into a single system through the "internetting" of their communications and control systems, "the targeting flexibility of the force as a whole" would be greatly enhanced. This proposed revision of the force structure was expected to cost only about $500 million more through F/Y 1969.[29]

In proposing such a small net quantitative addition to the Minuteman force, McNamara also stressed the operation of "the law of diminishing returns, where each additional increment of resources used produces a proportionately smaller increment of overall defense capability," particularly when a defense program was as large as the one that the U.S. had developed and procured.[30] Since the Democrats had assumed office in January 1961, McNamara pointed out,

> The number of weapons in the alert forces will have been increased about 2½ times and the megatonnage of these weapons almost 3 times, even though a large number of B-47s will have been phased out of the force during the same period.[31]

In regard to the Minuteman, McNamara testified that the approved program had the capability of fulfilling all the objectives of U.S. strategic policy even given the most pessimistic assumptions, and that "the results do not vary to any significant degree for alternative Minuteman forces greater than those I am recommending."[32]

In describing the theoretical underpinnings of the SRF procurement program, McNamara for the first time introduced the concept of "Damage Limitation." He explained this concept by juxtaposing the contending theories of "overkill" and "full first strike." According to McNamara,

> The proponents of the "overkill" theory would, in effect, restrict our strategic forces to those required for retaliation against cities only—with the calculation assuming near optimum conditions.[33]

28. Ibid., p. 6979.   29. Ibid., p. 6922.   30. Ibid., p. 6897.
31. Ibid., p. 6921.   32. Ibid., p. 6929.   33. Ibid., p. 6918.

Moreover, the "cities only" constrictions of "overkill" were considered by McNamara to be "dangerously inadequate." On the other hand, he believed a "full first strike" capability, which would limit damage to U.S. population and industry in any nuclear exchange to an "acceptable" level, to be "simply unattainable."[34] In terms of strategic forces, the damage-limiting posture would require something in between these two extremes—it could, for example, be "considerably larger than would be needed for a limited 'cities only' strategy." But studies of SRF alternatives showed "that forces in excess of those needed simply to destroy Soviet cities would significantly reduce damage to the United States and Western Europe," although he added that, of course, "there are some differences of judgment on just how large such a force should be."[35]

However, while McNamara conceded that the size and character of the Minuteman force would be important in reducing damage to the United States, he argued that "grave damage" could not be avoided, "no matter how many Minuteman missiles (within practical limits) . . . we were to add to our forces." And, furthermore, cost-effectiveness studies demonstrated "that a properly planned nationwide fallout shelter program would contribute far more to the saving of lives per dollar than an increase in Minuteman missiles beyond the level we recommend."[36]

The most important question discussed in relation to the SRF programs during the F/Y 1965 hearings was that of the reliability of U.S. missiles. This discussion was prompted by charges by Senator Goldwater to the effect that American missiles were "not dependable."[37] In his January 1964 posture statement, McNamara had pointed out that, as of mid-1964, "the number of ICBM and Polaris missiles will, for the first time, just about equal the number of manned bombers in the force." And because of the much greater vulnerability of the manned bomber force, "a higher proportion of the Minuteman force than of the B-52 force can be counted upon to reach targets in a retaliatory strike." In this sense, the Minuteman was "more dependable"

34. Ibid., p. 6920.   35. Ibid., pp. 6919–20.   36. Ibid., p. 6929.
37. *New York Times*, 10 January 1964.

than the B-52.[38] Goldwater took this as evidence of the administration's intention to further downgrade the manned bomber, however, and while producing no evidence, asserted that the "fire reliability" of U.S. ICBMs was only 38 percent.[39] McNamara did not offer any specific figures to refute these,[40] but stated that,

> Senator Goldwater's reported statement that the U.S. long-range missiles are not dependable is completely misleading, politically irresponsible, and damaging to the national security. There is no information, classified or otherwise, to support the false implication that our long-range missiles cannot be depended on to accomplish their mission.[41]

And he testified that those responsible for targeting "the war plan" had full confidence in the Minuteman system.[42] In any event, McNamara testified, any "mechanical unreliability" of the Minuteman missile had been compensated for by increased procurement so as to ensure its dependability in any of its mission objectives.[43]

As in previous years, McNamara reported that the U.S. estimate of Soviet forces had been "one of the major determinants of the size and character of our future strategic retaliatory forces." [44] But, as before, he gave no indications as to just how estimates and projections of Soviet strength in any concrete way affected the U.S. strategic-forces program, with one minor and only partial exception: it was argued that the administration's case for phasing out the "soft" missiles was partly based upon strategic developments within the Soviet Union.

The F/Y 1965 defense budget disclosed one other decision

38. House Armed Services Committee, *Hearings on Military Posture* (1964), pp. 6921–25.
39. *New York Times*, 29 February 1964.
40. "Cape Kennedy sources," however, were reported to have said that seven out of ten ICBM tests had been successful, and called only one out of ten outright failures (see the *New York Times*, 10 January 1964).
41. House Appropriations Committee, *Department of Defense Appropriations for 1965*, part 4, p. 158.
42. Ibid., pp. 164–65.
43. House Armed Services Committee, *Hearings and Military Posture* (1964), p. 6926.
44. Ibid., p. 6921.

relevant to the U.S. ICBM force. In a series of meetings between McNamara and the joint chiefs of staff between August and November 1963, it was decided to phase out the 27 Atlas D missiles during F/Y 1965. The Atlas E and Titan I missiles were also scheduled to be phased out, but a modernization program would allow this to take place "sometime later"; the actual schedule remained classified.[45]

The decision to withdraw these "soft," liquid-fuel missiles from the force was explained in a variety of ways. In his prepared posture statement, McNamara explained it in terms of the very unfavorable cost-effectiveness of the Atlases as compared with the rapidly increasing Minuteman force.[46] Before the Senate Appropriations Committee, in the face of fairly critical questioning, he stated that the decision was "based on the fact that the Minuteman is much more dependable than the Atlas D, is much less costly, and is coming in on schedule, as is the Polaris, very satisfactorily."[47] And before the same committee the next day, Dr. Harold Brown, assistant secretary of defense for research and development, explained the decision in terms of the increasing accuracy of Soviet missiles.[48]

At this time, the Atlas F was scheduled to remain in the force with the Titan II and the Minuteman indefinitely. However, all the Atlas E, Titan I, and Atlas F missiles were actually phased out before the end of F/Y 1965, within a few months of the Atlas D missiles. For some reason, the modification and modernization program which the Pentagon had judged worthwhile in late 1963 was not undertaken.[49] Incomplete "shakedown" tests and haste in bringing the Atlas F into operational status during the October 1962 Cuban Missile Crisis may have been responsible for the accelerated withdrawal of this missile from the force,[50]

45. Senate Appropriations Committee, *Department of Defense Appropriations for 1964*, pp. 50, 71.
46. House Armed Services Committee, *Hearings on Military Posture* (1964), p. 6922. The Atlases were slow reacting and very vulnerable, and their cost of operation and maintenance was about $1 million per missile per year, as compared with only about $100,000 for a Minuteman.
47. Senate Appropriations Committee, *Department of Defense Appropriations for 1964*, p. 50.
48. Ibid., p. 322.   49. Ibid., pp. 71, 318.
50. See John S. Tompkins, *The Weapons of World War III*, pp. 175–77.

but this does not explain the Atlas E and Titan I decisions. Most likely, for political reasons, McNamara simply waited until after the conclusion of the F/Y 1965 hearings before he announced his decision, thus avoiding interrogation by the many congressional supporters of the "big payload" missiles.

THE F/Y 1966 DEFENSE BUDGET DECISIONS:
CONFIRMING THE 1,000-MINUTEMAN CEILING

The defense budget for F/Y 1966, presented to Congress by Secretary of Defense McNamara in January 1965, included only $4.5 billion in TOA for strategic nuclear retaliatory forces, i.e., only 50 to 60 percent of the SRF funding of fiscal years 1962–64.[51] The most important decision in the strategic-weapons field was the decision to limit the Minuteman procurement program to the 1,000 missiles previously authorized in F/Y 1962–65.

Until this decision the Department of Defense had tentatively programmed a Minuteman force of 1,200 missiles by the end of the 1960s. This figure was originally presented by the DoD in McNamara's first posture statement, transmitted to Congress in January 1962 with the F/Y 1963 defense budget and F/Y 1963–67 defense program.[52] Under the McNamara Administration, the DoD kept a running five-year defense program; the figures for all years other than the current budgetary year, however, had no final approval associated with them—they were simply planning figures.

With the cancellation of the Skybolt ALBM program in December 1962, the DoD added another 100 Minuteman missiles to the F/Y 1963–68 five-year plan,[53] bringing the planned Minuteman force to 1,300 missiles. According to *Missiles and Rockets*, the DoD continued to plan on an eventual force of 1,300 Minuteman ICBMs until the fall of 1963.[54]

51. Senate Armed Services Committee, *Military Procurement Authorization, Fiscal Year 1966*, p. 74.
52. Testimony of Secretary of Defense Melvin Laird, Senate Appropriations Committee, *Department of Defense Appropriations for Fiscal Year 1970*, p. 585 (see also *U.S. News and World Report*, 22 January 1962, p. 22).
53. Testimony of McNamara, House Appropriations Committee, *Department of Defense Appropriations for 1964*, part 1, p. 319.
54. See *Missiles & Rockets*, 25 March 1963, p. 13 and p. 31; 6 May 1963, p. 32; 1 July 1963, p. 26; 29 July 1963, p. 91; 2 September 1963, p. 22; 4 November

In the F/Y 1965 defense budget, drawn up in late 1963 and sent to Congress on 21 January 1964, the DoD reverted to 1,200 as the F/Y 1969 planning figure.[55] Apparently there were at this time two alternative plans for reaching the 1,200 target. In his F/Y 1966 posture statement (February 1965), McNamara testified that "last year we had tentatively planned to fund another 100 Minuteman silos in each year F/Y 1966–67 (for a total of 1,200 missiles)."[56] *Missiles and Rockets* reported on 13 January 1964, however, that the administration had elected to procure 50 Minuteman missiles per year from F/Y 1966 through F/Y 1969 for a total of 1,200 missiles.[57] And in his interview with *U.S. News and World Report*, McNamara stated that the 1,200 figure was the "objective for the fifth year [F/Y 1969]."[58]

The decision to cut the tentative Minuteman program to 1,000 missiles was formally made by the DoD on 5 November 1964.[59] In a meeting with the joint chiefs of staff, Secretary McNamara, Deputy Secretary Vance, and BoB Director Kermit Gordon on 22 December 1964, President Johnson upheld this decision, and it was announced to the press immediately afterwards.[60] The estimated five-year cost of the 200 Minuteman II missiles cut from the Minuteman program was $1.3 billion, of which about $400 million would have been required in F/Y 1966. Fifty of the 200 missiles were to be sited at an existing wing, and the other 150 at a new (No. 7) wing.[61] In the face of very critical question-

1963, p. 22. These reports were confirmed in an interview with Dr. Henry Glass, 29 July 1970.

55. *Missiles & Rockets*, 13 January 1964, p. 14; and interview with Henry Glass, 29 July 1970.

56. Senate Armed Services Committee, *Military Procurement Authorization, Fiscal Year 1966*, p. 59.

57. *Missiles & Rockets*, 13 January 1964, p. 14.

58. *U.S. News and World Report*, 12 April 1965, p. 56.

59. Senate Preparedness Investigating Subcommittee, *Status of U.S. Strategic Power*, part 1 (April 1968), pp. 38, 114. This decision by the DoD was made just two days after the 3 November 1964 election, in which issues relating to the strategic missile force had been prominent. It is interesting to note that McNamara apparently waited until after the election before formally making the 1,000-Minuteman decision.

60. L. J. Korb, "The Role of the Joint Chiefs of Staff," p. 198; and interviews with Ellis Veatch, 6 February 1973, and Kermit Gordon, 8 February 1973.

61. Senate Armed Services Committee, *Military Procurement Authorization, Fiscal Year 1966*, pp. 56, 1033–34, 1067.

ing from members of the Senate Armed Services Committee, McNamara stated on 26 February 1965 that,

> The reason for the reduction is three-fold:
> First [*deleted*].
> Secondly, and most importantly, the capability of the Minuteman system has been increased by the introduction into the program of improvements in guidance and other features which increase its kill capability. . . .
> Thirdly, the decision was affected by the further studies that the Joint Staff and others have made of strategic nuclear war which outline the task to be accomplished by our forces and our capability for accomplishing it. As I tried to outline to you, we have basically two requirements for this strategic offensive force. One is to have such power that the Soviets will understand that they would be literally destroyed if they were to launch against us. That requires only a portion of the force. [*Deleted*]. The second requirement for the force is to assist in reducing the damage to our country, and these studies have shown that an additional 200 missiles would not have any material effect in reducing the damage to our Nation. Therefore I do not believe we should recommend them to you.[62]

From statements made elsewhere by McNamara and other members of the administration, it is possible to infer what the first reason was. General Gerrity, for example, stated before the Senate Armed Services Committee that the DoD decision was "based on what they consider the threat to be and the capability of the Minuteman II against that threat."[63] In reporting the Minuteman cutback, *Missiles and Rockets* disclosed that the Pentagon explained it partly in terms of "new U.S. intelligence indicating fewer Soviet ICBMs—about 200 in total—than previously estimated, and thus fewer targets" facing the U.S. force.[64] And in an interview with *U.S. News and World Report* on 12 April 1965, McNamara stated that one reason for the cutback was that, "Our estimates of the Soviet threat have changed. . . . We now estimate that the Soviet program will lag compared with what we previously estimated and this is what reduces our requirements."[65]

62. Ibid., p. 304.
63. Senate Armed Services Committee, *Military Procurement Authorization, Fiscal Year 1966*, pp. 1057–58.
64. *Missiles & Rockets*, 4 January 1965, p. 10.
65. *U.S. News and World Report*, 12 April 1965, p. 56.

McNamara, however, seems to have considered the increased capability of the Minuteman II far more important than the reduced estimates of Soviet missile deployment. In his prepared posture statement, for example, this was his only explanation of the Minuteman cutback. He testified that,

> On the basis of our analysis of the general nuclear war problem in the early 1970s, I am convinced that another 200 Minuteman silos are not required at this time. We now believe that we can markedly increase the "kill" capabilities of the Minuteman force through a number of qualitative improvements which now appear feasible. The Minuteman force presently planned for FY 1970 will have a total destruction capability of at least 30 or 40 percent greater than a force of the same size consisting only of Minuteman I. With the additional improvements which now appear possible, the destruction capabilities of the Minuteman force could be further increased in the future, if that appears desirable, by a factor of two compared with a force of the same size consisting only of Minuteman I.[66]

Throughout the F/Y 1966 hearings, McNamara and his chief aides emphasized that the 1,000-Minuteman force was still subject to change in the future if further missiles were thought necessary. Before the Senate Armed Services Committee and the Committee on Appropriations' subcommittee on defense, for example, McNamara stated:

> we can increase that total to 1,200 at a later date if it seems desirable . . . we can still reach 1,200 at the end of 1969 if it seems desirable to do so, by adding missiles at a later date. So I don't believe the decision should be thought final. We should review it each year, and raise it in the future if it seems necessary.[67]

And Deputy Secretary Vance testified before the House Armed Services Committee that the DoD was "preserving the option" of a 1,200-missile force "should we determine next year that it is desirable."[68] The Air Force, however, doubted that this would be done.[69]

66. Senate Armed Services Committee, *Military Procurement Authorization, Fiscal Year 1966*, p. 60.
67. Ibid., p. 385.
68. House Armed Services Committee, *Hearings on Military Posture* (1965), p. 202.
69. See, for example, testimony of Gen. McConnell, Senate Armed Services

In November 1964, when the Minuteman force size was under consideration in the F/Y 1966 budget discussions, most of the joint chiefs of staff favored the 1,200 total.[70] Within Congress the Air Force had a large number of prominent supporters of its 1,200-Minuteman position, particularly in the House and Senate Armed Services Committees. In the Senate, Senators John Stennis (Democrat, Mississippi, chairman of the preparedness investigating subcommittee), Richard B. Russell (Democrat, Georgia, chairman of the Committee on Armed Services and of the defense subcommittee of the Committee on Appropriations), and Strom Thurmond (then Democrat, South Carolina) were especially critical of the DoD's decision.[71] Some senators supported the 1,200-missile program because it would have meant an additional Minuteman wing, possibly in their own state. (Senators Cannon and Bible, for example, both Democrats from Nevada, contacted Secretary Zuckert with a view to having Stead AFB, Nevada, selected as the seventh Minuteman wing.)[72]

In early March 1965, however, the Air Force relaxed its earlier position. Testimony of Air Force generals on 12 March, for example, revealed that the Air Force now approved the OSD 1,000-missile ceiling on the Minuteman force, and accepted the 1,000 program as satisfactory.[73] At about the same time, the joint chiefs of staff were drawing up the JSOP setting out the requirements for the F/Y 1967 defense budget and the F/Y 1967–71 defense program, and in that plan the 1,000-Minuteman force was accepted as the JCS requirement.[74] And, during hearings on the F/Y 1967 budget in February 1966, the chairman of the joint chiefs, General Wheeler, testified that the JCS now unanimously accepted the 1,000 figure, and McNamara emphasized

---

Committee, *Military Procurement Authorization, Fiscal Year 1966*, p. 994, and testimony of Gen. Gerrity, p. 1056.

70. Ibid., p. 385.

71. Senate Armed Services Committee, *Military Procurement Authorization, Fiscal Year 1966*, p. 304; Senate Armed Services Committee, *Military Procurement Authorization for Fiscal Year 1967*, pp. 248, 252; Sen. Thurmond, *Congressional Record, Senate*, 12 May 1965, pp. 10369–70.

72. Senate Armed Services Committee, *Military Procurement Authorization, Fiscal Year 1966*, pp. 1009–10.

73. Ibid., pp. 1072–74, 1056.

74. Interview with F. S. Hoffman, 25 August 1970.

that both the secretary of the Air Force and the chief of staff (now General John P. McConnell) fully concurred in the decision.[75]

In retrospect there is little doubt that McNamara had little real intention of ever procuring more than 1,000 Minuteman ICBMs. Some former officials believe that he had actually settled on 1,000 some time in 1961;[76] others think that it was not until he was satisfied, some time in 1962, that the improved Minuteman (Minuteman II) would be an enormous qualitative improvement over the early Minuteman.[77] In any case, it was long before November 1964.

The higher figures were left in the OSD five-year program projections for two reasons. First, because McNamara was more interested in winning annual budget fights than fighting over the target for five years hence; and, second, because a higher end figure on paper gave him greater scope for bargaining. While it was in the plan, the higher figure(s) could be used as a "chopping block" to cut other programs (for example, the B-70); and the manipulation of the figure(s) allowed McNamara to cancel other programs while seemingly offering compensation (for example, the Skybolt cancellation).

The F/Y 1966 budget was simply the latest opportunity McNamara had of imposing the 1,000-Minuteman ceiling. And with President Johnson secure in office for a further four years, November–December 1964 was politically a very appropriate time for him to formally make the cut-off decision.

20 July 1970

75. Senate Armed Services Committee, *Military Procurement Authorization for Fiscal Year 1967*, pp. 248, 252. McConnell replaced Le May as Air Force chief of staff on 1 February 1965. This might partly explain the Air Force's reversal of position between January (1,200) and March (acceptance of 1,000). Before retiring, Le May made an urgent recommendation for approval of the 1,200 program (see *Missiles & Rockets*, 4 January 1965, p. 10). McConnell, however, appears to have been far more "reasonable" in his dealings with OSD.

76. Interviews with Dr. Alain C. Enthoven, 17 August 1970; Daniel Ellsberg, 24 August 1970; Gen. Curtis E. Le May, 16 August 1970; and Roswell Gilpatric, 20 January 1973.

77. Interviews with Henry Glass, 29 July 1970, and Neil Harlan, 21 July 1970.

part three

Explaining the
Strategic Missile Build-up

8 The Missile Build-up and Intelligence about Soviet Strategic Forces

With the deployment on station of the Polaris FBM submarine USS *Will Rogers* on 3 October 1967, the U.S. strategic ballistic missile force levelled off at 1,710 missiles. Only two weeks before this, in an address to the annual convention of United Press International editors and publishers at San Francisco on 18 September 1967, Secretary of Defense McNamara had stated that this missile force was "both greater than we had originally planned and in fact more than we require." He then went on to explain how this had come about:

> In 1961, when I became Secretary of Defense, the Soviet Union possessed a very small operational arsenal of intercontinental missiles. However, they did possess the technological and industrial capacity to enlarge that arsenal very substantially over the succeeding several years.

Now we had no evidence that the Soviets did in fact plan to fully use that capability. But as I have pointed out, a strategic planner must be "conservative" in his calculations; that is, he must prepare for the worst plausible case and not be content to hope and prepare merely for the most probable.

Since we could not be certain of Soviet intentions—since we could not be sure that they would not undertake a massive buildup —we had to insure against such an eventuality by undertaking ourselves a major buildup of the Minuteman and Polaris forces.

Thus, in the course of hedging against what was then only a theoretically possible Soviet buildup, we took decisions which have resulted in our current superiority in numbers of war heads and deliverable megatons.

Now let me be absolutely clear. I am not saying that our decision in 1961 was unjustified. I am simply saying that it was necessitated by a lack of accurate information.[1]

This remains the only "official" explanation of the Kennedy-McNamara missile build-up.

The belief that the Kennedy-McNamara missile program was an overreaction, produced by "conservative" planning, to the expectation of an impending missile gap favoring the Soviet Union is now a piece of conventional wisdom, accepted by strategists, former officials (from Herbert York to General Le May), journalists, and critics alike.[2] It is a belief which has never, however, been critically examined.

On 29 January 1964, in testimony before the House Armed Services Committee, McNamara in fact contradicted the substance of his argument of 18 September 1967—while acknowledging the inadequate intelligence available in 1959, 1960, and 1961, he denied that on the basis of the subsequent intelligence reappraisal the United States should have downgraded its own missile program. The following exchange took place between Congressman Becker and McNamara:

MR. BECKER: Now, let's get down to the intelligence estimates. We went ahead based upon certain overestimated intelligence information from 1960, 1961, on to the point of increasing our

1. Robert S. McNamara, "The Dynamics of Nuclear Strategy," pp. 445–46.
2. See, for example, Herbert F. York, "A Personal View of the Arms Race," p. 28; and Gen. Curtis E. Le May, *America is in Danger*, p. 43.

defense expenditures from $10 billion a year and increasing the building of missiles, during these years, because of a so-called improper or a lack of proper intelligence. Now, today we have good intelligence, so that we know we do not need so many missiles any more, we don't need to build so many, as Soviet Russia has nowhere near the amount of missiles we assumed they had from intelligence several years ago, this is part of your statement today, is that right?

SECRETARY McNAMARA: No, sir. I stated that the intelligence estimates of 1959, 1960 and 1961, when compared with the actual strength for the period which was included in those estimates, that is to say, mid-1963, had overestimated the strength. But I didn't state that this led this administration to act incorrectly in establishing a procurement program for missiles.[3]

On 7 April 1961, only some ten weeks after his taking office, McNamara was even more candid, in an exchange with Gerald Ford, of the House Appropriations defense subcommittee, on the effect on strategic planning of a downgrading of the Soviet threat:

MR. FORD: Mr. Secretary, if within the next two months or the next three months the Central Intelligence Agency should decide, based on new intelligence, that we had misjudged or miscalculated the ICBM threat from the Soviet Union, would that have any impact, material or otherwise, on the program you are submitting to us here today?

SECRETARY McNAMARA: I think it would depend on the degree of miscalculation and the time period that that miscalculation applied to.

MR. FORD: Your recommendations that we have before us now in this area are related to the intelligence summaries you now are working with?

SECRETARY McNAMARA: Essentially so, but I want to emphasize that the intelligence summaries, if we limit that term to mean the missile tables we discussed earlier, are not the only intelligence data that affect our force requirements.

MR. FORD: But if we had a 25 percent downgrading in the Soviet Union ICBM threat within the next several months, that would have a substantial impact on their total destructive force as far as we are concerned?

SECRETARY McNAMARA: Yes.

3. House Armed Services Committee, *Hearings on Military Posture* (1964), p. 6961.

MR. FORD: If that took place, would that have much impact, if any, on the program you are submitting to us?

SECRETARY McNAMARA: It would have some but no[t] much.

MR. FORD: That is all?[4]

To argue otherwise at this time would, perhaps, have made it politically more difficult to carry out the extensive changes in the U.S. defense posture that Kennedy and McNamara were so determined upon.

In January 1962 Senator Symington disclosed percentage figures which showed that national intelligence estimates of Soviet ICBMs had in fact been drastically downgraded during the previous 22 months—the September 1961 NIE was only 3.5 percent of the estimate of December 1959. Symington was obviously bemused by how seriously the Defense Department leadership took intelligence estimates:

> If you are figuring the needs of our Defense Department on our intelligence, it is difficult for me to see why there haven't been broader changes made. . . . I would ask you to file for the record the justification of your statement that intelligence is taken into consideration.[5]

McNamara sidestepped Symington's question, and failed to file anything for the record.

In each of McNamara's annual posture statements to Congress from January 1962 to January 1964, the secretary emphasized that the size and character of the Soviet strategic forces was a prime factor in determining U.S. strategic-forces requirements. For example, in his first posture statement, delivered to Congress in January 1962, he stated that

> obviously, the size and kind of forces we will need in the future will be influenced, in large part, by the size and kind of long-range nuclear forces the Soviets could bring against us and our allies and by the effectiveness of the Soviet defensive system.[6]

4. House Appropriations Committee, *Department of Defense Appropriations for 1962*, part 3, pp. 111–12.

5. Senate Armed Services Committee, *Military Procurement Authorization, Fiscal Year 1963*, pp. 49–50.

6. House Armed Services Committee, *Hearings on Military Posture* (1962), p. 3173.

He specified that a major factor in the calculations of the DoD had been

> the size, weight, and effectiveness of a possible enemy attack—based on estimates of the size and character of the enemy's long-range strategic offensive forces and the warhead yields, reliability, and accuracy of their weapon system.[7]

McNamara was aware that such estimates involved great uncertainties, but he believed that allowances could be made for these in the department's analyses. Again, in his first posture statement, he said:

> Clearly, each of these crucial factors involves various degrees of uncertainty. But these uncertainties are not completely unmanageable. By postulating various sets of assumptions, ranging from optimistic to pessimistic, it is possible to introduce into our calculations reasonable allowances for these uncertainties. For example, we can use in our analysis both the higher and lower limits of the range of estimates of enemy ICBMs and long-range bombers. We can assign to these forces a range of capabilities as to warhead yield, accuracy, and reliability.[8]

And during his testimony before the House Appropriations defense subcommittee on 29 January 1962, he said that

> in calculating the force requirements for our strategic nuclear delivery forces we took account of a series of cases ranging from what we would call the optimistic to the pessimistic. . . . we used a wide range of estimates because we were trying to determine under what circumstances would it be inadequate.[9]

However, McNamara gave no further details of these calculations or the relevant ranges of estimates; nor did he disclose how they gave rise to the assumptions about the Soviet missile program upon which the U.S. strategic-forces requirement was allegedly in part based.

The particular assumption that McNamara actually adopted in 1962 was "in fact . . . that the Soviet Union will eventually

7. Ibid., p. 3172.   8. Ibid.
9. House Appropriations Committee, *Department of Defense Appropriations for 1963*, part 2, p. 34.

build a large ICBM force." [10] This assumption largely ignored the 1960–61 downgrading of the NIE, the apparent difficulties that the Soviets were having in developing a second-generation ICBM or a submarine-launched ballistic missile, and the considerable evidence that Khrushchev had adopted a "minimum deterrence" strategic-forces posture.

McNamara stated again in January 1963 that "the size and character of our opponent's strategic forces and defense systems —now, and more importantly, in the future," were some of the major uncertainties faced by the administration in its planning. This was, moreover, complicated by the long lead-times involved in making strategic weapons operational for, because of these,

> we must plan for our forces well in advance of the time when we will need them and, indeed, we now project our programs at least 5 years ahead of the current budget year. For the same reason we must also project our estimates of the enemy's forces at least 5 years into the future, and for some purposes, even beyond. These longer range projections of enemy capabilities are, of course, highly conjectural, particularly since they deal with a period beyond the production and deployment leadtimes of enemy weapon systems. Therefore, we are, in effect, attempting to anticipate production and deployment decisions which our opponents, themselves, may not yet have made.[11]

The particular assumption made by McNamara about future Soviet strategic forces was that the Soviet Union would build a large ICBM force, which it would harden and disperse, and that it would acquire "a significant number of missile-launching submarines," a portion of which would be continually deployed at sea.[12] The grounds for this assumption were never publicly explicated. In fact, the NIE at this time, prepared in late 1962, represented a further downgrading in the projections of Soviet ICBM levels for mid-1967 as compared with the NIE of the previous year.[13]

10. House Armed Services Committee, *Hearings on Military Posture* (1962), p. 3173.
11. Senate Appropriations Committee, *Department of Defense Appropriations for 1964*, p. 40.
12. Ibid., p. 41.
13. *Statement of Secretary of Defense Robert S. McNamara before the House Sub-*

Furthermore, McNamara was often seemingly inconsistent in his explanations of how estimates and assumptions concerning the Soviet missile force related to the U.S. program. In one place, for example, he asserted that because it was U.S. policy to target Soviet strategic weapons, the growth of the Soviet force had increased American programs;[14] elsewhere, however, he stated that he was not predicating U.S. plans on estimates of the Soviet missile force.[15] McNamara was obviously playing very freely with the estimates of current and future Soviet strategic strength and its relevance to the U.S. strategic-forces program.

Again in January 1964, in testimony on the F/Y 1965 defense budget, the last budget to program additional strategic missiles, McNamara reported that the U.S. estimate of Soviet forces had been "one of the major determinants of the size and character of our future strategic retaliatory forces."[16] But, as before, he gave no indications as to just how the estimates and projections of Soviet strength affected, in any concrete way, the U.S. strategic-forces program.

Beneath the "shifting sands"[17] which characterized the McNamara strategy throughout his years as secretary of defense was a constant, although not always explicit, acceptance of a particular version of deterrence as a national strategic policy. This was the necessity for the United States to have the capability, at all times and under all circumstances, "of destroying the aggressor to the point that his society is simply no longer viable in any meaningful 20th-century sense."[18] In April 1961, some three months after he had taken office, McNamara stated that

> our objective has been to develop a strategic delivery system for nuclear weapons which will be able to survive an attack with suffi-

committee on Department of Defense Appropriations, the Fiscal Year 1964–68 Defense Program and 1964 Defense Budget, 6 February 1963, p. 29 (declassified 1975).

14. House Appropriations Committee, Department of Defense Appropriations for 1964, part 1, p. 328.

15. Senate Armed Services Committee, Military Procurement Authorization, Fiscal Year 1964, p. 131.

16. House Armed Services Committee, Hearings on Military Posture (1964), p. 6921.

17. See James R. Schlesinger, in Senate Committee on Government Operations, Planning, Programming, Budgeting (1970), p. 133.

18. McNamara, "The Dynamics of Nuclear Strategy," p. 444.

cient power to deliver *substantial destruction* to the attacker after that first strike.[19]

By February 1965 McNamara had defined "substantial destruction" to be "the destruction of . . . one-quarter to one-third of its [the Soviet Union's] population and about two-thirds of its industrial capacity."[20]

Two things should be noted about this formulation. In the first place, "such high assurance was not always a U.S. requirement"—certainty of such destructive capability would have been strategically unthinkable in the 1950s. Second, and more importantly, it is quite independent of whatever capacity for destruction might be possessed by the Soviet Union. As one critic has pointed out,

> It is questionable whether it is reasonable to consider deterrence as such as a function of some fixed, absolute assured destruction capability (as McNamara appears to do) without taking into consideration the magnitude of the threat to be deterred.[21]

In McNamara's overall strategy, of course, Soviet capabilities do enter into the U.S. strategic-forces requirement. In particular, Soviet first-strike offensive forces and strategic defensive forces must be considered. But, as McNamara himself has stated, Soviet capabilities in these respects are "but one of a series of factors, and not the most important by any manner of means" in the determination of U.S. missile and bomber requirements.[22] All this makes McNamara's rationale of 18 September 1967 extremely questionable.

It is clear from chapter 4 that by the late summer or early fall of 1961, if not immediately after taking office in January that year, the new administration found that the question of a possible missile gap was no longer relevant for policy and weapons-

19. House Appropriations Committee, *Department of Defense Appropriations for 1962*, part 3, p. 143. (Italics added.)
20. House Armed Services Committee, *Military Procurement Authorization, Fiscal Year 1966*, p. 44.
21. N. Petersen, in *Implications of Anti-Ballistic Missile Systems*, ed. C. F. Barnaby and A. Boresrup, p. 49.
22. Senate Armed Services Committee, *Military Procurement Authorization, Fiscal Year 1963*, p. 50.

procurement purposes. As Arthur Schlesinger has reported, the missile gap was no longer an issue by the time of the defense budget deliberations in November 1961.[23]

Virtually the whole of the Kennedy-McNamara strategic missile build-up was programmed after the Kennedy Administration had officially dismissed the missile gap—by about October 1961 at the latest. The F/Y 1963 defense budget, of which the missile requests were only made final in December 1961, added 200 Minuteman missiles and 192 Polaris missiles (12 FBM submarines) to the missile program, and McNamara's F/Y 1963–F/Y 1967 posture statement projected at least a further 400 Minuteman missiles. The F/Y 1964 and F/Y 1965 defense budgets provided the final authorization for 200 of these Minuteman missiles and six of the Polaris FBM submarines. This brought the U.S. strategic arsenal to 1,890 (including the 180 Atlas and Titan I) intercontinental and submarine-launched ballistic missiles—an increase of nearly 75 percent over the Eisenhower program in total long-range strategic missiles, and of just over 100 percent in numbers of second-generation strategic missiles.

Besides the Kennedy-McNamara strategic missile build-up of 1961–64, there were three other major long-range strategic missile decisions which bear on the question of the role of intelligence about the Soviet missile program in the U.S. missile build-up. First, there was the decision to cancel the mobile Minuteman program, finally made on 13 December 1961. During the course of his testimony on the F/Y 1963 and F/Y 1964 defense budgets, McNamara gave a variety of disparate reasons for the cancellation of this program. These included its increased development costs,[24] its lack of cost-effectiveness as an operational system when compared with Polaris and fixed-base Minuteman systems,[25] its minimal contribution to U.S. deterrent power,[26] and the planned development of a mobile medium-range ballistic

23. Arthur M. Schlesinger, Jr., *A Thousand Days*, p. 438.
24. Senate Armed Services Committee, *Military Procurement Authorization, Fiscal Year 1963*, p. 24.
25. Ibid., p. 25, and House Armed Services Committee, *Hearings on Military Posture* (1962), p. 3175.
26. House Appropriations Committee, *Department of Defense Appropriations for 1964*, part 1, p. 255.

missile.[27] Although at least two commentators[28] have attributed the cancellation of the mobile Minuteman program, at least in part, to the downgrading of the Soviet missile force by U.S. intelligence during 1961, this factor was never mentioned by McNamara.

The second ICBM program decision relevant here is that to phase out the 27 Atlas D missiles in the late summer and the fall of 1963 and the 99 Atlas E and F and the 54 Titan I missiles in late 1964. Again, a variety of reasons were given for this decision. The principal explanation, given by McNamara in his prepared F/Y 1965 posture statement, was the very low cost-effectiveness of these missiles as compared with the rapidly increasing Minuteman force.[29] In early 1966 McNamara was quite positive: "We took all the Atlas's out because they had practically no effective combat capability."[30]

There was little indication that estimates or projections of Soviet missile strength played any part in this decision. On 6 February 1964 Dr. Harold Brown, assistant secretary of defense for research and development, testified before the Senate Appropriations defense subcommittee that the increased accuracy of Soviet missiles had reduced any contribution which the Atlases and Titans could make to deterrence,[31] but this was the only reference made to the Soviets during the hearings on the Atlas and Titan phaseout.

This decision is perhaps best seen as the culmination of the policy decision early in 1961 by the Kennedy-McNamara administration to shift the basis of the U.S. strategic missile posture from the first-generation liquid-fuel Atlas and Titan missile program to the second-generation solid-fuel Polaris and Minute-

27. Senate Armed Services Committee, *Military Procurement Authorization, Fiscal Year 1963*, p. 25.
28. J. David Singer, *Deterrence, Arms Control and Disarmament*, p. 54; Jack Raymond, "Plan for Missile on Rails Killed in Favor of Underground Sites," *New York Times*, 14 December 1961, p. 20.
29. House Armed Services Committee, *Hearings on Military Posture* (1964), p. 6922; and Senate Appropriations Committee, *Department of Defense Appropriations for 1965*, p. 50.
30. Senate Armed Services Committee, *Military Procurement Authorization for Fiscal Year 1967*, p. 317.
31. Senate Appropriations Committee, *Department of Defense Appropriations for 1965*, p. 322.

man missile programs—a decision made and executed between 1961 and 1964 with apparently little regard to the development of the Soviet missile program.

Finally, there was the decision made in November 1964 to cut the projected Minuteman force from 1,200 to 1,000 missiles. In early 1963, about eighteen months or more after the demise of the missile gap myth, the Minuteman-force projection had in fact been *increased* by 100 missiles to 1,300 missiles, but the 1,200-missile program was reverted to by the DoD during the drawing up of the F/Y 1965 defense budget in late 1963. McNamara gave three reasons for further cutting the 1,200-missile Minuteman-force projection: firstly, a reduction in U.S. intelligence estimates of Soviet ICBMs;[32] "Secondly, and most importantly," qualitative increases in the kill capability of the Minuteman force; and, lastly, studies of strategic nuclear-war scenarios which showed "that an additional 200 missiles would not have any material effect in reducing the damage to our Nation." However, McNamara definitely considered the increased capability of the Minuteman II far more important than the reduced estimates of Soviet missile deployment.[33]

The official explanations given for these three decisions would seem to suggest that estimates and projections of Soviet missile strength played little part in determining the end size and character of the U.S. missile program. They certainly do not suggest, as McNamara did in September 1967, that if the United States had had better intelligence on the Soviet missile program earlier in the new administration it would have been a principal factor in the Kennedy-McNamara missile decisions.

All this, however, is not to suggest that the lack of adequate and agreed intelligence about the Soviet missile program during the missile-gap period had no effect on the Kennedy-McNamara missile build-up. In the first place, a direct consequence of the missile-gap debate was the legitimization within the U.S. defense planning establishment of arguments for large missile numbers.

32. Senate Armed Services Committee, *Military Procurement and Authorization, Fiscal Year 1966*, p. 304; interview with McNamara, *U.S. News and World Report*, 12 April 1965, p. 56; *Missiles & Rockets*, 4 January 1965, p. 10.

33. Senate Armed Services Committee, *Military Procurement Authorization, Fiscal Year 1966*, pp. 60, 229, 304.

For, just as the McNamara "assured destruction" criteria would have been unthinkable in the 1950s, arguments for more than a few hundred ICBMs would have been considered unreasonable before Sputniks I and II.[34] From about 1958 on, however, certain columnists, Air Force officers, congressmen, and Democratic politicians, etc., began talking in terms of missile forces numbering in the thousands. The missile-gap debate greatly extended the bounds of "realism," and made a build-up on the order of the subsequent Kennedy-McNamara Minuteman and Polaris programs appear quite "reasonable."

Secondly, the missile gap was always as much a projection of future Soviet and U.S. missile strengths as a comparison of current relative strengths. This meant, conceivably, that no matter what the U-2 and reconnaissance-satellite photographs showed of Soviet missile deployments in 1960–61, U.S. defense planners had to take into account projections of Soviet deployment rates.[35] But even granting this, the downgrading of the estimates of currently operational Soviet ICBMs in 1961 should have led to an adjustment of U.S. intelligence estimates of future Soviet missile production on two grounds. As George Quester has argued,

> Even if one still assumed that the Russians would hereafter produce all the missiles they could, the failure to produce expected numbers of missiles to date presumably reduced the maximum inventory they would be able to have for all future dates. Second, the Soviet failure thus far to produce up to known capacity suggested a lack of intention to produce at full capacity, and this intention might also be projected forward, again reducing estimates of likely inventories for specific future dates.[36]

Besides, with the doubling of Minuteman production capability and the extraordinary success of the Minuteman development and testing program in 1961, and with no evidence of the development of a second-generation mass-produceable ICBM by the Soviets, this projective consideration should not have been operative by the end of 1961.

34. Cf. Robert L. Perry, *The Ballistic Missile Decisions*, p. 14.
35. Interview with Roger Hilsman, 12 June 1970.
36. See George H. Quester, *Nuclear Diplomacy: The First Twenty-five Years*, p. 193.

And, finally, political factors would have made it difficult for McNamara and Kennedy to hold the U.S. missile program back even after the demise of the missile-gap myth. The Minuteman program authorized by the new administration in March 1961 involved a rapid build-up to a force of 600 missiles, with an end program of 800 Minuteman missiles projected. By the time a substantial consensus had developed within the U.S. intelligence community that a missile gap would not develop to the disadvantage of the United States (about September 1961), the money for the 600 authorized Minuteman ICBMs had been appropriated and committed to the industrial contractors, and the program had developed a considerable momentum of its own. To have cut it back at this time would have meant confronting not only the contractors, but large sections of the Air Force, parts of which (such as SAC) did not endorse or accept the September 1961 intelligence reappraisal; parts of the intelligence community, who would have leaked exaggerated contrary intelligence estimates; and the advocates of a large U.S. strategic superiority in Congress.[37] Moreover, even though there was a general acceptance by fall 1961 that no missile gap would develop, the Soviet Union was still deploying missiles, and many members of the administration believed that in the face of such Soviet action the administration could never have held a constant missile figure before Congress and the military, or even the American people, in the early 1960s.[38]

But McNamara relied on none of these arguments in his statement of 18 September 1967, quoted at the beginning of this chapter. On that occasion he attributed the initiation of U.S. strategic missile programs which, in his own words, were "in fact more than we require" to lack of information about Soviet intentions in 1961 and the existence of an inevitable action-reaction relationship between the forces on both sides. As has been shown, however, the role of the missile gap and inadequacies in intelligence about the Soviet missile program was a very indirect one after 1960–61. The Kennedy-McNamara missile build-up was programmed, essentially, after these inadequacies had been

37. Interview with Roger Hilsman, 27 May 1970.
38. Interview with Eugene Zuckert, 21 July 1970.

clarified; and the last of the missiles were not deployed until October 1967. Testimony by McNamara, his strategic policy and force planning assumptions, and his subsequent decisions on other aspects of the strategic missile program furthermore indicate that even if the United States had had perfect intelligence on the Soviet missile program before 1961, or inadequate intelligence after 1961, this would not have been a major factor in the Kennedy-McNamara missile program. The evidence suggests that estimates and projections of Soviet missile strength did not determine the size, character, and rate of build-up of the Kennedy-McNamara missile program.

9 Strategic Policy and the Missile Program

The Kennedy Administration began in 1961 with a complete and unequivocal rejection of the Eisenhower policy of "massive retaliation," which it chose to interpret as a wholly inflexible doctrine; but it was not until 1965–66, with the development and acceptance of the "assured destruction/damage limitation" posture, with primary emphasis on the former mission, that McNamara settled upon a strategy that was to sustain acceptance for any significant period of time. As James R. Schlesinger has written, referring to the period 1961–67, "shifting sands seems the best way to characterize the strategic rationales of recent years."[1]

1. Senate Committee on Government Operations, Subcommittee on National Security and International Operations, *Planning, Programming, Budgeting* (1970), p. 133.

Underlying these shifting sands was one basic U.S. strategic notion which was accepted throughout the Eisenhower and Kennedy Administrations and well into the Johnson Administration. This was the perceived need for U.S. superiority over the Soviet Union. This notion, by itself, however, could provide no guidance for force-structure decision making. That required the development and explication of more specific strategic policies.

The first part of this chapter describes the notion of superiority. The second describes the developments in (officially accepted) U.S. strategic policy from 1961 to 1965–66, with special regard to 1961–62. The last part then goes on to discuss the role of strategic policy and theory in determining the size and character of the U.S. missile program during the years 1961 to 1965–66.

THE NOTION OF SUPERIORITY

Throughout both the Eisenhower Administration of the 1950s and the Kennedy and Johnson Administrations of the 1960s, an enduring guiding principle governing the size of U.S. strategic nuclear forces was that of *superiority* over the Soviet Union. This was an assumption fundamental to the thinking of military and civilian strategists and politicians alike, with few exceptions.

"Massive retaliation," the basic national security policy of the Eisenhower Administration, for example, was keyed both for its credibility and its operational efficacy to U.S. strategic superiority. Although that policy was usually interpreted as requiring superiority in *all* major types of long-range nuclear delivery vehicles, there was one extremely important exception made by the Eisenhower Administration in 1959. A deliberate decision was made to produce only a minimum number of first-generation, liquid-fuel missiles, and to concentrate development efforts and production on the later-generation, more efficient and strategically viable solid-fuel missiles. If the Soviet Union concentrated on producing liquid-fuel ICBMs, however, this allowed the possibility of it achieving a temporary numerical advantage in this type of delivery vehicle—hence the possibility of a missile gap. As Secretary McElroy explained it, in a significant verbal exchange with Senator Symington before a joint hearing of the

Senate Committee on Armed Services and the Committee on
Aeronautical and Space Science in January 1959:

> It is not our intention or policy to try to match missile for missile
> in the ICBM category of the Russian capability in the next couple
> of years. Our position, Mr. Symington, is that our diversified
> capability to deliver the big weapon is what we are going to count
> on as our ability to deter general war.[2]

In the period before a large number of second-generation missiles became operational, the United States would rely primarily on its massive superiority in strategic bombers to prevent a
"deterrent gap."

This policy was the subject of a large number of attacks by the
Democrats in the presidential election year of 1960. During
his campaign, Senator Kennedy argued that the United States
needed "a policy which will keep America the strongest country
in the world,"[3] and declared that "the next President must
promptly send to Congress a special message requesting the
funds and authorization necessary to give us a nuclear retaliatory power second to none."[4] There was every reason to expect
that with Kennedy's accession to the presidency, the United
States would make efforts to ensure significant superiority in all
major types of strategic nuclear delivery vehicles.

Within the Kennedy Administration, the necessity for U.S.
strategic superiority was an assumption shared throughout the
defense establishment and other groups in the defense decision-
making process, virtually without exception. To the military, it
was, of course, an essential article of faith. As General Le May
has written: "Military men think that deterrence is only possible
in an atmosphere of [American] strategic superiority."[5] General
Power, the commander of SAC during the Kennedy Administration, was as terse and emphatic as possible: "I believe in the
preservation of military superiority."[6] General Samuel Phillips,

2. Senate Armed Services Committee and Senate Committee on Aeronautical
and Space Science, Joint Hearings, *Missiles and Space Activities* (1959), p. 46.
3. Speech at San Diego, California, 12 September 1960, cited in *Congressional Quarterly Weekly Report*, 13 January 1961, p. 32.
4. Speech at Washington, D.C., 20 September 1960, cited in ibid.
5. Gen. Curtis E. Le May, *America is in Danger*, p. 52.
6. Gen. Thomas S. Power, *Design for Survival*, p. 14.

the Minuteman program manager, claimed at the time of the missile build-up that "the real purpose of Minuteman is to get a true superiority in ICBMs."[7] Spokesmen from the other services also accepted the notion of strategic superiority.

Regardless of the various nuances of U.S. nuclear strategy during the years in which the Kennedy-McNamara missile build-up was programmed, the determination of the Pentagon to ensure strategic superiority was constant. Both the "second-strike counterforce" strategy of 1961–62 and the damage-limitation strategy of 1963–65 were predicated on the maintenance of strategic supremacy. At least until November–December 1964, when the 1,000-missile ceiling was imposed upon the Minuteman force, the "national strategic targeting and attack policy" still entailed the preservation of U.S. strategic superiority and "war-winning capability."[8]

In his first posture statement in January 1962, McNamara reported to the Senate Armed Services Committee that, "there is no question but that, today, our strategic retaliatory forces are fully capable of destroying the Soviet target system, even after absorbing an initial surprise attack." According to McNamara, this meant "that the United States has nuclear superiority. We are determined to maintain that superiority."[9] During testimony on his F/Y 1964 budget statement a year later, McNamara referred several times to "our current strategic nuclear superiority over the USSR," and he argued that U.S. policy and budgetary actions could only be interpreted as "a series of actions designed to maintain the military strength and superiority of this Nation."[10]

The need for strategic nuclear superiority was also accepted by the State Department. For example, in August 1963, during hearings on the Limited Test Ban Treaty, Secretary of State Rusk was asked by Senator Jackson whether effective deterrence required that the United States have a margin of strategic superiority. Rusk replied, "Senator, I believe that the United States

7. *Time*, 29 December 1961, p. 12.
8. Power, *Design for Survival*, p. 189.
9. Senate Foreign Relations Committee, *Nuclear Test Ban Treaty* (1963), p. 98.
10. Senate Armed Services Committee, *Military Procurement Authorization, Fiscal Year 1964*, pp. 90, 108.

must maintain in its own security interests a very large overall nuclear superiority with respect to the Soviet Union."[11]

Even the U.S. Arms Control and Disarmament Agency (ACDA) appeared to accept American superiority as a necessary strategic requirement. The principal arms-control proposal of the Kennedy-Johnson Administration, that calling for a "freeze" on strategic nuclear delivery systems by the United States and the Soviet Union, which was presented at Geneva in 1964, 1965, and 1966, and which had originated with ACDA, implicitly accepted the maintenance of U.S. strategic superiority. The proposal was dropped by the United States following the beginning of the rapid build-up of the Soviet ICBM force in the latter half of 1966.

Within Congress and U.S. industry, the need for strategic superiority went unquestioned.[12] Indeed, the very committees in Congress with authorization and appropriation powers in the military field were the most vocal in the call for the expansion of U.S. military strength.[13] And American industry was certainly willing, and had the capacity to undertake the build-up.

The articulated justifications for strategic superiority were severalfold. In the first place, the United States was assumed to be on the defensive against communist aggression. As McNamara explained it in a speech in Chicago on 17 February 1962, to deter "Soviet aggression" and "to meet the kind of military challenges that Khrushchev has announced he has in store for us," it was necessary for the United States to maintain "a larger stockpile of nuclear weapons" than the Russians.[14]

11. Senate Foreign Relations Committee, *Nuclear Test Ban Treaty* (1963), p. 45.

12. Even George McGovern, who led congressional moves to cut back the U.S. nuclear weapons programs, believed in the necessity of "American strategic superiority" (see *Congressional Record, Senate*, 2 August 1963, p. 13987.

13. The four principal relevant committees are the Senate and House Armed Services and Appropriations committees. During the years of the Kennedy-McNamara strategic missile build-up these were headed, respectively, by Richard B. Russell (Democrat, Georgia), Carl Vinson (Democrat, Georgia), Sen. Robertson (Democrat, Virginia), and George H. Mahon (Democrat, Texas), all elderly, conservative Southerners, and all "superhawks" (see Seymour Hersh, "The Military Committees," *The Washington Monthly*, 1 April 1969, pp. 84–92).

14. See William W. Kaufmann, *The McNamara Strategy*, pp. 74–75.

Second, the United States was seen to require "a margin of safety and superiority . . . in view of Soviet secrecy."[15] Because too little was known about Soviet capabilities and intentions, strategic superiority would provide some "insurance" against the "many uncertainties and variables in the [Soviet] military threat."[16]

Third, the military looked upon strategic superiority as an "umbrella" under which, or a "shield" behind which the United States could take the initiative in local conflicts. As General Le May argued before the Senate Appropriations Committee in early 1962, "You cannot fight a limited war except under the umbrella of strategic superiority. . . . So, I believe that your strategic power comes first."[17]

Fourth, the United States needed strategic superiority to offset the supposed communist advantage in manpower. As Barry M. Goldwater has written:

> Our own first resolve must be to retain—and enhance—our military superiority. Mere equality in this field will not do. Since we could never match the Communists in manpower, our equipment and weapons must more than offset their advantage in numbers.[18]

Fifth, the United States needed strategic superiority because SAC was responsible for the defense not only of the United States, but also of the nation's allies in the Free World. According to McNamara, U.S. strategic superiority was the "best" way to "pursue the interests of the United States, our allies, and the rest of the Free World."[19] Strategic superiority was seen as necessary to enhance the credibility of the nuclear deterrent among the NATO allies in Europe, where the possibility of a missile

15. Senator Jackson, Senate Foreign Relations Committee, *Nuclear Test Ban Treaty* (1963), p. 45.

16. Power, *Design for Survival*, pp. 121–22.

17. Senate Appropriations Committee, *Department of Defense Appropriations for 1963*, p. 186.

18. Barry M. Goldwater, *Why Not Victory?*, p. 42. Although McNamara's staff, and especially the Systems Analysis Office, eventually succeeded in discrediting the notion of Soviet manpower superiority, it remained extant during the years of the Kennedy-McNamara missile build-up (see Alain C. Enthoven and K. Wayne Smith, *How Much is Enough?*, chap. 4).

19. Speech at Chicago, 17 February 1962, cited in Kaufmann, *The McNamara Strategy*, p. 75.

gap had raised serious doubts about that deterrent in the late
1950s. Superiority in long-range nuclear delivery vehicles was
also necessary if the United States was to target the Soviet's
IRBMs and MRBMs aimed at Europe.

Finally, many in the U.S. defense establishment sought strategic superiority to provide the United States with a first-strike
option. Many Air Force generals were quite explicit about their
desire for such a posture. General Power, for example, argued
that a first-strike option was necessary if only to compound Soviet planning problems and hence detract from the Russians'
offensive strength.[20] And General Le May saw "the capability
of a first-strike—of initiating nuclear war...[as] absolutely
necessary if the United States is to prevail."[21]

Many congressmen also argued that the United States must
"reserve to ourselves the initiative to strike first."[22] Several other
members of Congress also called upon the Defense Department
to accept a first-strike policy.[23] And, in the report on the Defense Appropriations Bill for 1961, the powerful House Appropriations Committee stated, in effect, that the United States
should be willing to take the initiative in the use of nuclear weapons. It said:

> In the final analysis, to effectively deter a would-be aggressor, we
> should maintain our armed forces in such a way and with such an
> understanding that should it ever become obvious that an attack
> upon us or our allies is imminent, we can launch an attack *before
> the aggressor has hit* either us or our allies. This is an element of
> deterrence which the United States should not deny itself. No oth-
> er form of deterrence can be fully relied upon.[24]

There is also some evidence that in 1961 and 1962 Secretary
McNamara was considering heading the United States toward a
position where a successful preemptive first strike was an option,

20. Power, *Design for Survival*, p. 83.
21. Le May, *America is in Danger*, p. 63.
22. Congressman Melvin R. Laird, *A House Divided*, p. 79. (Laird was later
secretary of defense in the Nixon Administration.)
23. See James Roherty, *Decisions of Robert S. McNamara*, p. 121; and Edgar M.
Bottome, *The Balance of Terror*, p. 73.
24. *Report of the House Appropriations Committee on the Defense Appropriations
Bill for 1961* (1962), cited in Laird, *A House Divided*, p. 81. (Italics in original.)

although this does not, of course, necessarily constitute a determining reason for the Kennedy-McNamara strategic missile
build-up.

Overwhelming strategic superiority over the Soviet Union was
clearly projected at the time when the key U.S. strategic ballistic-
missile decisions were made. For example, in late 1961, when the
five-year program included a Minuteman force of 1,200 ICBMs,
the NIE projected a Soviet ICBM force for mid-1967 of only
350 to 650 missiles. In late 1962, when the planned Minuteman
force was 1,200 or 1,300 missiles, the NIE was actually somewhat
lower, with 300 to 600 Soviet ICBMs projected for mid-1967. In
other words, the United States was planning for a superiority in
ICBMs of between 2:1 and 4:1.[25]

However, despite the fact that the principle of strategic superiority was accepted throughout the U.S. defense decision-
making community, it could not, by itself, serve as a concrete
guide to the establishment of finite strategic force levels. There
was, for example, no agreement as to the yardstick by which
"superiority" could be measured. Was it to be by total number of
strategic nuclear delivery vehicles, number of relatively invulnerable and alerted vehicles, number of ICBMs, number of
SLBMs, number of warheads, or total deliverable megatonnage?
Was the relative balance of strategic defensive forces to be taken
into account? How were relative differences in command and
control and communications arrangements and qualitative differences in weapons technology to be dealt with in the strategic
equation?

In the particular case of ICBMs, the quest for superiority
could have been satisfied during this period by the deployment
of 700 Minuteman missiles, or 1,000, 1,200, 2,000, or more. The
criteria for deciding on the appropriate force level had to be
derived from some more specific policy.

THE DEVELOPMENT OF U.S. STRATEGIC POLICY
(1961 TO 1965–1966)

In his years as a senator, Kennedy showed a great personal interest in matters relating to peace, defense, strategy, and foreign

25. *Statement of Secretary of Defense Robert S. McNamara before the House Sub-*

policy. For almost a decade, he was a persistent critic of the defense policies of the Eisenhower Administration. During the two years immediately preceding his election to the presidency, his particular target had been the reliance of the United States on the country's nuclear arsenal for "massive retaliation" as the beginning and the end of formal strategy. As Kennedy saw it, the Eisenhower Administration had driven the United States "into a corner where the only choice is all or nothing at all, world devastation or submission."[26] By the time of his election, Kennedy's strategic thinking had matured to the point of insisting that the United States must essentially do two things to its defense posture: it must expand and protect its nuclear forces as a deterrent, and it must expand and modernize its non-nuclear forces for response to provocation short of nuclear war.[27] However, as Bernard Brodie has pointed out, Kennedy was a "busy politician who had to have an all-round approach to the nation's problems [and] we may be sure that [his] basic strategic ideas were derived from others and not developed in any detail."[28] The detailed development, planning, and operation of U.S. strategy was to be left to McNamara and the DoD.

When McNamara accepted the position of Kennedy's secretary of defense, he had been away from the military for more than fourteen years.[29] The knowledge of defense and strategy that he brought to his job at the Pentagon was meager; offhand, he could recall, on taking up his position, having read only one recent military book—*The Question of National Defense* by Oskar Morgenstern.[30] But, apparently, McNamara had a natural predisposition toward the strategy of flexible response, with the "options" that it contained.[31]

---

committee on Department of Defense Appropriations, the Fiscal Year 1964–68 Defense Program and 1964 Defense Budget, 6 February 1963, p. 29.

26. Speech delivered at Lake Charles, Louisiana, 16 October 1959, in John F. Kennedy, The Strategy of Peace, p. 226.

27. Henry L. Trewhitt, McNamara, p. 6.

28. Bernard Brodie, A Review of William W. Kaufmann's "The McNamara Strategy," p. 9.

29. McNamara served for three years with the U.S. Army Air Forces during World War II (see William W. Kaufmann, The McNamara Strategy, pp. 44–45).

30. Richard Fryklund, in The New Frontiersmen, ed. Public Affairs Press, p. 69; Time, 15 February 1963, p. 12.

31. Kaufmann, McNamara Strategy, p. 53.

When the new administration took office in January 1961, the debate over the appropriate nuclear strategy to be adopted had reached a new level of intensity. The Democratic critique of "massive retaliation" during the 1960 election campaign had provided both the opportunity and the forum for a wider public debate. The publication of Herman Kahn's *On Thermonuclear War*, Oskar Morgenstern's *The Question of National Defense*, Henry Kissinger's *The Necessity for Choice*, and of the special fall 1960 issue of *Dædalus* on *Arms Control, Disarmament, and National Security* was evidence of this renewed and enlivened interest in questions of national strategy. The deployment on station of the first Polaris submarines in the fall of 1960 brought active Navy interest in the targeting of the United States' long-range nuclear delivery vehicles.[32] The assumption of office by President Kennedy in January 1961 was taken by the services as an occasion and an opportunity to represent their particular strategies to the administration and the public.

McNamara was introduced to "counterforce" strategy, including the RAND–Air Staff findings on "no-cities" nuclear-war scenarios, in a formal briefing by William Kaufmann within a week of his taking office. He was immediately impressed with this particular strategy.[33] Much of the January–March 1961 defense reappraisal was concerned with what relative weights to give conflicting Air Force, Army, and Navy strategies, what mix of weapons to procure for these, and the preparation of new, comprehensive, integrated war-contingency plans.[34] A decision was made within the first two weeks of the reappraisal to increase the emphasis on limited-war forces, and this was taken by many commentators as evidence that the administration had adopted a posture much closer to the recommendations of the Army and the Navy.[35] But although the Air Force certainly

32. A Joint Strategic Targeting Planning Staff was established by Secretary Gates on 17 August 1960; the first integrated (Navy and SAC) master list of global strategic targets was completed and approved by Gates, in mid-December 1960.

33. Interviews with Richard Fryklund and Al Goldberg, 20 July 1970; and Dr. Marvin Stern, 21 August 1970. Alain Enthoven and Marvin Stern were also present at the briefing.

34. *New York Times*, 7 and 11 February 1961.

35. See, for example, *Missiles & Rockets*, 6 March 1961, pp. 14–15.

failed to persuade the Kennedy Administration to adopt its version of "counterforce" strategy, the Army-Navy "minimum" or "finite deterrent" argument was also rejected.

As early as February 1961, McNamara testified to his predilection for a "controlled response" strategy. He explained to the House Armed Services Committee that the U.S. nuclear force must be able to be used "in a cool and deliberate fashion and always under the complete control of the constituted authority."[36]

On 6 March 1961 McNamara ordered the preparation of a draft memorandum revising basic national-security policies relating to nuclear weapons, including an examination of "the assumptions relating to 'counterforce' strikes." The joint chiefs were also ordered to "prepare a 'Doctrine' which, if accepted, would permit controlled response and negotiating pauses in the event of thermo-nuclear war."[37] President Kennedy's special message to Congress on 28 March 1961 reflected the administration's decision that the U.S. defense posture "be both flexible and determined," and that the response to a Soviet attack would be controlled and discriminating.[38]

Work on revising the Eisenhower BNSP began in late March 1961, largely under the supervision of Paul Nitze, assistant secretary of defense for international security affairs. It was at this stage undertaken largely by Henry Rowen, William Kaufmann, and Daniel Ellsberg—all members or former members of the RAND Corporation. The first draft was completed by 7 April 1961, and the final draft by mid-May 1961. It stressed the im-

36. Testimony of McNamara before the House Armed Services Committee, cited in Kaufmann, *McNamara Strategy*, p. 53.

37. *New York Times*, 25 March 1961. This was project no. 2 of McNamara's original "76 Trombones." The joint staff paper for project no. 2, which argued for strategic flexibility and graduated options, was prepared by Lt. Col. Robert P. Lukeman (USAF). The JCS were, however, divided on acceptance of the doctrine—although all the chiefs accepted the necessity for flexibility and were agreed on the utility and advisability of such a doctrine, the Air Force insisted that it be a mandate for action, i.e., a basis for force procurement and command and control programs, but neither Gen. Lemnitzer nor Adm. Burke were prepared to support such action, and project no. 2 was therefore shelved.

38. *Special Message*, pp. 2–4. Kennedy's concern that he have a capability "to exercise discrimination and control should nuclear conflict come" was partly a response to a briefing on U.S. nuclear war plans by a joint chiefs of staff team early in his administration which had left him less than satisfied (see W. W. Rostow, *The Diffusion of Power, 1957–1972*, pp. 172–73).

portance of non-nuclear forces, and the need to resist major aggression with conventional forces, if possible, and to have various options prepared so as to give the president a range of choices in the event of nuclear war.[39]

Despite the efforts of ISA, President Kennedy rejected all moves to have the revised BNSP adopted as the formal national-security posture.[40] Instead, McNamara issued a series of guide-lines, in accordance with which the Office of the Secretary of Defense revised the SIOP.[41] The JSCP inherited by the new administration (to which the SIOP is in effect an annex) had contained only one plan, under which the United States would launch all its strategic nuclear delivery vehicles immediately upon the initiation of nuclear war with the Soviet Union. The single JSCP target list predominantly included Soviet and satellite cities; no strategic reserves were to be retained; and there was no provision for the preservation of command and control. As Daniel Ellsberg has recently observed, "If the SIOP [of 1960–61] were activated, we would have hit every city in the Soviet Union and China in addition to all military targets."[42] Expected Soviet, Chinese and satellite fatalities were placed by the JCS at 360 to 425 million.[43]

In place of this single option, a new strategic policy was drawn up which was rather more flexible. For example, China and the

39. Under the direction of Henry Rowen, the section of the revised BNSP on limited (or conventional) war was prepared by William Kaufmann, and the draft on "objectives and general war" by Daniel Ellsberg. Walt W. Rostow later took responsibility for the final direction of the study (interviews with Malcolm W. Hoag, 19 August 1970; Paul H. Nitze, 7 February 1973; Daniel Ellsberg, 24 August 1970 and 8 October 1972; Charles J. Hitch, 11 August 1970; and Henry S. Rowen, 25 August 1970).

40. While McNamara supported the reemphases in strategic thinking, neither he nor Gilpatric saw the need for any "abstract plan." Adoption of the revised BNSP was also opposed by Richard Neustadt, who managed to persuade President Kennedy that a BNSP would limit his flexibility. Opposition also came from McGeorge Bundy (interviews with Paul Nitze, 7 February 1973; McGeorge Bundy, 18 December 1972; Daniel Ellsberg, 14 August 1970; Henry S. Rowen, 25 August 1970; Charles J. Hitch, 11 August 1970; and Malcolm W. Hoag, 19 August 1970; see also Col. James A. Donovan, *Militarism, U.S.A.*, p. 223).

41. Interview with Daniel Ellsberg, 24 August 1970. The "Guidelines for Planning," which included a draft "Policy Guidance on Plans for Central War," embodied the principle of "options" as developed in project no. 2 (interviews with Daniel Ellsberg, 8 October 1972, and Gen. Robert Lukeman, 12 February 1973).

42. *International Herald Tribune*, 9 May 1978.

43. Interview with Dr. Marvin Stern, 21 August 1970.

satellite countries were separated from the Soviet Union for targeting purposes; Soviet strategic forces were separated from Soviet cities on target lists; strategic reserves were to be held by the United States; U.S. command and control systems were to be protected, to allow "controlled response"; and Soviet command and control was to be preserved, at least in the initial stages of any nuclear exchange.

With regard to any nuclear exchange with the Soviet Union, the SIOP was given five options, plus various suboptions, with U.S. attacks to proceed along the following spectrum:

1. Soviet strategic retaliatory forces—missile sites, bomber bases, submarine tenders, etc.
2. Soviet air defenses away from cities—for example, those covering U.S. bomber routes.
3. Soviet air defenses near cities.
4. Soviet command and control centers and systems.
5. If "necessary," all-out "spasm" attack.

Suboptions included such things as provision for the use of clean or "dirty" bombs, larger or smaller warheads, air- or ground-burst weapons, etc.[44]

Initial work on the revised SIOP, done mainly by Daniel Ellsberg and Frank Trinkl, under the direction of Alain Enthoven (all RAND alumni), was completed by late summer 1961. It was then taken up by Henry Rowen and General Maxwell Taylor, and formalized in the fall of 1961. The JCS studied and approved the strategic change in late 1961, and it was officially adopted in January 1962.[45] To provide the Soviet Union with the option of fighting a "controlled" nuclear war, Moscow was taken off the list of initial targets in late 1961.[46] The final nuclear-war target list was adopted by the joint strategic target planning staff in June 1962.[47]

44. Interviews with Daniel Ellsberg, 24 August 1970, and 8 October 1972; Col. Donald Martin, 29 July 1970; and Dr. Marvin Stern, 21 August 1970; see also Richard Fryklund, "U.S. War Plan Shift Would Spare Cities," *Washington Star*, 17 December 1961, pp. 1–2.
45. Interviews with Daniel Ellsberg, 24 August 1970, and 8 October 1972; and Dr. Marvin Stern, 21 August 1970; see also Richard Fryklund, "U.S. War Plan Shift," and *100 Million Lives*, pp. 32–33.
46. *Newsweek*, 27 November 1961, p. 17; and interview with Richard Fryklund, 2 February 1973.
47. *Newsweek*, 2 July 1962, p. 11.

While targeting plans were being revised, work was also under way on redesigning the U.S. strategic posture to make it compatible with the new nuclear-war fighting strategy. In the spring of 1961, the net evaluation subcommittee (NESC) of the National Security Council under General Hickey was directed to integrate strategic-force requirements with the revised targeting plans.[48] The study continued during the summer and fall of 1961.[49] According to Dr. Alain Enthoven:

> The study group developed a list of all strategic targets and, using the best available intelligence and their own judgement projected the growth of these target lists over the next ten years. They then estimated the performance and operational characteristics of the various available weapon systems and calculated how many would be needed for destruction of 75 percent and 90 percent of the targets in each of the next ten years.[50]

The Hickey study (formally designated Sec Def Project 12, 1961), concluded that the currently programmed strategic force was inadequate to accomplish the objectives of the National Strategic Targeting and Attack Policy (NSTAP). It recommended a Minuteman program of 150 missiles in 1963, growing to 2,000 by 1971. Of that latter number, 1,950 would have been an "advanced" model with much improved CEP and a yield of 5–10 Mt., and 50 would have been mobile (5 trains with 10 missiles each). One hundred and fifty additional Minuteman ("advanced" model) ICBMs would have been added to the 2,000 by 1971 if the Soviet threat developed to include an extensive ABM system. By that date 60 Titan ICBMs would have been in the force, including 54 "advanced" models with yields of over 50 Mt. The

48. The NESC was established by President Eisenhower in the mid-1950s. In 1960 it produced a study, NESC 2009, which developed the targeting policy of "sequential options." The 1961 NESC study group was formally directed to "determine the force levels necessary to accomplish the objectives of the NSTAP [National Strategic Targeting Attack Policy]" (interview with Dr. Marvin Stern, 31 August 1970).

49. The Hickey committee was directed by McNamara to produce two reports, the first by June–July 1961, and the second by December (interview with Dr. Alain Enthoven, 17 August 1970). According to Gen. Burchinal, the "Hickey study" lasted nine months (see House Appropriations Committee, *Department of Defense Appropriations for 1963*, part 5, p. 335).

50. Senate Committee on Government Operations, *Planning, Programming, Budgeting* (1970), p. 249.

1971 force also would have included 150 RS-X reconnaissance strike bombers (of the RS-70 type, with 18 glide missiles each, fully reprogrammable and with very high kill probabilities against any target), and from 230–370 Skybolt ALBMs on the B-52 force. Finally, the Hickey study recommended a Polaris FBM submarine force of some 40 to 47 submarines (including an "advanced Polaris A-4," with improved accuracy and three yield options from kiloton to multi-megaton range).[51]

In April 1961 a task force was set up, under USAF Brigadier-General L. G. McCallum, to study the field of command and control. Later, in September 1961, this was subsumed into a major committee headed by General Partridge. The Partridge task force on presidential command and control included service officers, representatives of the director, Defense Research and Engineering (DDR&E), and RAND consultants; and General Taylor and McGeorge Bundy from the White House also studied the question. Its report, completed late in November 1961, contained plans for a national command and control system designed to survive nuclear attack and give the president instantaneous command over vital U.S. military forces.[52]

This policy change from "massive retaliation" to the strategy of "controlled flexible response" required major changes in the Minuteman missile system. In mid-1961, the Fletcher Committee was set up by the Secretary of the Air Force, Eugene Zuckert, and given verbal orders on 30 July 1961 to review the safety and the flexibility of the system.[53] The recommendations of the

51. Interview with Dr. Alain Enthoven, 17 August 1970; see also testimony of Gen. Wheeler, Senate Armed Services Committee, *Status of U.S. Strategic Power* (1968), part 1, p. 18. The "Hickey study" was, however, very inadequate as a basis for designing a strategic forces posture (see testimony of Dr. Alain Enthoven, Senate Committee on Government Operations, *Planning, Programming, Budgeting* [1970], p. 249).

52. *Aviation Week & Space Technology*, 17 April 1961, p. 25; 11 September 1961, p. 21; 18 September 1961, p. 28; and 4 December 1961, p. 25; Daniel Ellsberg, *Papers on the War*, p. 15; and interviews with Ellsberg, 24 August 1970 and 8 October 1972. (Ellsberg was a member of the Partridge Committee.)

53. House Appropriations Committee, *Department of Defense Appropriations for 1963*, part 4, pp. 415–16; and interview with George W. Rathjens, 11 July 1970. Members of the Fletcher Committee included Dr. James C. Fletcher, chairman, Space Electronics Corp.; Dr. Charles Lauritsen, California Institute of Technology; Dr. M. P. Wilson, Bell Telephone Laboratories; Dr. William Graham and others from the RAND Corp.; Dr. Hendrick Bode; Brig. Gen.

Fletcher Committee, submitted on 27 September 1961, "were thoroughly reviewed by the Air Force and schedules [were] developed for their incorporation"; they were responsible for major "ground rules changes in the Minuteman program."[54] The change in U.S. strategic posture from "massive retaliation" to "controlled flexible response" in the summer of 1961

> required changes in the command and control electronics so that the operational concept of the Minuteman force would enforce that national policy. Force improvement such as selective launch and stop launch, increase[d] target selection capability, lighter guidance and control packages, safety, refinements in propulsion, and a new re-entry system (Mark-II) were developed.[55]

These changes increased the cost of the Minuteman program by some $840 million, or approximately 15 percent of the cost of the entire 800-missile Minuteman I program.[56]

By the end of 1961, after about eight months of intensive work, the United States had developed a new nuclear-war-fighting strategy. U.S. strategic targeting plans had been redesigned, though the selection of the specific targets had not been completed, and the redesigning of the Minuteman missile, the Minuteman-force program, and the national command and control system to fit into this strategy had begun. Throughout this preparatory work, the military had been in full consultation with the Office of the Secretary of Defense, and military expertise had been used wherever OSD thought it applicable. The civilian principals in the work were, however, virtually without

Ariel W. Nielson (JCS); Dr. Harvey Brooks, Harvard University; Dr. George Rathjens, Advanced Research Projects Agency (ARPA); and Dr. Herbert Scoville, Jr. (CIA).

54. House Appropriations Committee, *Department of Defense Appropriations for 1963*, part 4, p. 415; and interview with Harvey Brooks, 15 January 1973.

55. Testimony of Gen. Schultz, House Appropriations Committee, *Department of Defense Appropriations for 1970*, part 4, pp. 650–51. In the original plans Minuteman could be programmed with a single target and launched in squadrons of fifty. But in summer 1961 the Minuteman force was given a longer range and a selective, individual launch capability; and the Minuteman II (LGM-30F) missile, operational in 1965, had a selection capability of eight targets. (Interviews with Dr. Marvin Stern, 21 August 1970; Harvey Brooks, 15 January 1973; and George W. Rathjens, 8 December 1972.)

56. House Appropriations Committee, *Department of Defense Appropriations for 1970*, part 4, pp. 650–51. The Minuteman I program was costed out at $6,052,400,000.

exception, members and former members of the RAND Corpo-
ration—Henry Rowen, Charles Hitch, Alain Enthoven, Daniel
Ellsberg, Frank Trinkl, Andrew Marshall, William Kaufmann,
David McGarvey, and William Graham.

In January 1962 McNamara's F/Y 1963 defense budget statement revealed, publicly and officially for the first time, that the
first steps towards the "no-cities" version of the counterforce
strategy were being taken. On the question of "counterforce"
McNamara stated in his prepared statement that, "A major mission of the strategic retaliatory forces is to deter war by their
capability to destroy the enemy's warmaking capabilities."[57] Under questioning by Congressman Minshall (Republican, Ohio),
McNamara said that U.S. weapons were being deployed so that
cities could be either spared or destroyed.[58] He argued that a
strategic posture designed to give both the United States and the
Soviet Union the option of sparing cities in the event of nuclear
war required a larger strategic force than would otherwise be
the case. After detailing two alternative strategic postures—that
of a "city destruction force only" and that of a "second strike
salvo capability"—McNamara contended that a third option,
"which would permit you to launch in waves a second strike and
a second strike prime, one against their military targets and the
other against their urban centers," and which was then favored
by the administration, called for the largest force of all: it required "greater numbers than either of the other two."[59] And
he testified that

> we are basing our weapons system design, development, and pro-
> curement and our communications system design, development,
> and procurement upon this higher requirement. It has affected
> the appropriations which we request for fiscal year 1963.[60]

A month later, in Chicago on 17 February 1962, McNamara
spelled out the new U.S. nuclear-war-fighting strategy in detail.

57. House Appropriations Committee, *Department of Defense Appropriations for 1963*, part 2, p. 13.
58. Ibid., pp. 249–50.
59. House Armed Services Committee, *Hearings on Military Posture* (1963), pp. 571–72.
60. House Appropriations Committee, *Department of Defense Appropriations for 1963*, part 2, p. 250.

He began by arguing that a wide range of threats had to be taken into account by the United States, and multiple capabilities maintained. To deter "Soviet aggression" it was necessary for the United States to maintain "a larger stockpile of nuclear weapons" than the Russians. This, however, was not enough.

> In a world in which both sides may be capable of inflicting severe damage on each other, we must have machinery for the command and control of our forces which is itself able to survive an attack and to apply the surviving forces in consonance with national security objectives. To this end we are providing alternate command posts at sea and in the air, with communications links to all elements of our strategic force. With this protected command and control system, our forces can be used in several different ways. We may have to retaliate with a single massive attack. Or, we may be able to use our retaliatory forces to limit damage done to ourselves, and our allies, by knocking out the enemy's bases before he has had time to launch his second salvos. We may seek to terminate a war on favorable terms by using our forces as a bargaining weapon—by threatening further attack. In any case, our large reserve of protected firepower would give an enemy an incentive to avoid our cities and to stop a war. Our new policy gives us the flexibility to choose among several operational plans, but does not require that we make any advance commitment with respect to doctrine or targets. We shall be committed only to a system that gives us the ability to use our forces in a controlled and deliberate way, so as best to pursue the interests of the United States, our Allies, and the rest of the Free World.[61]

And a month later again, on 15 March 1962, Deputy Secretary of Defense Gilpatric stated that, "It might not . . . be our objective to inflict maximum damage on the enemy." Instead, he said, the United States might try to knock out "the enemy's bases before he has had time to launch his second salvos and at the same time force him to meet our terms by threatening to destroy his cities in future attacks."[62]

Early in May 1962, McNamara described the "no-cities" strategy at a secret session of NATO in Athens. This audience was reportedly incredulous.[63] Then, on 16 June 1962, he distilled

61. Cited in Kaufmann, *McNamara Strategy*, pp. 74–75.
62. *U.S. News and World Report*, 26 March 1962, p. 12.
63. See Henry L. Trewhitt, *McNamara*, p. 114.

his Athens lecture into his landmark commencement address at
the University of Michigan at Ann Arbor.[64] He began by asserting that "the Alliance has over-all nuclear strength adequate to
[meet] any challenge confronting it," and expressing his confidence in the adequacy of "our current nuclear programs," and
then went on to outline current U.S. strategy for "the terrible
contingency of nuclear war":

> The U.S. has come to the conclusion that to the extent feasible,
> basic military strategy in a possible general nuclear war should be
> approached in much the same way that more conventional military
> operations have been regarded in the past. That is to say, principal
> military objectives, in the event of a nuclear war stemming from
> a major attack on the Alliance, should be the destruction of the
> enemy's military forces, not of his civilian population . . . we are
> giving a possible opponent the strongest imaginable incentive to
> refrain from striking our own cities.[65]

In the week following this speech, Secretary of State Rusk
made a three-day tour of six Western capitals to explain the new
U.S. policy to Western Europe's leaders. But he met with frus-
tration; the NATO allies were obviously unwilling to accept the
implications of the "no-cities" strategy, especially those for small,
independent European nuclear capabilities.[66]

Within the United States, the reaction was similarly unfavorable. In particular, there was much criticism of the first-strike
implications of the counterforce strategy. As one former McNamara aide is reported to have said,

> there could be no such thing as primary retaliation against mili-
> tary targets after an enemy attack. If you're going to shoot at mis-
> siles, you're talking about first strike.[67]

64. The Athens speech had been primarily drafted by William Kaufmann,
and he himself strongly opposed its declassification. McNamara was persuaded
to make the public address by Adam Yarmolinsky, his special assistant, who then
prepared a "sanitized" version of the Athens speech for delivery at Ann Arbor.
However, public release of that version was opposed by Daniel Ellsberg, who
was then authorized to write the final Ann Arbor version. Ellsberg's draft was
closer to the original speech than Yarmolinsky's had been. (Interviews with
Daniel Ellsberg, 24 August 1970 and 8 October 1972; and Adam Yarmolinsky,
10 July 1970.)
65. Kaufmann, *McNamara Strategy*, pp. 114–20.
66. On the European reaction to the "no-cities" strategy, see *Newsweek*, 2 July
1962, pp. 10–11; and Trewhitt, *McNamara*, pp. 171–72.
67. Trewhitt, *McNamara*, p. 115.

The first-strike implications received particular attention because of the controversy which had followed an article in the *Saturday Evening Post* early in March, written by Stewart Alsop, in which Alsop cited President Kennedy's belief that "Khrushchev must NOT be certain that, where its vital interests are threatened, the United States will never strike first."[68] Although Kennedy had hastened to explain, at a press conference on 22 March 1962, that what he had envisaged was striking first with nuclear power only if a vital area was already under conventional attack—and, he said, Western Europe was such a vital area—the misinterpretations that followed the Alsop article remained.[69]

Almost immediately, McNamara apparently began backtracking from his Ann Arbor position. During the summer and fall of 1962 he edged steadily closer to an acceptance of the prospects for nuclear parity with the Soviet Union. During a television appearance in September 1962, he acknowledged that,

> The value of our nuclear security may decline over time. We can, for a long time to come, we believe, maintain nuclear superiority over any possible opponent. What is doubtful, though, is that we can maintain the kind of superiority we have now and will have for at least the next few years.[70]

In a November interview with Stewart Alsop of the *Saturday Evening Post*, he voiced something approaching the ultimate heresy for the times. Asked whether the Soviets also would reach full retaliatory power he answered "Indeed, yes." He seemed, in fact, to think it was a good idea. "When both sides have a sure second-strike capability," he said, "then you might have a more stable balance of terror. This may seem a rather subtle point, but from where I'm sitting it seems a point worth thinking about."[71]

By this time, of course, the Cuban missile crisis of October 1962 had occurred, and as George Quester has pointed out,

> American actions in the Cuban crisis weakened any notion of general war without annihilation of populations. During the crisis, which had erupted so soon after the Ann Arbor speech, U.S. B-47 aircraft were deployed to civilian airfields (thus perhaps denying

68. *Newsweek*, 9 April 1962, p. 32.   69. Ibid.
70. Cited in Trewhitt, *McNamara*, p. 115.   71. Ibid., p. 116.

the Soviets a counterforce "no-cities" option), and President Kennedy had threatened a "full retaliatory strike" against the Soviet Union, seemingly if any missiles from Cuba were fired at any target. The declaratory policies which had seemed desirable when general war was a more abstract question appeared to have lost their appeal when a contest of wills had begun.[72]

In January 1963, however, when McNamara presented his second posture statement to Congress with the F/Y 1964 defense budget, he was still publicly accepting and justifying the "no-cities" version of counterforce strategy. When questioned by Senator Smith of the Senate Armed Services Committee, for example, he expressly certified his continued adherence to "the position I took in Ann Arbor."[73] In his prepared statement, McNamara gave the rationale for the U.S. strategic nuclear retaliatory forces:

> These forces—the long-range bombers, the land-and-sea based strategic missiles and their command and control systems—are designed to carry the burden of battle in general nuclear war. Their immediate purpose, however, is to deter war by their capacity to destroy an enemy's warmaking potential, including not only his nuclear strike forces and military installations, but also, if necessary, his urban and industrial society.[74]

He then outlined the current U.S. nuclear strategy behind the administration's F/Y 1964 strategic-forces budget request:

> What we are proposing is a capability to strike back after absorbing the first blow. This means we have to build and maintain a second strike force.
>
> Such a force should have sufficient flexibility to permit a choice of strategies, particularly an ability to (1) strike back decisively at the entire Soviet target system simultaneously, or (2) strike back first at the Soviet bomber bases, missile sites, and other military installations associated with their long-range nuclear forces to reduce the power of any follow-on attack—and then if necessary strike back at the Soviet urban and industrial complex in a controlled and deliberate way.
>
> Now the foregoing is not to say that we can forecast the nature

72. George H. Quester, *Nuclear Diplomacy*, p. 246.
73. Senate Armed Services Committee, *Military Procurement Authorization, Fiscal Year 1964*, p. 317.
74. Senate Appropriations Committee, *Department of Defense Appropriations for 1964*, p. 6.

of a nuclear attack upon the United States. In talking about global nuclear war, the Soviet leaders always say that they would strike at the entire complex of our military power including government and production centers, meaning our cities.

If they were to do so, we would, of course, have no alternative but to retaliate in kind.

But we have no way of knowing whether they would actually do so.

It would certainly be in their interest as well as ours to try to limit the terrible consequences of a nuclear exchange. By building into our forces a flexible capability, we at least eliminate the prospect that we could strike back in only one way; namely, against the entire Soviet target system including their cities.

Such a prospect would give the Soviet Union no incentive to withhold attack against our cities in a first strike. We want to give them a better alternative.[75]

McNamara explained that because of the decision to provide the "no-cities" option, the U.S. weapons system

should have two characteristics that weapons systems designed to meet other situations might not have. The first is that it must be invulnerable, because my set of premises require that we hold back a certain portion of our force, even under attack by the Soviet Union, which means that it must be able to survive that attack. So it must be invulnerable.

Secondly, the force must be larger than would otherwise be the case. Because since no force can be completely invulnerable, we will lose a portion of it under those circumstances and we must buy more than we otherwise would buy.[76]

If the United States had not decided to assume the possibility of "no-cities" nuclear exchanges, then

there would be strong reasons to reduce the forces which we are requesting funds to procure.

It is this particular assumption, as outlined on page 31 of the classified statement, that leads to procurement requirement for missiles and other forces as large as those which we are proposing for fiscal 1964.[77]

But on the other hand, McNamara rejected the option of a "full counterforce" capability. He believed that to destroy "any

75. House Armed Services Committee, *Hearings on Military Posture* (1963), p. 309.
76. Ibid., p. 332.   77. Ibid.

very large portion of the fully hard ICBM sites" would be unfeasible; and he judged this to be so "regardless of how large or
what kind of strategic forces we build."[78] Even a force "two,
three or several times larger than the force we recommend"
would not destroy all Soviet nuclear capability.[79] And, even with
"an extensive missile defense system and a much more elaborate
civil defense program than has thus far been contemplated . . .
we could not preclude casualties counted in tens of millions."[80]
As William Kaufmann has reported, "To the anguish of the Air
Force, this meant placing a limit on the size of the [U.S.] strategic
offensive forces."[81]

In the Pentagon, in fact, McNamara had by this time actually
moved further away from counterforce and "no-cities" strategy
than his public testimony implied. His 1962 draft presidential
memorandum (DPM) on strategic forces, finally drafted by Alain
Enthoven in late 1962, represented a distinct retreat from his
earlier position—stating, for example, "We do not want a comprehensive damage limitation posture."[82] According to aides
who drafted his F/Y 1964 posture statement of January 1963, it
included several passages on the planning of counterforce and
"no-cities" contingencies simply to make it consistent with the
F/Y 1963 statement and speeches by McNamara and other
administration spokesmen during 1962, especially the Ann
Arbor speech.[83] McNamara was also unwilling, at that particular time, to admit to Congress and the public the prospect of
Russia effectively catching up with the United States in strategic
strength. According to Henry Trewhitt, "There is no question
that for a time McNamara deliberately obscured the outlook for
an eventual nuclear stand-off, long after he understood the
prospect himself." And that was probably the fall of 1962.[84] In

78. Senate Armed Services Committee, *Military Procurement Authorization,
Fiscal Year 1964*, pp. 40–41.
79. House Appropriations Committee, *Department of Defense Appropriations
for 1964*, part 1, p. 234.
80. Senate Armed Services Committee, *Military Procurement Authorization,
Fiscal Year 1964*, p. 40.
81. Kaufmann, *McNamara Strategy*, p. 95.
82. Interviews with former aides to McNamara, 12 February 1973, 13 February 1973 and 22 February 1973.
83. Interview with Henry Glass, 29 July 1970.
84. Trewhitt, *McNamara*, p. 115.

January 1963, moreover, some dozen Air Force generals were given a briefing to the effect that they were no longer to take the avowed U.S. strategy as a criterion for strategic-force proposals.

The third annual DPM on strategic forces in August 1963 retreated even further from pure counterforce than had the second, and there was great agitation at the highest levels in the Pentagon about "what was referred to as McNamara's backsliding." There was particular concern within the Air Force that McNamara would even change the 1962 SIOP, which the Air Force had now come around (even eagerly) to accepting.[85]

It was not until the fall of 1963 that the DoD had, in fact, developed precise criteria on which U.S. strategic-forces procurement could be based. In the summer of 1962, McNamara authorized a Defense Department analysis, which came to be known informally as the Kent study, after General Glenn A. Kent (USAF) who headed the study group, to analyze the various alternative strategies which were available to the United States, and the weapons systems and force levels which each implied. The results of a pilot survey were ready in July 1963, and were very important in shaping the rationale for the administration's F/Y 1965 defense request. At this stage, the most significant contribution of the Kent study was the development of the strategy of "Damage Limitation."[86]

In his F/Y 1965 posture statement, submitted to Congress in January 1964, McNamara stated that

> comprehensive studies of alternative U.S. strategic retaliatory force structures employed in a nuclear exchange with a wide range of possible Soviet forces and under a wide variety of assumptions pertaining to the outbreak of war and United States and Soviet operational factors [have] found that forces in excess of those needed simply to destroy Soviet cities would significantly reduce damage to the United States and Western Europe. And the extent to which damage to ourselves can be reduced depends importantly on the size and the character of our own forces, particularly by the

85. Interviews with former aides to McNamara, 9 July 1970 and 13 February 1973.
86. Interview with Gen. Kent, 16 July 1970. The relevant document here is *Damage Limitation: A Rationale for the Allocation of Resources by the U.S. & USSR*, a study prepared for the director of defense research and engineering, 21 January 1964.

surface-to-surface missiles such as MINUTEMAN that can reach their targets quickly. . . . While a cities-only strategic retaliatory force would, in our judgment, be dangerously inadequate, a full-first-strike force, as I defined it earlier, is, on the basis of our estimates of the Soviet nuclear strike forces in the fiscal year 1967–69 period, simply unattainable. . . . Thus, a damage-limiting strategy appears to be the most practical and effective course for us to follow. Such a strategy requires a force considerably larger than would be needed for a limited cities-only strategy. While there are still some differences of judgment on just how large such a force should be, there is general agreement that it should be large enough to insure the destruction, singly or in combination of the Soviet Union, Communist China, and the Communist satellites as national societies, under the worst possible circumstances of war outbreak that can reasonably be postulated, and, in addition, to destroy their war-making capability so as to limit, to the extent practicable, damage to this country and to our allies.[87]

In a memorandum dated 12 March 1964, McNamara asked for an amplification of the January damage-limitation study, and requested "that the Services conduct studies during the next six months that would focus attention on 'damage limitation' and 'assured destruction.'" These studies were integrated by WSEG in August 1964, and the project was formally completed in September.[88] It had reportedly found that "the presently planned inventory of strategic missiles is approximately correct in this time period, whether by accident or good intuitive planning."[89] The analysis also showed that

further expansion in numbers of ICBMs would provide much less damage-limiting capability, compared with spending the same resources elsewhere. This includes anti-submarine warfare, improved surveillance and early warning of ICBM attack, fallout/

87. Senate Appropriations Committee, *Department of Defense Appropriations, 1965*, pp. 31–32.
88. The WSEG study was WSEG No. 79, *Analysis of General Nuclear War Postures for Strategic Offense and Defense Forces*, 2 vols., August 1964; and the final study in the project was *A Summary Study of Strategic Offense and Defense Forces of the U.S. & USSR*, prepared for the director of defense research and engineering, 8 September 1964. This account of the damage-limitation project is based on the latter document; an interview with Gen. Kent, 16 July 1970; and *Aviation Week & Space Technology*, 9 November 1964, pp. 23–24.
89. *Aviation Week & Space Technology*, 9 November 1964, p. 24. (This report was confirmed in an interview with Gen. Kent, 16 July 1970.)

blast shelters and perhaps a limited Nike X [ABM] missile deployment.[90]

The Kent study formed the basis of McNamara's discussion of U.S. strategic policy in his F/Y 1966 defense budget statement.[91] McNamara stated:

The strategic objectives of our general nuclear war forces are:
1. to deter a deliberate nuclear attack upon the United States and its allies by maintaining a clear and convincing capability to inflict unacceptable damage on an attacker, even were that attacker to strike first;
2. in the event such a war should nevertheless occur, to limit damage to our populations and industrial capacities.

The first of these capabilities (required to deter potential aggressors) we call "Assured Destruction," i.e., the capability to destroy the aggressor as a viable society, even after a well planned and executed surprise attack on our forces. The second capability we call "Damage Limitation," i.e., the capability to reduce the weight of the enemy attack by both offensive and defensive measures and to provide a degree of protection for the population against the effects of nuclear detonations.[92]

Furthermore, the Kent study provided a rationalization for limiting the Minuteman force to 1,000 missiles.[93]

Since 1965, of course, the avowed U.S. strategic policy has continued to change. By the time McNamara left office, in 1968, the "assured destruction" aspects of U.S. strategic capability received full emphasis.[94] Under Secretary Schlesinger, who held office from July 1973 to November 1975, however, there was something of a return to the McNamara policies of 1961–62.[95]

90. Ibid. The RAND counterforce study, which Kaufmann had begun in 1959, and which was critical in shaping the U.S. posture in 1961–62, was completed by F. S. Hoffman in 1963. Under Hoffman it came to much the same conclusions as had the Kent study. See Fred Hoffman et al., *Counterforce and Damage-Limiting Capability in Central War* (Santa Monica: RAND Corp., R-420-PR, August 1963).

91. Interview with Gen. Kent, 16 July 1970.

92. Senate Armed Services Committee and Senate Appropriations Committee, *Military Procurement Authorization, Fiscal Year 1966*, p. 43.

93. Interview with Gen. Kent, 16 July 1970.

94. McNamara's *The Essence of Security*, published as a record of "the principles and philosophy by which I have directed the activities of the Defense Establishment" (p. x), contains not a single mention of "Damage Limitation"; it is all "Assured Destruction."

95. See Desmond Ball, *Déjà Vu.*

The Schlesinger doctrine has more recently been reaffirmed in Presidential Review Memorandum (PRM) 10 and Presidential Directive (PD) 18 of the Carter Administration.[96] Current U.S. strategic policy is very similar to that which McNamara introduced in 1961–62 but was later to disavow.

STRATEGIC POLICY AND THE U.S. MISSILE PROGRAM (1961 TO 1965–1966)

The argument that the strategy adopted by the United States in the 1960s explains the U.S. missile posture has taken two principal forms. First, some commentators argue merely that there was a direct connection between strategic policy and strategic-forces procurement, with the implication that the McNamara strategic posture was "rationally" based.

These include those who saw in the U.S. missile program the hardware realization of strategic theories they had supported or developed, and especially McNamara's former colleagues and supporters, those who argue that one of his prime contributions to the management and design of the U.S. strategic posture was the development of a credible strategy and its use as a criterion for the designing of the U.S. strategic posture. William Kaufmann, for example, seems to believe that the McNamara "revolution" in the design of U.S. military and strategic forces can be explained entirely in terms of, and by a simple description of, "The McNamara strategy."[97]

A number of critics go further than this, and argue that not only was the U.S. strategic posture shaped by strategic and national-security policy considerations, but that the particular strategies adopted throughout the first half of the 1960s, the particular shifts in avowed strategy, and especially the peculiar progression through them, were responsible for the "excessive" levels of the missile build-up. From this position, that build-up was a mistake.[98]

However, in neither case has any direct or precise connection

96. See *New York Times*, 26 August 1977; and *Aviation Week & Space Technology*, 6 March 1978, p. 16.
97. Kaufmann, *The McNamara Strategy*.
98. See, rather ironically, James R. Schlesinger, in Senate Committee on Government Operations, *Planning, Programming, Budgeting* (1970), p. 133.

been established between strategic considerations and the size and characteristics of the U.S. strategic-forces posture. The first missile decisions of the Kennedy-McNamara Administration were made before that administration had decided, in any but the most general terms, what particular strategic and national security policy it would adopt. From the beginning there was, of course, an acceptance of the concept of deterrence. And, underlying the task forces' recommendations which formed the basis of the 28 March 1961 defense moves, there was the strategic assumption that the second-strike strategic forces must be specially designed to survive a first strike. According to Dr. Alain Enthoven, for example,

> the dominant influence [on the early 1961 decisions] was views about strategy. We speeded up the Polaris and Minuteman program because we believed that it was terribly important to have an invulnerable retaliatory force.[99]

But details of nuclear-war-fighting strategy and decisions on targeting had to be worked out, and national-security policy had yet to be explicated. And, of course, the need for a retaliatory force capable of surviving by itself implied little as far as the size of the strategic-forces requirement was concerned.

By the time of the strategic decisions of late 1961, the Defense Department had progressed a long way towards formulating a nuclear strategy, designing the necessary hardware, including command and control systems, and drawing up target lists. The progress made in only eight months was, in fact, very impressive, but the work was still six months from completion. Although a series of general options and guidelines for nuclear-war-fighting contingencies had been delineated within the U.S. SIOP by the late fall of 1961, the new SIOP was not officially adopted until January 1962,[100] at least a month after the F/Y 1963 defense budget had been prepared, and specific targets to accord with it had not yet been designated. Only in the last week of June 1962, at a meeting at SAC headquarters between McNamara, his deputy Gilpatric, and the most senior U.S. military officers, was final

99. Ibid., p. 295.
100. Interviews with Richard Fryklund and Al Goldberg, 20 July 1970.

approval given to specific targets, and ground-zero areas marked and specific bombs and missiles allocated to the targets.[101]

Similarly, work on the revised U.S. BNSP was not completed until June 1962.[102] Final drafting of this document was taken over by Walt W. Rostow (a White House defense aide until December 1961, and then chairman of the State Department's Policy Planning Board) in mid-1961.[103] A draft had been finished and circulated throughout the Pentagon and other top security agencies for "emendation and recommendations" in April 1962,[104] and by the time of its completion in June 1962 the revised BNSP had seen five major attempts to reach agreement by top military and civilian leaders.[105] It was never approved, but remained the major guideline for U.S. strategic policy.[106] Without a formal statement of basic national-security policy, McNamara had no basis for determining force levels and military structure for the F/Y 1963 defense budget other than very general ad hoc views on national strategy.[107]

All this meant that, while the strategy accepted by McNamara

101. *Newsweek*, 2 July 1962, p. 11.

102. The revised "Basic National Security Policy," a document of 286 pages, was presented to the National Security Council and the president in mid-June (see Mr. Hall, *Congressional Record, House*, 2 July 1962, p. 12616). Kennedy stated on 27 June 1962 that he had still "not studied the paper; the Secretary of State has it" (see Kennedy's press conference of 27 June 1962, in *Kennedy and the Press*, ed. Chase & Lerman, p. 279).

103. Interviews with Henry S. Rowen, 25 August 1970, and Malcolm W. Hoag, 19 August 1970.

104. *Newsweek*, 9 April 1962, pp. 32–33.

105. There were apparently seven issues which could not be resolved during the drafting of the revised BNSP, including the question of nuclear strategic doctrine and the role of tactical nuclear weapons (see Rostow, *The Diffusion of Power*, pp. 174–76; Col. James A. Donovan, *Militarism, U.S.A.*, p. 223, and interview with Paul Nitze, 7 February 1973).

106. In the late fall of 1961, in a document signed for Kennedy by McGeorge Bundy, his special assistant for national security affairs, it was decided that the administration would not adopt a single BNSP (interview with Adam Yarmolinsky, 10 July 1970). For contents of the Rostow BNSP, see *Newsweek*, 9 April 1962, pp. 32–33; *Congressional Record, Senate*, 18 June 1962, pp. 10757–60; 20 June 1962, pp. 11081–82; 26 June 1962, pp. 11670–72; and *Congressional Record, House*, 2 July 1962, pp. 12615–19.

107. See Donovan, *Militarism, U.S.A.*, pp. 223–24. McNamara preferred to rely on Draft Presidential Memoranda and speeches, both public and classified, of top administration personnel for basic national security policy, but these were of little use in designing a complex national security posture (interview with Henry S. Rowen, 25 August 1970).

at the time was interpreted by him as requiring larger strategic forces "than would otherwise be the case,"[108] only very rough estimates could as yet be made; and McNamara's subordinates had difficulty in following his interpretations.[109] General Burch-inal, for example, denied that "the new concept of target-ing" would require more missiles than the "massive retaliation" policy.[110]

By the time the final decisions were made on the F/Y 1964 defense budget in late 1962, McNamara had begun backtracking somewhat from his late-1961–mid-1962 position on national strategic policy. He had rejected the extremes of his previous "no-cities" position, but had not yet settled on a single, consistent strategic policy. Moreover, the posture statement on which the strategic nuclear retaliatory forces requirement was allegedly based did not reflect his true position.[111]

Again during the development of the F/Y 1965 defense bud-get, although some preliminary work had been done on devel-oping strategic criteria as a foundation for strategic-weapons procurement, it had not proceeded to the point of providing any specific basis. As McNamara testified, there were "still some dif-ferences of judgment" on what the size of the U.S. missile force should be.[112] By the time such criteria had been fully worked out, with the completion of the Kent study in September 1964, the decision had been made to limit the Minuteman program to 1,000 missiles. The Kent study did provide some (strategic-theoretical) justification for the imposition of this ceiling, but it was only one of several relevant factors, and the ceiling would probably have been imposed even if it had come to different conclusions. The Kent study's main concern was to provide an internal structure, in terms of strategic missions and the char-

108. Testimony of McNamara, House Armed Services Committee, *Hearings on Military Posture* (1963), p. 332.

109. Interview with Henry S. Rowen, 25 August 1970; see also Rostow, *The Diffusion of Power*, p. 176.

110. House Appropriations Committee, *Department of Defense Appropriations for 1963*, part 2, p. 529.

111. Interview with Henry Glass, 29 July 1970; see also Trewhitt, *McNamara*, p. 115.

112. Senate Appropriations Committee, *Department of Defense Appropriations, 1965*, p. 32.

acter of the U.S. missile program, for a force whose size had been determined on the basis of several other factors.[113] As such, it could provide little more than a rationalization of the predetermined force level.

Thus, three things are apparent in the relationship between strategic policy and missile numbers. First, strategic policy was not determining with regard to the size and characteristics of the U.S. missile program, except in a very tenuous and general way. The sophisticated strategic calculus, largely originating in the RAND Corporation, which argued the necessity for a second-strike retaliatory force capable of surviving a nuclear attack, showed itself in the early-1961 decisions to accelerate the Polaris and hard-silo Minuteman programs. Throughout the early 1960s there was an almost universal acceptance of the necessity for strategic superiority over the Soviet Union, but it was never made clear just how this superiority was to be measured. By themselves, principles of "survivability" and "superiority" could not serve as guides to the establishment of finite force levels. The major missile decisions were made before the administration had worked out an internally consistent strategy and compatible targeting plans. U.S. strategic policy was continually in a state of flux—"shifting sands"—and never stood still long enough to provide a precise basis for determining the strategic-forces requirement. Strategic policy never served as a direct criterion for deciding U.S. missile numbers.

One might, of course, consider this to be obvious. That 1,000 missiles—no less and no more—should be the precise requirement of a particular strategy would surprise most critics, especially since the targeting structure has never remained constant. But this is not the point. Few strategic analysts would claim that strategic calculations alone *can* indicate a precise force requirement. Enthoven, for example, has written that "no set of calculations alone can logically imply that the United States should have 'X' divisions or 'Y' ICBMs."[114] The eventual decision

113. Interview with Gen. Kent, 16 July 1970.
114. Senate Committee on Government Operations, *Planning, Programming, Budgeting* (1970), p. 285. Secretary McNamara has also testified that "the shape of the [marginal offensive capability] curve is generally agreed upon, and what it

always remains a political and necessarily somewhat arbitrary one. The "shifting sands" undercut any attempt to reduce this arbitrariness.

The second significant point is that from 1961–62 to 1965–66, U.S. strategic policy shifted from the extreme "no-cities" version of counterforce to the doctrine of "assured destruction," with its necessary emphasis on urban targeting. The procurement requirements of the former, no matter how imprecisely formulated, obviously need not be those of the latter; some aspects of the required strategic posture might even be incompatible with those of other postures.

By 1965–66, when the United States did adopt a strategy which could claim official acceptance over a substantial time period (that of "assured destruction"), the major missile decisions had been made. One argument which follows from this is that of James Schlesinger:

> In 1961 the suicidal implications of massive retaliation were underscored: the United States would be faced with a choice between humiliation or holocaust. Interest then developed in damage-limiting and coercion. But there has been little willingness to invest money in either. Since 1965 the merits of Assured Destruction have been emphasized—with little attention paid to the suicidal implications found so distressing in prior years. The principal rationale for the current emphasis on Assured Destruction reflects certain recently-developed notions of arms control. It clearly falls within the province of the decisionmakers to adopt a strategy of measured response to any Soviet buildup with the long term objective of preserving U.S. Assured Destruction capabilities. One should note, however, that to accept this particular guide to action, implies that the buildup of the Minuteman force in 1961–62 was a mistake.[115]

---

says is that if we had 300 Minuteman missiles we could achieve this level of destruction of their force or their cities. If we had 600 missiles we could achieve this level. If we had 1,200 we could achieve this level. I think there is general agreement on the shape of the curve, but there is not always agreement at what point on the curve you should stop increasing the force" (Senate Armed Services Committee and Senate Appropriations Committee, *Military Procurement Authorization, Fiscal Year 1966*, p. 250). See also Charles J. Hitch, *Decision-Making for Defense*, p. 51.

115. Senate Committee on Government Operations, *Planning, Programming, Budgeting* (1970), p. 133.

If the administration had delayed the missile build-up until after its period of experimentation with various strategic policies had been concluded, this "mistake" might have been avoided. However, the evidence appears to show that any relationship between purposive strategic theory and U.S. weapons procurement is too tenuous to support such an argument. Moreover, other factors in the decision-making process are, in any case, much too weighty. In particular, the sorts of political pressures confronted by the administration required accommodation on their own terms.

Finally, it is apparent that strategic policy provided a *rationalization* for the missile decisions. At the time of great superiority over the Soviet Union in strategic strength, the United States could adopt a counterforce strategy within both feasibility and credibility; as this superiority declined, some of its strategic forces could still be allocated to the damage-limitation mission; but once it had disappeared, the counterforce factor in U.S. strategic policy lost its credibility. Strategic policy was, in essence, forged by the given international military and technological situation.

At the most, the peculiar and not necessarily inevitable progression of strategic theories accepted by the administration allowed a rationalization of the large Kennedy/McNamara missile build-up at each stage in the missile decisions, and allowed decisions which other strategic theories would have foreclosed.

10 The Missile Build-up and Alternative Strategic Nuclear Delivery Systems

Throughout the years of the Kennedy-McNamara missile build-up of 1961–64, the major controversy confronting the administration and its secretary of defense—more intense by far than the controversy over missile numbers—was that over the continuation of manned strategic systems, and their relative role in the U.S. nuclear deterrent force structure.

One of the first decisions made by the new administration in early 1961 was that intercontinental and submarine-launched ballistic missiles were superior to manned bombers as strategic nuclear delivery vehicles. The most important immediate consequence of this general decision was the decision to countermand the development and production of the B-70 manned bomber—designed as the supersonic (Mach 3) successor to the B-52—as a full weapons system. This was followed in late 1962 by the decision to cancel the Skybolt ALBM program, one which the Air Force considered to be necessary if the subsonic B-52s were to have a capability of operating effectively in the environment of the late 1960s and 1970s.

It is often argued that this decision to downgrade the role of manned delivery systems was responsible for the build-up of U.S. strategic long-range ballistic-missile systems. This argument has taken two principal forms. The first derives from the point that the decision to downgrade the role of the manned bomber meant confronting the Air Force, its industrial allies, Congress, the aviation press, and large sections of the general media.

A number of former White House staff members contend that the Kennedy-McNamara missile build-up was, at least in part, a direct consequence of this confrontation. Arthur Schlesinger, for example, has argued that neither Kennedy nor McNamara personally favored a large increase in the U.S. missile force:

> But he [McNamara] was already engaged in a bitter fight with the Air Force over his efforts to disengage from the B-70, a costly, high-altitude manned bomber rendered obsolescent by the improvement in Soviet ground-to-air missiles. After cutting down the original Air Force missile demands considerably, he perhaps felt that he could not do more without risking public conflict with the Joint Chiefs and the vociferous B-70 lobby in Congress. As a result, the President went along with the policy of multiplying Polaris and Minuteman missiles.[1]

The first part of this chapter is an examination of that contention.

The second line of argument derives from the point that in the McNamara defense establishment, the complementary role of long-range bombers and missiles in the U.S. strategic offensive forces was made explicit. As defined by Secretary McNamara, strategic retaliatory forces included "the long-range bombers, their air-to-ground and decoy missiles, and their tankers; the land-based and submarine-based strategic missiles; and

---

1. Arthur M. Schlesinger, Jr., *A Thousand Days*, p. 438.

the system for the command and control of the forces."[2] Hence, it has been argued, the deployment of additional ICBMs was necessary to provide a functional replacement for the down-graded manned delivery systems. In particular, it was argued in 1963 that a portion of the Minuteman program could be explained in terms of the cancellation of the Skybolt air-launched ballistic missile program, and the functional ("defense suppression") replacement of the programmed Skybolt missiles by Minuteman missiles.

The second part of this chapter argues that it is uncertain if any Minuteman missiles were in fact deployed as a functional replacement for the cancelled Skybolt missiles. Even granted that some were procured for that purpose ("defense suppression"), it is argued that this was unnecessary, because (a) the Skybolt program was regarded, at least everywhere outside the U.S. Air Force, as being of dubious value in terms of national security; and (b) other programs, particularly the "Hound Dog" air-breathing missile, were sufficient for the "defense suppression" task.

This chapter also serves as a transition between the more "rational" explanations discussed in the previous two chapters and the more "political" explanations discussed in the following chapter.

THE B-70 AND THE KENNEDY-McNAMARA
STRATEGIC MISSILE BUILD-UP

The B-70 program began in the mid-1950s, at about the time when the development of the Atlas and Titan first-generation ICBMs was recommended and authorized. In December 1957, in the immediate aftermath of the first Sputniks, development of the B-70 was given high (1-A) priority, second only to the ballistic missile and Vanguard satellite programs. In January 1958, the Air Force's first definite program plans for the B-70 proposed that a combat wing be ready in August 1964, with the bomber's maiden flight scheduled for December 1961. At this time, the Air Force planning estimate for the 1965-75 period

2. House Appropriations Committee, *Department of Defense Appropriations for 1963*, part 2, p. 13.

was for 250 B-70s, at an estimated program cost of $6.4 billion (or an average cost of $24.6 million each).[3]

Throughout 1958, 1959, and the first half of 1960, however, there was little support for the B-70 program within the Eisenhower Administration. The program was only minimally funded, the earliest possible operational date was extended to 1967, and in October 1959 the program was almost cancelled entirely.[4]

Then during the 1960 Kennedy-Nixon presidential campaign the B-70 was given a new lease on life. In August, with the beginning of the campaign following the party conventions, F/Y 1961 B-70 funding was more than doubled;[5] and just days before the presidential election the DoD announced that sufficient funds would be released for the production of twelve B-70 prototypes, at least four of which would be prototypes of a "usable weapons system." A production program of 200 aircraft was planned. Eisenhower's F/Y 1962 defense budget, transmitted to Congress in January 1961, contained $358 million for the B-70, which although $217 million less than the $575 million requested by the Air Force would have continued the development of the B-70 as a complete weapons system.[6]

In February 1961 the whole question of the manned strategic bomber in the U.S. nuclear deterrent posture was considered as part of the defense reappraisal of the new administration. On 28 February 1961 the JCS reviewed the B-70 program, and the Army and the Navy recommended that the B-70 "be retained in R&D indefinitely"; it was not considered by the joint chiefs in a program context.[7] Then in March, during the preparation of the revised (Kennedy) F/Y 1962 defense budget, McNamara, Jerome Wiesner, then Kennedy's science adviser, Herbert York, director of defense research and engineering, David Bell, the

3. Ed Rees, *The Manned Missile*, pp. 35, 106.
4. Ibid., pp. 116, 119–21, 123.
5. *Missiles & Rockets*, 15 August 1960, p. 16.
6. Herbert F. York, *Race to Oblivion*, pp. 55–56. The new program was formalized as Schedule W-27R, dated 9 December 1960. See *Congressional Record, Senate*, 16 March 1961, pp. 4118–21.
7. Senate Armed Services Committee, *Military Procurement Authorization, Fiscal Year 1962*, p. 351.

new director of the BoB, "and a few others" met with President Kennedy, and it was decided to cut the B-70 program back. According to York, the "most important" reason behind this decision was that "the new Administration had confirmed the claims of the prior one that the missile gap for all practical purposes did not exist."[8] Kennedy also joined with McNamara in March in rejecting a 15th wing of B-52s which the Air Force had also recommended; and the decision was made to accelerate the phaseout of the B-47 medium-bomber wings.[9]

The revised F/Y 1962 defense budget, announced to Congress by Kennedy on 28 March 1961, cut $138 million from the Eisenhower B-70 budget, leaving approximately $220 million. Kennedy stated that the development of the B-70 "as a full weapons system at this time [is] unnecessary and economically unjustifiable." The cut-back stemmed from the decision that the B-70 would not contribute anything to the U.S. deterrent force over and above the capacity of the ICBMs and the B-52 bomber fleet. The B-70 would not have become available in operational numbers until 1968, and by that time the United States expected to have "large numbers" of ICBMs fully tested and in place. To preserve future options, however, the B-70 was to be carried on, essentially as a Mach-3 bomber experimental program.[10]

Numerous protests were made to Air Force Secretary Zuckert by advocates of the manned bomber, but Congress initially seemed quite quiescent—and this despite the fact that contracting for a full weapons system would have been spread through many states. As soon as congressional hearings opened on the revised F/Y 1962 defense budget, the Air Force began a drive to have the B-70 reinstated as a full weapons system, making it clear that it was first on its list of priorities for restoration.[11] However, the Armed Services Committees of both Houses of Congress, while adding more funds for the B-52 and B-58

8. York, *Race to Oblivion*, p. 57.

9. See House Armed Services Committee, *Authorizing Appropriations for Aircraft, Missiles and Naval Vessels for the Armed Forces* (1961), pp. 1564–65, 1577.

10. President Kennedy, *Special Message*, p. 11.

11. *Aviation Week & Space Technology*, 3 April 1961, p. 25; House Appropriations Committee, *Department of Defense Appropriations for 1962*, part 3, pp. 467–68.

manned bombers than the administration had requested, refused to heed Air Force pleas to restore the money for the B-70. Congressman Vinson, chairman of the House Armed Services Committee, explained that,

> This cut in the B-70 program caused the committee some concern at first, but we found that the Kennedy program will permit an orderly development of the B-70, and will provide an opportunity to find out a great many things about the B-70 which must be known before the final decision on its complete development can be made.[12]

In July, however, General Le May personally took the Air Force case for the B-70 to the Senate's defense appropriations subcommittee, where he recommended spending $448 million in F/Y 1962 and $500 million annually the following "three or four" years on its development. The Senate committee approved the recommendation, and in August Congress transmitted its approved F/Y 1962 defense budget to the president, with $400 million (or $180 million more than Kennedy had requested) for the B-70.[13]

McNamara continued to oppose spending the extra funds, and Kennedy was faced with the choice "of over-riding McNamara or inviting trouble on Capitol Hill."[14] Kennedy accepted McNamara's recommendation to stand firm on his position on impounding the extra $180 million, though he waited until Congress had adjourned for the Christmas 1961 break before he revealed his decision.[15] And by the end of the year the chairman of the House Appropriations Committee's defense subcommittee, which had carried the burden of the congressional argument, had accepted this decision.[16]

McNamara's biggest, and most bitter, fight over the B-70 occurred in February–March 1962, over his decision to request no new money (NOA) for the bomber in the F/Y 1963 defense budget. In testimony before the House Armed Services Committee on 24 January, McNamara said, "We have again re-studied

12. *Aviation Week & Space Technology*, 8 May 1961, p. 26.
13. Ibid., 24 July 1961, pp. 32–33; and 14 August 1961, p. 30.
14. Ibid., 18 September 1961, p. 25.   15. Ibid., 6 November 1961, p. 28.
16. Ibid., 15 January 1962, p. 25.

the role of the B-70 in our strategic retaliatory forces . . . and again have reached the conclusion that the B-70 will not provide enough of an increase in our offensive capabilities to justify its very high cost." [17] And later, at a news conference on 15 March, he stated that the strategic retaliatory forces programmed through 1967 could "achieve practically complete destruction of the enemy target system even after absorbing an initial nuclear attack," and the addition of 200 B-70s or 150 RS-70s "either of which would cost about $10 billion, would not appreciably change this result." [18] McNamara also reaffirmed his decision to restrict the B-70 program to two or three flight-demonstration prototypes.[19]

The initial Air Force B-70 submission to the secretary of defense for the F/Y 1963 defense budget was made on 16 August 1961. It called for the release by the Defense Department of the additional $180 million appropriated by Congress for F/Y 1962 and for a funding level of $574 million in F/Y 1963, with the ultimate object of establishing a first wing of 45 aircraft. This proposal was again submitted, in greater detail, with the Air Force's F/Y 1963 defense budget submission of 23 October 1961. On 1 November an alternative plan—"the optimum for the earliest operational date"—was submitted by the Air Force, proposing $675.8 million in F/Y 1963.[20] However, as General Ferguson explained to the House Appropriations defense subcommittee:

> Subsequent to the November 1 submission it has become apparent in the refinements of the 1963 program that the DOD was not proposing to accept the recommendations. Therefore the Air Force extracted elements, important elements, of the November 1 plan, and submitted once again to the Department of Defense a modified plan dated January 12 [1962].[21]

This plan called for a B-70 funding of $491 million in F/Y 1963 (or $320 million over that requested by the administration). This money was to be used to reorient that B-70 program toward the

---

17. House Armed Services Committee, *Hearings on Military Posture* (1962), p. 3177.
18. *Aviation Week & Space Technology*, 19 March 1962, p. 38.
19. Ibid., 22 January 1962, p. 27.
20. House Appropriations Committee, *Department of Defense Appropriations for 1963*, part 5, pp. 326–31.
21. Ibid., p. 326.

RS-70, or reconnaissance-strike version of the aircraft. This expanded development program would have led to a first wing (45
aircraft) of RS-70s operational by about 1968 at a cost of about
$5 billion.[22]

Throughout this period, the Air Force's maneuverings, in
terms of changes in both funding requests and in program des-
ignations and mission rationales, were obviously designed to
improve the chances of a successor manned strategic bomber in
the U.S. deterrent. This opportunism was characteristic of the
Air Force during the preparation of defense budgets in the fall
and winter of each year.

None of these Air Force submissions on the B-70 was ever
considered in a "program context," by the JCS as a whole. The
official positions of the various chiefs remained as they were on
28 February 1961.[23] As President Kennedy stated in a press
conference on 7 March 1962, the majority of the joint chiefs
(General Lemnitzer, chairman; Admiral Anderson, CNO; and
General Decker, Army) supported the administration's position
—that the B-70 program be retained in R&D and, for F/Y 1963,
be funded $180 million appropriated by Congress for F/Y 1962;
only the Air Force chief of staff, General Le May, supported a
development and production program. McNamara had no need
to fear that the joint chiefs of staff would unite against him over
the B-70. President Kennedy also stated that he himself strongly
supported the position of his DoD.[24]

In the first week of March 1962 the House Armed Services
Committee not only accepted the Air Force's plea for $491 mil-
lion for the RS-70, but on the initiative of Chairman Vinson
voted to test congressional authority over the DoD by *ordering*
the Air Force to spend the full amount authorized.[25] McNamara
was incredulous, and on 14 March he appeared before the committee in a closed session with the intention of "straightening
Vinson out."[26] On 20 March the president himself intervened in

22. Ibid., p. 331.   23. Ibid., p. 327.
24. Harold W. Chase and Allen H. Lerman, eds., *Kennedy and the Press*,
pp. 199–200.
25. *Aviation Week & Space Technology*, 12 March 1962, p. 310.
26. See Charles J. V. Murphy, "The Education of a Defense Secretary,"
p. 105.

the quarrel, which had become a test of strength between the legislative and executive branches of the government, a test desired neither by Kennedy nor the Democratic leadership in Congress. After a walk in the White House rose garden, a compromise was worked out between Kennedy and Vinson. The latter was persuaded to withdraw his stern language from his committee's bill, replacing the word "directed" with "authorized," and was assured that McNamara would bring an open mind to a new appraisal of the RS-70 program, which the secretary had ordered on 12 March.[27]

Ironically, as it turned out, Congress was not fully behind the Vinson committee. On the recommendation of the House Appropriations defense subcommittee, the House added only $52.9 million to the administration's program, rather than the $491 million which Vinson (and the Air Force) had wanted.[28] The Senate accepted the Air Force's $491 million recommendation, and after a conference between House of Representatives and Senate defense-appropriations representatives, both Houses agreed in July to a $362 million allocation (or $191 million more than the administration had requested) for six test RS-70 aircraft. During 1962 the Defense Department released $50 million of these additional funds, for the development of radar components for the reconnaissance-strike version, but $140 million was still left impounded.[29]

For F/Y 1964, the Air Force asked for $363.7 million to build five RS-70 prototypes.[30] Secretary McNamara refused to ask Congress for new funds, however, intending to use only $81 million from earlier appropriations to continue the development of three prototypes and system components.[31] In his opinion, "neither the B-70 nor the RS-70 would contribute enough to the Strategic Retaliatory Forces already planned to justify their great costs."[32] This year, however, McNamara had only minority sup-

27. *Aviation Week & Space Technology*, 26 March 1962, p. 11; see also Theodore C. Sorensen, *Kennedy*, p. 385.
28. *Aviation Week & Space Technology*, 16 April 1962, p. 26.
29. Ibid., 30 July 1962, p. 16; and 3 December 1962, p. 32.
30. *Congressional Quarterly Almanac*, 1963, p. 419.
31. *Aviation Week & Space Technology*, 21 January 1963, p. 28.
32. Senate Appropriations Committee, *Department of Defense Appropriations for 1964*, p. 8.

port within the joint chiefs. On 29 September 1962, in fact, the JCS had unanimously recommended developing the RS-70; and after General Taylor became chairman of the JCS in October, all but he "supported the development of the RS-70 at a substantially higher level of development than that currently planned under the program of the Secretary of Defense."[33] Largely upon the initiative of Senator Richard B. Russell (Democrat, Georgia), chairman of the Senate Armed Services Committee, Congress went ahead and voted the $363.7 million requested by the Air Force for F/Y 1964, although it was generally conceded that McNamara probably would not spend the money.[34] This was largely a pro forma action; Congress evinced little will to fight the administration again.

The draft F/Y 1965 defense budget circulated throughout the Pentagon in December 1963 included *no* funds for the (now) XB-70. But, probably as a result of the intervention of President Johnson, McNamara released $100 million to complete the construction of two of the prototype aircraft.[35] By this time, the Air Force was no longer interested in the deployment of the B-70/RS-70/XB-70 as a manned strategic system; it had, by 1964, taken up a further follow-on manned bomber, the advanced manned strategic strike aircraft (AMSS, later AMSA). And although the AMSA issue was before him until his resignation in 1968, there was no question but that by 1964 McNamara had won.

However, the fact that in every year of the Kennedy-McNamara missile build-up (F/Y 1962 to F/Y 1965 inclusive) Congress supported the Air Force against the administration's bomber requests is at least circumstantial evidence in favor of the arguments of some former White House staff members as described at the beginning of this chapter. But a close examination of the foregoing review makes claims for any direct connection between the administration's missile and bomber decisions (in terms of intramural bargaining) difficult to sustain.

During the first half of 1961, the administration's decisions

33. *Aviation Week & Space Technology*, 18 March 1963, p. 39.
34. Ibid., 22 April 1963, p. 26.
35. Ibid., 16 December 1963, p. 30; and 27 January 1964, p. 26.

against the manned bomber and in favor of the relatively invulnerable silo-based intercontinental and submarine-launched ballistic missile were opposed only by the Air Force. The White House staff and the key civilian officials of the DoD (McNamara, Gilpatric, York, Hitch, Enthoven) were virtually unanimous in their position: they were supported by the Army and the Navy, and Air Force Secretary Zuckert was not enthusiastic in representing the Air Force's position, while the Democratic-controlled Congress at that time either supported or acquiesced to the administration's decision.

In the fall of 1961, when the administration's F/Y 1963 missile proposals were being drawn up, there was the possibility of a confrontation with Congress over the B-70. But the administration did not announce its decision on the F/Y 1962 funds appropriated by Congress for the B-70 until Congress had adjourned, and in the event the final F/Y 1963 missile decisions were not made until December 1961. During November and December the Air Force was arguing for a large ($675.8 million) F/Y 1963 B-70 budget allocation, but it was apparently fairly easily induced to cut this to $491 million itself.[36] In some ways, the fact that the Air Force wanted to play "the budget game" made it easier for McNamara to take an absolute stand on the B-70 and stick to it. McNamara's biggest and bitterest fight over the B-70 occurred, as has been shown, in February–March 1962, but by this time all but 200 of the eventual U.S. ICBM force had been programmed, and in January 1962 the administration was in fact projecting some 400 more Minuteman missiles.[37]

It might have been, of course, that the expectation of a confrontation with Congress in 1962 induced Kennedy and McNamara to program more missiles "than national security required" in fall 1961.[38] But apart from the actions of the House Appropriations Committee in August 1961, the administration had no basis for such an expectation; and the confrontation which did eventuate in February–March 1962 was largely with

36. House Appropriations Committee, *Department of Defense Appropriations for 1963*, part 5, pp. 326–31.
37. The F/Y 1963–F/Y 1967 strategic-forces program, transmitted to Congress in January 1962, projected an end-program of 1,200 Minuteman missiles.
38. Schlesinger, *A Thousand Days*, p. 438.

the House Armed Services Committee, which had accepted the administration's view the previous year. This confrontation, which developed into a test of strength between the legislative and executive branches of the government, could have provided a basis for large, politically induced missile requests in later years; but if so, the lesson was lost. In the three ensuing defense budgets (F/Y 1964–66), the administration not only continued to refuse to develop the B-70 as a full weapons system, but also slowed down the missile build-up, and finally cut the projected Minuteman program back to 1,000 missiles.

Moreover, if McNamara actually feared to confront Congress over both the B-70 and Minuteman numbers, he could have made more extensive use of the technique which he did in fact use somewhat in cutting back the B-70—the manipulation of Minuteman program projections:[39] for example, a lower F/Y 1963 Minuteman procurement coupled with a higher projected Minuteman end program; the end figure could then have been reduced subsequently.

By June 1963 the administration had moved to counter the B-70 advocates directly. President Kennedy decided to commit the United States to an accelerated and expanded supersonic transport (SST) program, which although a commercial program would provide many of the technological advances that were expected from the B-70 prototypes. Pressure from within the Air Force, Congress, and industry shifted from the B-70 to the SST.[40] But other supersonic military aircraft programs (e.g., the A-11, later redesignated the SR-71) had been under way in the United States since the late 1950s. These were already well known to key congressmen and aircraft manufacturers, and this move to counter the B-70 could have been made in 1961–62 had the administration really feared Congress and the Air Force's industrial allies on this issue.

Throughout the Kennedy Administration, the Democrats held substantial majorities in both the House and the Senate, and Democrats chaired both appropriations committees (House

39. Interviews with Dr. Albert Wohlstetter, 16 August 1970 and 18 November 1972.
40. H. L. Nieburg, *In the Name of Science*, pp. 324–29.

and Senate) and both armed services committees. Although this did not mean that Congress would invariably comply with the policies of the administration—as shown in the congressional B-70 appropriations—it did mean that, as leader of the majority party, Kennedy had available to him a variety of sanctions sufficient to prevent congressional "revolt," as evinced by the Kennedy-Vinson "walk in the Rose Garden."

There were, then, no overriding political necessities for the administration to procure and deploy more missiles as a political quid pro quo to the Air Force and Congress for the cancellation of the B-70 as a weapons system. And there is little to suggest, apart from the reconstruction of the former White House staff members, made from their peculiar and necessarily delimited vantage point and from the purely circumstantial evidence, that this was in fact the case. Temporal juxtaposition of the respective missile and B-70 decisions would, indeed, appear to suggest that any relationship between the two was extremely tenuous. By themselves, the political pressures engendered by the cancellation of the B-70 would not have been sufficient to have forced an "excessive" strategic missile build-up.

THE SKYBOLT CANCELLATION AND THE PROGRAMMING OF MINUTEMAN FOR "DEFENSE SUPPRESSION"

The Skybolt ALBM program was officially cancelled in December 1962. Under McNamara, this missile had been programmed for a sole mission—that of "defense suppression," or the destruction of Soviet air defenses, to prepare the way for attacks on primary Soviet targets by U.S. manned bombers.[41] In explaining the cancellation of the Skybolt program to Congress during the F/Y 1964 defense budget hearings, McNamara asserted that there were ways of destroying Soviet air defenses other than by Skybolt missiles, "specifically, the Hound Dog and Minuteman missiles which we added to the program for that purpose."[42] In his prepared statement, McNamara stated:

41. Senate Appropriations Committee, *Department of Defense Appropriations for 1964*, p. 175.
42. Ibid.

We propose, then, that to the extent ballistic missiles are required for defense suppression, they be Minuteman. I can assure you, moreover, that the missile program I am recommending is fully adequate to the defense suppression task.[43]

McNamara testified several times during the F/Y 1964 hearings that 100 additional missiles had been added to the Minuteman program as a functional replacement of the cancelled Skybolt missiles. Throughout the hearings, various other witnesses also used this figure.[44] But the actual position is much less clear than this F/Y 1964 testimony would suggest. In the first place, there was some confusion as to whether these 100 Minuteman missiles were approved for procurement in the F/Y 1964 defense budget, or whether they were an addition to the longer-range Minuteman program. The F/Y 1964 budget contained funds for 150 new Minuteman missiles, and Dr. Brown testified that 100 of these were for defense suppression.[45] On the other hand, Secretary McNamara testified that the extra 100 Minuteman missiles were added "to the longer-range [Minuteman] program,"[46] and at this time 100 Minuteman missiles were added to the F/Y 1964–68 program, bringing the projected force to 1,300 missiles. But if this was the case, were these 100 Minuteman missiles still programmed for the defense-suppression role when the long-range Minuteman program was reduced from 1,300 to 1,200 missiles in fall 1963?

More importantly, there is inconsistency in McNamara's own F/Y 1964 testimony. In his prepared explanation of the Skybolt

43. Senate Armed Services Committee, *Military Procurement Authorization, Fiscal Year 1964*, p. 46.

44. See, for example, testimony of Secretary McNamara, House Appropriations Committee, *Department of Defense Appropriations for 1964*, part 1, p. 319; testimony of Gen. Friedman, House Appropriations Committee, *Department of Defense Appropriations for 1964*, part 5, p. 1001; testimony of Dr. Harold Brown, Senate Armed Services Committee, *Military Procurement Authorization, Fiscal Year 1964*, p. 449; and testimony of Gen. Le May, House Armed Services Committee, *Hearings on Military Posture* (1963), p. 1129; see also Alain C. Enthoven and K. Wayne Smith, *How Much is Enough?*, p. 259.

45. Senate Armed Services Committee, *Military Procurement Authorization, Fiscal Year 1964*, p. 449.

46. Senate Appropriations Committee, *Department of Defense Appropriations for 1964*, p. 175.

cancellation, he stated that the total saving from the cancellation of the Skybolt program was $2 billion, even after considering the cost of the additional Minuteman missiles required for the defense-suppression role previously envisaged for the Skybolt missiles. In other places in his testimony, however, McNamara stated (a) that the Skybolt program would have cost nearly $3 billion, not counting the additional cost of warheads, and (b) that "the incremental initial investment cost for a Minuteman missile, complete with its blast resistant silo . . . would approximate $4 million per missile."[47] This suggests that at least 250 Minuteman missiles were to be produced for the defense-suppression task.[48]

But whatever the compensatory additional Minuteman procurement figure was (100, 250, or more—or even, after the manipulation by McNamara of the Minuteman end-program figure, finally zero), the decision to add Minuteman missiles begged the question about that sort of replacement action. The Skybolt program was, from its inception in January 1959, reckoned by many analysts to be of dubious value. The concept of an air-launched ballistic missile had originated in 1958 as an Air Force answer to the Navy's Polaris FBM system, rather than as a national-security requirement in its own right.[49] Throughout 1959 and 1960, the Fletcher Committee, an independent ad-

47. House Appropriations Committee, *Department of Defense Appropriations for 1964*, part 1, pp. 115, 463.

48. The figure of 250 is derived by subtracting the savings involved in substituting Minuteman for Skybolt ($2 billion) from the cost of the Skybolt program ($3 billion) and dividing the resultant $1 billion by the cost of each Minuteman missile ($4 million). This calculation ignores the cost of Skybolt warheads, the inclusion of which in the equation must necessarily raise the Minuteman figure figure well above 250 missiles. Enthoven and Smith (*How Much is Enough?*, p. 225) estimate the cost of warheads for the Skybolt program as "in the hundreds of millions of dollars." $1 billion would be the approximate order of magnitude for 1,000 Skybolt warheads. The Minuteman figure would then be 500 missiles. If, as the administration claimed, the additional Minuteman procurement was only 100 missiles, then assuming the correctness of McNamara's figures for (i) the cost of a Minuteman missile ($4 million), (ii) the total cost of the Skybolt program ($3 billion plus the cost of warheads), and (iii) the savings involved in the substitution of the 100 Minuteman ICBMs for the Skybolt program ($2 billion), the cost of Skybolt warheads is minus $600 million! In other words, McNamara's figures are internally inconsistent.

49. See "Bold Orion: AF Answer to Polaris," *Missiles & Rockets*, 1 December 1958, p. 11.

visory committee established by the director of defense research and engineering to continuously review and evaluate the Skybolt program, recommended that it be discontinued; in 1960 another independent scientific advisory group made a similar recommendation; and WSEG No. 50 also suggested that it be dropped.[50] Cancellation of the program was seriously considered during the F/Y 1962 defense-budget review in fall 1960. The program was not cancelled, however, though no NOA was included in the (Eisenhower) F/Y 1962 budget for it. But any firm plans for the deployment of the Skybolt missile were deferred indefinitely.[51]

When the new administration entered office in January 1961, it, too, seriously considered cancelling the program immediately. But, according to Herbert York, domestic political factors and relations with the British forced the administration to continue it.[52] McNamara himself believed that because of the money which had been spent to date, the highly uncertain strategic situation, and the fact that, despite increasing cost projections, Skybolt seemed competitive with other systems, the program should be continued, and $50 million was included for it in the revised (Kennedy) F/Y 1962 defense budget.[53]

During the development of the F/Y 1963 defense budget, the Skybolt project was carefully reviewed by McNamara. According to Schlesinger, several top administration officials, as well as McNamara's scientific advisers, cautioned against the program, but McNamara decided to go ahead, presumably because "he had enough fights on his hands with the Air Force already."[54] In early 1962, however, OSD placed Skybolt on the "suspect

50. Enthoven and Smith, *How Much is Enough?*, pp. 253–54; and interviews with George W. Rathjens, 11 July 1970, and Laurence B. Dean, 27 July 1970.

51. York, *Race to Oblivion*, p. 155.

52. Ibid. The Skybolt program is an excellent example of the effect of alliance politics on the Kennedy Administration's policy for procuring weapons. Its eventual cancellation caused a "crisis in Anglo-American relations . . . superficially as sharp as that of Suez" (see Richard E. Neustadt, *Alliance Politics*, chap. 3, "The Skybolt Affair").

53. Enthoven and Smith, *How Much is Enough?*, pp. 254–55. In an interview on 17 August 1970, Dr. Enthoven described this decision as "a curious mistake."

54. Schlesinger, *A Thousand Days*, p. 731.

list,"[55] and by August 1962 rising costs and remaining technical difficulties convinced McNamara that further investment in the program would be a mistake. On 7 November 1962 he formally recommended to Kennedy that the program be cancelled.[56] By this time, Skybolt's cost had increased 300 percent over the initial estimates, its performance had been downgraded by about 66 percent compared with the original objectives, and it was not expected to be operational in any significant sense until 1966.[57] The missile was nearly as far away from its scheduled operational date as it had ever been.

At the time of its cancellation, the Skybolt program involved the procurement of 1,012 missiles.[58] Before the House Armed Services Committee in February 1963, General Le May stated with angry bemusement that he did not know how 100 Minuteman missiles could replace over 1,000 Skybolt missiles, and the basis for the trade-off remains a mystery.[59] Certainly, the Minuteman figure—unlike those for Skybolt—does not suggest any precise calculation.

It has been estimated that in the early 1960s there were over 200 Soviet defense suppression targets which would have had to be destroyed to assure the penetration of U.S. manned bombers to their primary targets. These defense suppression targets (mainly SA-2s) were completely vulnerable not only to ballistic missiles, but also to the Hound Dog air-breathing missiles. According to Enthoven and Smith,

> There were, in fact, not enough productive defense suppression targets to occupy the entire alert force of Hound Dogs.... The number of Hound Dogs on alert status was scheduled to increase from 280 to approximately 400, and all of them could be assigned

55. House Appropriations Committee, *Department of Defense Appropriations for 1964*, part 5, p. 969.

56. Schlesinger, *A Thousand Days*, p. 732. McNamara decided, however, to postpone any announcement of the decision until after Congress had adjourned in late November.

57. Senate Appropriations Committee, *Department of Defense Appropriations for 1964*, p. 177; and Enthoven and Smith, *How Much is Enough?*, p. 257.

58. Testimony of McNamara, Senate Armed Services Committee, *Military Procurement Authorization, Fiscal Year 1964*, p. 45.

59. House Armed Services Committee, *Hearings on Military Posture* (1963), p. 1229.

to defense suppression targets. This would have permitted multiple attacks against [Soviet anti-bomber defense systems].[60]

There was simply no strategic need for any Minuteman compensation for the Skybolt cancellation.[61]

The relating of additional Minuteman missiles to the cancelled
Skybolt program is an excellent example of the way McNamara
manipulated weapons-systems programs in order to cut back
other programs and projects when he believed he would otherwise face unrelenting opposition. The Skybolt missile was already much less cost-effective than incremental Minuteman
missiles when the F/Y 1963 defense budget was being prepared.
Only before June 1961 were the Skybolt cost estimates competitive with those of incremental Minuteman missiles. From the
July 1961 cost estimate on, the Minuteman gained the cost advantage, and later estimates greatly increased this.[62] And, on
the effectiveness side of the calculation, apparently much fewer
than 408 Minuteman missiles were needed to perform the same
mission.[63] But OSD did not put the Skybolt program on the
"suspect list" until after the F/Y 1963 budget had been passed by
Congress in early 1962.[64]

The only explanation for Skybolt being left in the program at
this time is that given by Schlesinger—that McNamara was not

60. Enthoven and Smith, *How Much is Enough?*, p. 258.
61. In planning for a force of about 1,000 Skybolt missiles in addition to the
Hound Dog air-to-ground missiles, the USAF was perhaps intending to use Skybolt against the primary targets within the Soviet Union (rather than against
SAMs). Such action, from stand-off range, would in fact nullify the air defenses
anyway, by destroying the targets they are defending. But this would simply
duplicate the function of the Minuteman. Confining Skybolt to defense suppression was perhaps McNamara's first step in cancelling the program.
62. Of the 1,000 or so Skybolt missiles programmed for procurement most
were development models and spares. Only 408 missiles were to be deployed,
four aboard each of 102 B-52-H bombers. The incremental cost of 408 Minuteman missiles was just over $1,600 million. The June 1961 cost estimate for the
Skybolt program was the last to be below this figure. See Enthoven and Smith,
How Much is Enough?, p. 255.
63. McNamara testified that 100 Minuteman missiles would be "adequate to
the defense suppression task." See House Appropriations Committee, *Department of Defense Appropriations for 1964*, part 1, pp. 116, 319.
64. House Appropriations Committee, *Department of Defense Appropriations
for 1964*, part 5, p. 969.

prepared to face another fight with the Air Force.[65] Leaving Skybolt in the U.S. strategic-weapons program at that time did, moreover, give McNamara a lever in his fight to cancel the B-70 —the deployment of Skybolt aboard the B-52-Hs seemingly gave evidence of his intention of keeping the manned bomber in the U.S. strategic arsenal into the 1970s. Herbert York has written that he once heard President Kennedy remark that he needed Skybolt "to shoot down the B-70."[66] And, in February 1963, Richard B. Russell, chairman of the Senate Armed Services Committee, stated that,

> this committee has placed great store by the Skybolt program. We were comforted with a lollipop that the Skybolt would assuage our concern over the cutback of the RS-70 or the B-70, and now we have had that lollipop taken from us without any compensating factor, except a few extra Minuteman.[67]

The best explanation of the linking of the Minuteman missiles with the Skybolt cancellation by the administration in early 1963 is, indeed, in terms of "lollipops." There seems to have been no national-security requirement for it,[68] the administration's testimony is spuriously reasoned, and the basis for the particular trade-off described by McNamara defies discovery. Further, the civilian heads of the Department of the Air Force at the time deny any relationship between the F/Y 1964 Minuteman authorization and the cancellation of Skybolt.[69]

McNamara was apparently using the Minuteman as a "chopping block" upon which he could cut the Skybolt program. By

65. Schlesinger, *A Thousand Days*, p. 731.
66. York, *Race to Oblivion*, p. 155.
67. Senate Armed Services Committee, *Military Procurement Authorization, Fiscal Year 1964*, p. 1020.
68. Dr. Alain Enthoven has testified that "a month after it [Skybolt] was cancelled, everybody agreed that the Secretary of Defense did the right thing" (Senate Committee on Government Operations, *Planning, Programming, Budgeting* [1970], p. 244). In 1965 Charles J. Hitch wrote: "No responsible military or civilian official within our Defense Department . . . would argue in favor of the Skybolt today" (Hitch, *Decision-Making for Defense*, p. 56). In late 1962 President Kennedy suggested that Skybolt was "militarily worthless" (George H. Quester, *Nuclear Diplomacy*, p. 255).
69. Interviews with Neil A. Harlan, 21 July 1970; Eugene M. Zuckert, 21 July 1970; and Gen. Maxwell D. Taylor, 27 July 1970.

manipulating the programmed Minuteman figures, he was able to carry out an action which he did not think he could otherwise get away with. Like the B-70 program, the Skybolt program only related to the Minuteman program because McNamara manipulated the latter in order to cancel other strategic-weapons programs and projects. The Kennedy-McNamara strategic missile build-up was certainly not made necessary by the cancellation of either of these alternative delivery systems.

11 Pressures on Kennedy and the Missile Build-up

This chapter attempts to place the Kennedy-McNamara strategic missile build-up and the decisions which related to it in the broader context of the workings of politics and government. It explicitly recognizes that in defense policy making, as in other areas of policy making, presidents "can very rarely command. Mainly they maneuver, persuade and pressure, using all the levers, powers and influences they can muster to get the people concerned to come around."[1] The essential reason for this is that there are, in the U.S. policy-making process, a multiplicity of actors, or "quasi-sovereignties," both inside and outside the

1. Roger Hilsman, *The Politics of Policy Making in Defense and Foreign Affairs*, pp. 5–6.

government, each with various perspectives and interests. Many have developed and articulated positions on the subjects and issues at hand, and have a quasi-autonomous political power base from which to press their respective positions. As Roger Hilsman has pointed out:

> In a political process the relative power of these participating groups is as relevant to the final decision as the cogency and wisdom of the arguments used in support of the policy adopted. Who advocates a particular policy may be as important as what he advocates.[2]

In discussing the pressures which these participating groups, or quasi-sovereignties, are able and willing to bring to bear upon the president, the formal institutional approach (Executive, Congress, Press, etc.) is eschewed. Instead, this chapter is simply concerned with identifying the *sources* of the particular pressures which confronted Kennedy and McNamara in making the strategic missile decisions of the early 1960s.

To some extent these pressures were self-generated. The Kennedy Administration's major changes in the strategic-forces program, including the strategic ballistic missile build-up, were virtually all made within a year of that administration's assuming office. The election to the presidency of John F. Kennedy had followed a campaign in which questions of defense and foreign policy had been principal issues, and in which Kennedy had campaigned on a platform of, inter alia, strengthening the U.S. strategic posture. Kennedy eagerly accepted campaign support and the material for his critiques of Eisenhower's defense and strategic policies from people who wanted a much greater defense effort. The expectation within Congress, industry, and the military, and among the American people at large, was that on taking office the Kennedy Administration would make substantial changes in U.S. strategic posture. In view of Kennedy's 1960 campaign charges, it would have been politically very difficult for the new president to adhere to Eisenhower's F/Y 1962 defense budget and not to commit the United States to an expanded missile program. The first section of this chapter dis-

---

2. Roger Hilsman, "The Foreign Policy Consensus," p. 365.

234 Explaining the Strategic Missile Build-up

cusses the role of these self-generated pressures in the Kennedy-McNamara strategic missile build-up.

Secondly, there were pressures generated from inside the government. In particular, the military services had developed positions on the strategic-forces "requirement" which were different from the personal predilections of either Kennedy or McNamara, and they had quasi-autonomous power-political bases from which to press for their different positions. The reconciliation of these different positions was necessarily a political process, involving bargaining, negotiation, and compromise between various groups and personalities, and the manipulation of threats as a means of coercion. For political reasons, no less than in the interests of military efficiency, it is incumbent upon the president to keep high military officers in the Pentagon from making public displays of discontent.[3] A discussion of the bargaining with the military through which this was attempted forms the second section of this chapter.

Thirdly, pressures are generated on any U.S. administration by outside groups allied with elements within the bureaucracy. One principal source of such pressures in the area of defense policy making is the power-political base of "military-industrial capitalism." A discussion of industrial pressures and economic factors which were relevant to the Kennedy-McNamara strategic missile build-up completes this chapter.

KENNEDY'S 1960 ELECTION COMMITMENTS

Throughout Senator Kennedy's 1960 presidential campaign, the "missile gap" was one of the prime charges made by Kennedy against the Eisenhower Administration, and the expansion of the U.S. missile program was one of Kennedy's principal campaign policies.

From the summer of 1958, Senator Kennedy supported those Democrats who argued the existence and the possible fateful consequences of a missile gap. During 1960 Kennedy stated at least half a dozen times that the United States was behind the Soviet Union in numbers of long-range missiles, and that, unless

3. Hilsman, *The Politics of Policy Making*, p. 6.

drastic steps were taken, this gap would grow even larger in the future.[4]

Kennedy pledged himself, if elected, to undertake these drastic steps. In the two months before the 8 November 1960 election, he argued that the United States must, inter alia, step up its Polaris and Minuteman programs; step up the Atlas production and base-building efforts; provide SAC with a continuous airborne alert capability; and expand and modernize its conventional forces.[5] Kennedy further pledged that, if elected, he would "promptly send to Congress a special message requesting the funds and authorization necessary to give us a nuclear retaliatory power second to none,"[6] and in a letter to *Missiles and Rockets* he stated specifically that, if elected, he would act "in January."[7]

Ralph E. Lapp has argued that, having made these charges and pledges, it was politically impossible for Kennedy, once elected, to stick with the Eisenhower F/Y 1962 defense budget; that he obtained reliable intelligence on the Soviet missile program on taking office, "but it was not politically expedient to admit this fact"; and that, having campaigned on a missile gap platform, "Kennedy apparently found it politically necessary to commit the nation to more missiles."[8]

However, in the U.S. political scene few candidates and party leaders ever consider themselves bound by their campaign speeches or platform commitments when elected. These speeches, the party platform, campaign literature, etc., are electioneering documents, not blueprints for action. They may indicate the general direction of movement sought by the candidate and the dominant elements of the party, but for both practical

4. *Congressional Record, House*, 11 April 1962, p. 6396.
5. See, for example, *Congressional Quarterly Weekly Report*, 13 January 1961, p. 32; *New York Times*, 19 October 1960, and *Aviation Week & Space Technology*, 24 October 1960.
6. *Congressional Quarterly Weekly Report*, 13 January 1961, p. 32.
7. *Missiles & Rockets*, 10 October 1960, p. 13.
8. Ralph E. Lapp, *The Weapons Culture*, pp. 60, 184. Lapp was one of Kennedy's advisers during the 1960 campaign. Other writers who argue that Kennedy's campaign charges (among other factors) committed the new administration to a missile build-up include Herbert F. York, "A Personal View of the Arms Race," p. 28; George H. Quester, *Nuclear Diplomacy*, p. 206; and Harvey Sapolsky, *The Polaris System Development*, p. 9.

and theoretical necessities they ordinarily leave wide latitude for discretion once the election is won. As V. O. Key has argued, lines of action can rarely be spelled out in advance of the time of action; many political scientists would argue that the attempt *should* not be made; few would expect it.[9]

In a major speech two weeks after Kennedy's election, Senator Dodd (Democrat, Connecticut) argued that any elected representative had the right, indeed the duty, to violate any campaign commitments, party platforms, etc., "should his reason lead him to do so in the national interest." This speech was widely interpreted in the press as providing President-elect Kennedy with an escape hatch by which he could conveniently disregard his own and the Democratic party's pledges of 1960—and some even advised that Kennedy should "avail himself of the opportunity to start backpedalling."[10]

Senator Kennedy's 1960 statements were neither legally nor politically binding. According to a list compiled by *Congressional Quarterly* from all of Kennedy's speeches, letters and statements, he made some 220 statements of policy which he implicitly or explicitly promised to carry out if he were elected president, ranging from national security (15 promises), through (for example) agriculture (21 promises), to the judiciary (35 promises), between his acceptance speech on 15 July 1960 and the eve of his election on 8 November 1960.[11] Even a very cursory examination of this list reveals that many of these promises were disregarded after 20 January 1961.

During the campaign Kennedy was not averse to making statements which would bring him votes, but which he knew he would not act upon. As Congressman Gubser has stated:

> Political considerations caused Candidate Kennedy to speak glowingly of the B-52 near the Boeing plant in Seattle, to draw applause with his ringing commendation of the B-58 at the Convair plant in Fort Worth, Tex., and to emphatically condemn the Eisenhower cutback of the B-70 program in San Diego.[12]

9. V. O. Key, Jr., *Politics, Parties and Pressure Groups*, p. 421.
10. *Congressional Record, Senate*, 5 January 1961, pp. 205–12.
11. *Congressional Quarterly Weekly Report*, 13 January 1961, p. 32.
12. *Congressional Record, House*, 11 April 1962, p. 6394.

In fact, Kennedy criticized Eisenhower three times in speeches during the 1960 campaign for not pushing the B-70, and in San Diego on 2 November 1960, he stated, "I endorse wholeheartedly the B-70 manned aircraft."[13] Kennedy aides also advised *Missiles and Rockets* in October 1960 that Kennedy was in favor of building the B-70.[14] His vice-presidential running mate, Lyndon B. Johnson, was also a vocal supporter of the B-70.[15] And at least twice during 1960 Kennedy argued that the United States must "step up our production of Atlas missiles."[16]

But in his first major recommendations to Congress on the F/Y 1962 defense budget, the special message of 28 March 1961, Kennedy did not propose any funds for the further procurement of either B-52 or B-58 manned bombers; the B-70 program was severely cut back; and, although Atlas base-building was accelerated, no further Atlas missiles were programmed for deployment. Throughout his whole administration, President Kennedy unreservedly, determinedly, and successfully resisted congressional and Air Force pressures for continued production of B-52s and B-58s, and for development of the B-70 as a weapons system. But throughout this struggle, it was never a major argument against Kennedy that he had reneged on his 1960 campaign promises.

If Kennedy had chosen to retreat from those 1960 charges and pledges which specifically related to the U.S. missile program, his position as perceived by his personal staff was such as to allow him to so move without inviting charges of dishonesty. Many of his personal staff believe that he did not push a specific missile gap charge very strongly—and, therefore, should have had little compunction at reneging on such a charge. Sorensen, for example, has stated that,

In his primary and autumn campaigns he referred sparingly and for the most part cautiously to the Soviet missile "advantage," avoiding precise dates and numbers, quoting non-partisan experts

13. *Congressional Record, Senate*, 21 March 1962, pp. 4703, 4706.
14. *Missiles & Rockets*, 31 October 1960, p. 7.
15. *Congressional Record, Senate*, 21 March 1962, p. 4706.
16. *Congressional Record, Senate*, 29 February 1960, p. 3802; and *Aviation Week & Space Technology*, 24 October 1960, p. 21.

and emphasizing that the United States was still the stronger military power although danger lay ahead.[17]

While this is in fact not exactly the case, it was a position which had some truth—Kennedy had avoided setting precise dates and numbers on the missile gap, and had refused to place a specific price-tag on his defense recommendations—and one which would have allowed the administration to proceed with a more cautious missile program while still believing in its own consistency.

Some critics can undoubtedly argue that while campaign charges and promises are neither legally nor politically binding, a man of integrity might consider himself so bound. But if Kennedy sincerely believed that a major defense effort was urgently and vitally needed for the security of the United States, there were opportunities for him to act in 1960 and put integrity above the political calculus. During the pre-election "catch-up" session of Congress in August 1960, for example, Kennedy and Johnson could have attempted to force a large defense money bill through the Democratic-controlled Congress. Kennedy did seriously consider this, but to do so he would have had to persuade the powerful Senate Appropriations Committee to reverse the position it had taken in June 1960, when it rejected individual Democratic proposals to increase defense spending.[18] It is possible that Kennedy could have so persuaded that committee. To have made the attempt would have exposed him to charges of opportunism, however, and to have failed could have damaged his image as a potential president—while to succeed would have made the committee vulnerable to charges of inconsistency or worse. Kennedy proved unwilling to face the political risks involved.

Moreover, most political commentators would probably, like Senator Dodd, consider it more noble for a president to violate his campaign commitments "should his reason lead him to do so in the national interest," than to follow a policy based upon elec-

17. Sorensen, *Kennedy*, p. 676.
18. *Missiles & Rockets*, 8 August 1960, p. 8; *Aviation Week & Space Technology*, 25 July 1960, p. 25.

tion promises, no matter how sincerely made.[19] Finally, it might be argued that, having made various pledges during the campaign, Kennedy was required to keep trust with the American people. However, he received no sweeping defense mandate in the election. His was an extremely narrow victory (a plurality of less than 0.2 percent), and defense issues were far from decisive in that victory. By 1960, only 21 percent of Americans polled thought "too little" was being spent on defense, while 18 percent thought "too much."[20]

Historians have not been hard on Kennedy for his extravagant charges during the 1960 campaign that the Eisenhower Administration had been remiss about the missile program. As William Carleton has pointed out, "Presidents are rated in history by the records they make in office, not by how they wage their campaigns." As Carleton predicted, Kennedy's zeal has been put down as no more than excessive campaign oratory; ironically Eisenhower has been blamed for failing to "nail" Kennedy and tell the nation bluntly the true state of its defenses, and for missing the opportunity to add credibility to America's nuclear deterrent.[21] Liberal historians, impressed by Kennedy's domestic promises, and believing his foreign policy to have been more liberal than Nixon's would have been, have not been prone to hold Kennedy accountable for the alarmist flavor of his campaign. Kennedy, who had an unusual appreciation of history and historians, would not have considered that promises made during his 1960 campaign alone committed him to a missile build-up in 1961–62, when on taking office he found that his allegations of a missile gap lacked substance. It would seem, therefore, that fidelity to a campaign pledge is an inadequate explanation for his actions in respect of the missile program during those years.

Rather than being moral or legal, any commitments for an

19. *Congressional Record, Senate*, 5 January 1961, p. 206.
20. John J. Harrigan, "Foreign Affairs and the Presidential Election of 1960" (Ph.D. diss., University of Chicago, 1965), pp. 91–95; and Helen Gaudet Erskine, "The Polls," p. 485.
21. William G. Carleton, "Kennedy in History," reprinted in *The Politics of John F. Kennedy*, ed. Edmund S. Ions, p. 204.

expanded missile program which were derived from the 1960 campaign were purely political. Kennedy could not break with his campaign supporters, nor deny the expectations he had generated within Congress, industry, and the military.

BARGAINING WITH THE MILITARY

The decision by the Kennedy-McNamara Administration to procure 1,000 Minuteman missiles and 41 Polaris FBM submarines was, in essence, the outcome of a political process, involving bargaining, negotiation, and compromise between groups and personalities both inside and outside the administration, each with distinct perceptions and interests.

This process was, of course, extremely complex. In the first place, it was not limited to specific weapons systems but was, rather, an overall process in which particular weapons systems were manipulated and used in order to enhance the position of the services or the administration as a whole. At one level, the trade-off between various weapons systems was made explicit by the McNamara Defense Department. It was, for example, evinced in the decisions to reduce the Titan II program by two squadrons and to cancel the mobile Minuteman and Skybolt ballistic missile programs, with the administration positing compensatory action in the build-up of the fixed Minuteman missile force. At another level, the Air Force missile and bomber-force proposals were obviously not prepared in isolation, but with a view to enhancing the Air Force's overall position. And McNamara was prepared to manipulate the force projections for the Minuteman program in order to keep the B-70 from production as a full weapons system, and to downgrade the role of the manned bomber in general in the U.S. strategic retaliatory force.

Secondly, the process is, even when unidirectional—or concerned with the promotion, or denial, of a particular weapons system or program—multifaceted. Besides the direct, formal submission of its requests to the administration, the Air Force worked through sympathetic congressmen, journalists and others, and dependent industries, to get its position accepted. The development, dissemination, and propagation of particular strategic policies, including the articulation of the "necessity" for U.S. strategic superiority, though more subtle and indirect, was also used.

However, at this level of complexity, it is not possible to work through the relationship between the relative positions of the services and the administration, a relationship of intramural bargaining and mutual appeasement, at anything less than a level of great generality. This section therefore concentrates on the particular compromise over missile numbers; some of the more general relationships are described and expounded in the conclusion of this study.

There is no statement on the public record of what particular missile force level Kennedy and McNamara would have themselves personally favored. Among those who participated in the missile decisions of the Kennedy-McNamara Administration there is, however, a fairly widespread assumption, supported by anecdotes and recollections of informal conversations, that both Kennedy and McNamara personally believed that national-security considerations alone required less than a 1,000-missile Minuteman force. According to a former (sympathetic) member of the JCS, for example, "both Kennedy and McNamara thought 1,000 missiles was 'excessive.'"[22] And McGeorge Bundy has stated that both Kennedy and McNamara "intellectually agreed [that] there was no persuasive case" for a missile build-up.[23] Among the former top civilian and military officers of the Kennedy-McNamara defense establishment whom I interviewed in 1970, 1972–73, and 1975, virtually all believed that McNamara would himself personally have favored "about 800 Minuteman ICBMs."[24] President Kennedy is reported to have had "a certain sympathy" with the view of his White House staff, who

22. Interview with General Maxwell D. Taylor, 27 July 1970.
23. Interview with McGeorge Bundy, 18 December 1972.
24. Interviews with George Rathjens, 11 July 1970; Adam Yarmolinsky, 10 July 1970; Eugene Zuckert, 21 July 1970; Richard Fryklund, 20 July 1970; and Bernard Brodie, 14 August 1970. There were only two exceptions—a former assistant secretary of the Air Force and a former director of the Budget Bureau, both of whom believed McNamara would have preferred 900 Minuteman missiles. Interviews with Neil A. Harlan, 21 July 1970, and Kermit Gordon, 8 February 1973.

believed the F/Y 1963 Minuteman program of 800 missiles was "more missiles than national security required."[25]

The service positions have proved much easier to document and to explicate than the personal predilections and motives of Kennedy and McNamara. In particular, the Navy had by the beginning of 1960 firmly settled upon a program goal of 45 Polaris FBM submarines. This figure of 45 had itself involved the resolution of various conflicting budget claims and alternative hardware postures within the Navy, especially between the Special Projects Office and the other, more traditional, offices of that service. This, together with the acceptance throughout the Navy (including the Special Projects Office) of the concept of "minimum" or "finite" deterrence as a nuclear strategic posture, meant that the Navy was effectively circumscribed in its bargaining with the Air Force and the Department of Defense over numbers of Polaris submarines. The Special Projects Office itself, essentially a research and development office, was ill-positioned and ill-equipped to fight its case at the top DoD decision-making levels.

During most of 1961, the Navy's efforts were principally directed towards ensuring an orderly and even scheduling of Polaris submarine procurement and deployment. From April 1961 through the summer and fall of that year, this meant securing the authorization of long-lead-time items for the 30th and subsequent Polaris submarines, which the administration was not then prepared to grant. The Navy's case was taken up, ironically, by the Republican party in the House of Representatives.[26] In the House Armed Services Committee, Congressman Gubser (Republican, California) proposed adding long-lead-time items for six more submarines to the ten submarines al-

25. Arthur M. Schlesinger, Jr., *A Thousand Days*, p. 438.
26. From 1957 to 1960 it had been the Democratic Party in Congress which had supported the Polaris program most strongly. Throughout this period, the Democrats proposed, and succeeded in persuading Congress to fund, approximately 50 percent more Polaris submarines than the administration had requested. Congress funded 21, while the administration had only agreed to requesting 14 (and at least three of these 14 were undoubtedly a result of congressional pressure). See *Congressional Record, House*, 1 September 1960, pp. 19239–40.

ready included by the administration in the F/Y 1962 defense budget. This move would have tentatively committed the administration to building 35 Polaris submarines; but the committee voted 25 to 3 against the proposal. Gubser then persuaded the House Republican Policy Committee to support his proposal on the House floor, and on 24 May 1961, he moved in amendment to the F/Y 1962 defense budget, "an additional $697,500,000 for the acquisition of an additional six SSB(N) submarines." The House rejected the amendment by 105 to 58. The opposition to the GOP motion was largely Democratic, with Congressman Kilday (Democrat, Texas) and Congressman Vinson (Democrat, Georgia), chairman of the House Armed Services Committee, carrying the burden of the argument.[27]

McNamara's position at this time was that the question of whether there would be more than 29 Polaris submarines in the program "is part of a study which is now under way covering the entire field of requirements for strategic delivery systems" and that any decisions would await the completion of that study.[28] The Hickey study, to which McNamara was undoubtedly referring, suggested a Polaris force on the order of 40 to 47 submarines,[29] and on 22 September 1961, McNamara decided on the figure of 41 submarines.[30] The choice of a low figure within the recommended range not only allowed McNamara to increase the Polaris submarine fleet in future years, but also gave him a position for later bargaining with the Navy.[31] In November 1961 the Navy apparently made a move to get its goal of 45 submarines accepted by the Defense Department—it proposed a Polaris force of 50 submarines,[32] presumably to give itself some

27. *Missiles & Rockets*, 22 May 1961, p. 9, and 29 May 1961, p. 27; *Congressional Record, House*, 24 May 1961, pp. 8826–27.
28. *Congressional Record, House*, 24 May 1961, p. 8826.
29. Interview with Dr. Alain Enthoven, 17 August 1970; testimony of McNamara, Senate Armed Services Committee, *Military Procurement Authorization, Fiscal Year 1963*, p. 61; and testimony of Gen. Wheeler, Senate Armed Services Committee, *Status of U.S. Strategic Power* (1968, part 1), p. 18.
30. *Polaris and Poseidon Chronology*, p. 7.
31. According to McNamara, 41 was not a "final decision" (House Appropriations Committee, *Department of Defense Appropriations for 1963*, part 2, p. 26).
32. *Missiles & Rockets*, 27 November 1961, p. 13, *Aviation Week & Space Technology*, 11 December 1961, p. 38.

bargaining leeway. McNamara refused to shift from his 41-submarine decision, however, and no proposals for further Polaris submarines have subsequently been made by the Navy.

Unlike the Navy, the USAF never developed a missile-force goal that was accepted right throughout the service or over any substantial period of time. Within the Air Force views on the size of the ICBM force needed by the United States ranged widely. From the beginning of the Minuteman program, it was assumed that there would be a minimum production run of some 600–800,[33] but some Air Force proposals suggested force goals of as many as 10,000. Official Air Force recommendations were never below 1,700 to 1,800 Minuteman missiles; the formal requests in the early 1960s were usually for about 1,000 more than the Defense Department was willing to authorize. Always for more missiles than the administration saw fit to grant, the actual requests of the Air Force reflected, more than anything else, its own assessment of internal political factors and of its own bargaining position at every point at which a decision was made or in the process of being made. For example, in order to take advantage of the increased receptiveness of the new administration, after January 1961, to proposals for increases in strategic-forces programs, the Air Force at that time doubled its recommendation on the Minuteman "requirement" (from 1,450 missiles in January to 2,915 in July).[34]

One technique used by the Air Force in its bargaining with the DoD was the development and propagation of "wish lists."[35] These generally ranged from about 3,000 to about 10,000 Minuteman missiles. There was never any real expectation within the Air Force that they would be approved, but they did provide a position from which to bargain. The Air Force's 3 July 1961 Central War Offensive Forces package proposal, calling for 3,190 long-range strategic ballistic missiles in addition to the 126 Atlases already programmed (and the 1,319 Skybolts programmed in July 1961) represented something of such a "wish

33. Interviews with Gen. Robert C. Richardson, 25 July 1970, and Robert A. Kilmarx, 22 July 1970.
34. For further details of the Air Force's position, see the relevant section of chapter three.
35. Interview with Eugene M. Zuckert, 21 July 1970.

list." This proposal was reduced to a more "realistic" figure (1,700 to 1,950 Minuteman missiles) once actual negotiations on the size of the F/Y 1963 defense budget were begun.

Perhaps the major constraint on the setting of missile-force goals within the Air Force was the desire to ensure the future position of the manned bomber in the U.S. strategic-forces posture. In terms of Air Force priorities, continued production of the B-52 (at least to an additional wing) and development of the B-70 (RS-70) as a full weapons system usually rated at least as high as more missiles.[36]

By 1964 some civilians and officers in the Air Force had begun to believe that the propagation of "wish lists" and the submission of "unrealistic" initial recommendations for the purpose of bargaining was, perhaps, counterproductive in the McNamara DoD. It seemed the Air Force would receive a better overall deal if it were more "reasonable" in its missile requests,[37] and with reluctance and, in some cases, anger, the administration's position had been accepted by that service by early 1965.

In compromising their initial position with that of the Air Force, it is not clear whether the responsibility rests with President Kennedy or with Secretary McNamara. On the one hand, most of the former White House staff (e.g., Kaysen, Schlesinger, Wiesner, Rathjens) argue that Kennedy wanted fewer Minuteman ICBMs but that McNamara said he "could not live in the Pentagon" with less than 1,000;[38] and, according to Schlesinger, the president "was not prepared to overrule McNamara's recommendation." McNamara had already cut down

36. See testimony of Gen. White, House Appropriations Committee, *Department of Defense Appropriations for 1962*, part 3, pp. 467–68; and testimony of Sec. Zuckert, House Appropriations Committee, *Department of Defense Appropriations for 1963*, part 2, p. 504.

37. This was the prevailing reasoning at a meeting between Neil A. Harlan (then assistant secretary of the Air Force for financial management), Sec. Zuckert, and Gen. Le May, in late 1963, at which it was agreed that since McNamara was not going to approve more than about 1,000 Minuteman ICBMs at that stage, the Air Force would get a better overall deal if it reduced its F/Y 1965 Minuteman request to 1,000 missiles (interviews with Charles J. Hitch, 11 August 1970, and Neil A. Harlan, 21 July 1970).

38. Interviews with Morton Halperin, 20 August 1970; George Rathjens, 11 July 1970; and Jerome Wiesner, 20 February 1973. Halperin pointed out to me the differences in position of former Pentagon officials and former White House staff members on this question.

the original Air Force missile demands considerably [and] he perhaps felt that he could not do more without risking public conflict with the Joint Chiefs and . . . Congress. As a result, the President went along with the policy of multiplying Polaris and Minuteman missiles.[39]

Similarly, Jerome Wiesner has written of the meeting between Kennedy and McNamara and their aides on 9 December 1961, during the preparation of the F/Y 1963 budget, that McNamara recommended

950 new Minuteman missiles. McNamara thought this was modest, since the Air Force wanted 3,000. . . .

The only understandable explanation given by Secretary McNamara for his recommendation was that because the Air Force recommended 3,000 Minuteman missiles, 950 was the smallest number he could imagine asking Congress for and, in his words, "not get murdered." Ultimately the President was convinced of this too, and reluctantly agreed to the Secretary's proposal.[40]

On the other hand, some former Pentagon officials (e.g., Adam Yarmolinsky) argue that McNamara and "most of the civilian staff in the Department of Defense" were prepared to hold the numbers down, but that Kennedy believed he could not face Congress or gain support for his other political commitments and programs with less than 1,000 Minuteman missiles; and McNamara went along.[41]

But in contrast to the position of most of the White House staff, there is much less unanimity among former Pentagon officials on this. Both Roswell Gilpatric and Norman Paul, for example, are prepared to credit McNamara with the responsibility for the build-up.[42] It is likely, of course, that at least to some

39. Schlesinger, *A Thousand Days*, p. 438.

40. Jerome B. Wiesner, "Arms Control," p. 6; and Joseph Alsop, "The Secretary was Supported," *Washington Post*, 20 December 1961, p. A17. Further details were obtained in interviews with Roswell Gilpatric, 30 January 1973; Jerome B. Wiesner, 20 February 1973; Carl Kaysen, 19 December 1972; Marcus Raskin, 6 February 1973; and a telephone conversation with Dr. Vincent McCrae (formerly of the president's Office of Science and Technology), 20 February 1973.

41. Interview with Adam Yarmolinsky, 10 July 1970.

42. Interviews with Roswell Gilpatric, 30 January 1973, and Norman S. Paul, 9 February 1973.

Pressures on Kennedy 247

extent fears both of "an Air Force revolt"[43] and of an antago-
nistic and uncooperative Congress were involved, and that they
influenced both Kennedy and McNamara.

The actual process was apparently somewhat more subtle, and
even ironic, than the alternative positions of the former White
House staff and McNamara aides would suggest. Both Kennedy
and McNamara would have personally preferred a smaller missile force; the actual decision in favor of 1,000 Minuteman
ICBMs was made by McNamara, however, and then agreed to
by the president. That McNamara took the initiative in giving
way to this higher figure was partly due to his fear of a possible
"Air Force revolt." Military morale would suffer, cooperation on
other issues involving limitations on military programs would
be more difficult, and the joint chiefs might even have exercised
their peculiar statutory prerogative under the National Security
Act of 1947 to take their case directly to Congress. But apparently "McNamara was not aware of any pressures upon himself
from Congress."[44]

There is, nonetheless, "no question that there was lots of Congressional pressure. . . . The Air Force used every trick in the
book to have pressures exerted from Congress."[45] These pressures were aimed at the president, and usually took the form of
personal contacts between congressional leaders (such as Senators Jackson and Russell and Congressmen Mahon and Vinson)
and members of the White House staff like Lawrence O'Brien.
But they account principally for McNamara's initiative in giving
way. McNamara expected opposition from Congress if the Air
Force missile requests were cut too much. According to his deputy, Roswell L. Gilpatric, McNamara was

> convinced that a decision on numbers could be overridden on the
> Hill. . . . Out of loyalty to the President, McNamara made sure
> that the Administration's request would not be overridden. . . . It
> was better to shorten sail ahead of time rather than to catch the
> blast in full rig.[46]

43. Interview with George Rathjens, 11 July 1970; see also Adam Yarmolinsky, "Some Lessons of Vietnam," p. 89.
44. Interview with Norman S. Paul, 9 February 1973.
45. Ibid.
46. Interview with Roswell L. Gilpatric, 30 January 1973.

Or in the less colorful words of Norman S. Paul in explaining McNamara's concession,

> McNamara was intensely loyal to the President, and to avoid any possibility of the President being over-ruled by Congress, to that extent he would take account of pressures before taking the budget to the President. . . . He wanted to keep this kind of issue off the President's desk as much as possible.[47]

It was not so much McNamara's worry about his own skin as his concern to see that the president's budget request to Congress would not be rebuffed and Kennedy placed in an embarrassing and politically difficult position.

As it happened, Congress proved fairly willing to accept the administration's strategic-missile recommendations. In particular, there was no strong body within Congress which from 1961 supported a larger Polaris program. The attempts by the House Republicans in May 1961 to increase the F/Y 1962 Polaris procurement were easily defeated by the Democratic majority;[48] and although in February 1963 the House Armed Services Committee intimated that it was willing to consider any Navy requests for a 45-submarine program,[49] there was no evidence that it would have supported such a request, or that Congress would have authorized funds for the Polaris program in addition to the administration's official F/Y 1964 defense budget (6-submarine) request.

The Air Force's lobby in Congress was much stronger, but it was primarily interested in the future of the manned bomber. Whereas in every fiscal year, from F/Y 1962 to F/Y 1966 inclusive, Congress authorized and approved funds for the B-52 and/ or B-70 (later RS-70 and AMSS in F/Y 1965 and F/Y 1966) programs over and above those requested by the administration, it always went along with the administration's strategic-missile requests.[50]

47. Interview with Norman S. Paul, 9 February 1973.
48. *Congressional Record, House*, 24 May 1961, p. 8827.
49. House Armed Services Committee, *Hearings on Military Posture* (1963), pp. 1081–82.
50. In March 1962 the House approved an additional $10 million to fund the procurement of long-lead-time items for 100 additional Minuteman missiles, but this was rejected by the Senate in April (Senate Appropriations Committee,

It might be presumed, however, that if Congress had not decided to fight the administration over the manned bomber, it would have taken up the Air Force's missile case, particularly if the U.S. missile program had not been increased in the F/Y 1962, 1963, 1964, and 1965 defense budgets. As Schlesinger has disclosed, the administration may have given way somewhat on the question of missiles in order to enable it to fight the bomber question.[51] McNamara apparently believed not so much that there would be less congressional opposition to a cancellation of a major weapons system (whether it be mobile Minuteman, the B-70, or nuclear-powered aircraft) than to a cut in missile numbers, but he "was convinced that a decision on numbers could more easily be over-ridden on the Hill."[52]

The threat of a "revolt" by the Air Force (as several Army officers had "revolted" under Eisenhower) was apparently more real, at least as perceived by Kennedy and McNamara. The latter, in his quest for unanimous military support of the administration's defense program and posture, might be expected to have been worried by this; and Kennedy would presumably have been embarrassed by the resignation of any of his military chiefs. Despite the fact that the administration increased the defense budget by over $6 billion in 1961 (of which the Air Force received over $2 billion in additional total obligational authority),[53] McNamara demoralized the Pentagon by challenging the right of the services to determine for themselves how they would spend the money made allowable to them. Only two months after he entered office, McNamara was being accused of by-passing the service chiefs in making major defense decisions.[54]

Department of Defense Appropriations for 1963, p. 948). In 1963 the Senate actually approved a $67.6 million cut in the Minuteman F/Y 1964 appropriation, though this was later restored by a House-Senate conference (*Congressional Quarterly Almanac*, 1963, p. 423). In 1965 the Air Force had a large number of prominent congressional supporters of its 1,200-Minuteman position, particularly in the House and Senate Armed Services Committees, but there was no attempt made to authorize or fund the additional 200 Minuteman missiles.

51. Schlesinger, *A Thousand Days*, p. 438.

52. Interview with Roswell Gilpatric, 30 January 1973.

53. House Appropriations Committee, *Department of Defense Appropriations for 1964*, part 1, p. 212.

54. *New York Times*, 18 March 1961.

And his relations with bomber generals like Le May were always very strained.

In 1963 McNamara twice admitted that he was being subjected to pressures from the military. In a speech in April of that year he acknowledged that, "Every hour of every day the Secretary is confronted by a conflict between the national interest and the parochial interests of particular industries [and] individual services."[55] And in January 1963, when testifying before the House Appropriations Committee, he disclosed that there were pressures from the military for more missiles. According to McNamara,

> the pressure on me from external sources, the public, certain of the military Departments, Congress, is to . . . get there more quickly. . . . The forces we see and observe and normally confront are all forces to push us to higher [missile] levels more rapidly.[56]

McNamara himself was fairly adept at bureaucratic bargaining and at handling the inevitable pressures of any political process. In particular, he manipulated weapons systems and weapons programs in order to resist the military pressures. For example, on 19 January 1962, he told the Senate Armed Services Committee that the most important factor in the decision to cancel the mobile Minuteman program was "a new mid-range ballistic missile project which we are proposing but have not yet discussed with your Committee."[57] However, serious study of the mobile medium-range ballistic missile (MMRBM) concept within the DoD had only begun in October 1961,[58] and, as the House Appropriations Committee pointed out, the Air Force was not "authorized to undertake the development of a MMRBM but is only authorized to initiate a program leading to the development of such a missile."[59] The project was cancelled in 1965, but the mobile Minuteman was not reinstated. In 1962 McNa-

55. Robert S. McNamara, *The Essence of Security*, pp. 103–4.
56. House Appropriations Committee, *Department of Defense Appropriations for 1964*, part 1, p. 235.
57. Senate Armed Services Committee, *Military Procurement Authorization, Fiscal Year 1963*, p. 25.
58. *Missiles & Rockets*, 16 October 1961, p. 9.
59. Report of House Appropriations Committee, cited in *Missiles & Rockets*, 23 April 1962, p. 14.

mara approved an eventual Minuteman force level of 1,200 missiles, and used this figure together with the Skybolt program to justify his refusal to develop the B-70. In December 1962 he cancelled Skybolt, and the projected Minuteman program was increased by 100, to 1,300 missiles; when the Skybolt and B-70 decisions had been more widely accepted, the Minuteman program was cut back to 1,000 missiles.

The actual occasion at which the decision was made to limit the Minuteman program to 1,000 missiles provides a further interesting example of bureaucratic political maneuvering. Meeting on 22 December 1964 on the F/Y 1966 defense budget at President Johnson's ranch in Texas, Secretary McNamara and General Le May became involved in an apparently unresolvable argument as to whether 1,000 or 1,200 Minuteman missiles should be procured. In an attempt to relieve the tension, President Johnson asked BoB Director Kermit Gordon to enter the argument, knowing from a meeting with Gordon in early November that he favored only 900. Gordon's entry into the argument had the desired effect—he was "jumped on" by both McNamara and Le May, and Johnson was able to get 1,000 accepted as a compromise.[60]

The eventual Air Force–administration compromise at a figure of 1,000 for the Minuteman program was the result not only of the relative adeptness at bargaining and negotiation of the various participants in the decision-making process, but also of their relative power. For, as Roger Hilsman has pointed out, "in a political process the relative power of [the] participating groups is as relevant to the final decision as the cogency and wisdom of the arguments used in support of the policy adopted."[61] That the eventual figure of 1,000 was much closer to McNamara's initial position than to the requests of the Air Force is a reflection both of his own personal strength and of the greater support he was able to muster within the administration. In particular, McNamara was "keenly conscious of his accounts with . . . the President," and by purposefully and determinedly

60. Interviews with Kermit Gordon, 8 February 1973, and Ellis Veatch, 6 February 1973.
61. Roger Hilsman, "The Foreign Policy Consensus," p. 365.

keeping these in order he was able to hold the support of Kennedy, and for some time afterwards of President Johnson.[62]

To describe the missile decisions of the Kennedy Administration in terms of bureaucratic bargaining, negotiation, and intramural appeasement, and of the relative power of the various participants in the decision-making process, therefore, goes far in explaining the rate of build-up and the eventual force level of the U.S. missile program. As Roswell Gilpatric has said about the Minuteman figure, "1,000 was really just a horse trade."[63]

MILITARY-INDUSTRIAL CAPITALISM

Industrial Pressures. In January 1961, along with his attempt to dispel what he believed was the fiction of a missile gap, President Eisenhower gave his now famous warning of the dangers of the "military-industrial complex." Eisenhower admonished the American people:

> In the councils of government we must guard against the acquisition of unwarranted influence, whether sought or unsought, by the military-industrial complex. The potential for the disastrous rise of misplaced power exists and will persist.[64]

Since then much has been written on "the economics of militarization" and the relationships between the U.S. corporate economy and military and political institutions. Very little of this has, however, been serious research—besides the obvious difficulties in documenting the degree of untoward pressure from defense industries on congressmen, the Pentagon, and the administration, there are serious conceptual problems when operating on that level of abstraction and complexity of interactions. But this does not obviate the need to look for evidence of the role played by industrial pressures or the perceived mutuality of military, industrial, and political interests.

In 1962 Victor Perlo wrote *Militarism and Industry: Arms Profiteering in the Missile Age*, a book in which he attempted to show

62. Morton H. Halperin, *National Security Policy-making*, p. 119.
63. Interview with Roswell Gilpatric, 30 January 1973.
64. *New York Times*, 18 January 1961.

that the impetus for the U.S. missile program came from industrial interests. According to Perlo, "groups reaping profits from armaments and war, rather than an external enemy, bear much of the responsibility" for the American postwar arms build-up, not excluding the missile program.[65] And a study in 1964 by a Senate subcommittee chaired by Senator Joseph Clark concluded that certain firms, especially in the aerospace industry, suffered from an overcapacity that drove them to insist on more missiles than the nation needed.[66] During the Eisenhower Administration there was, in fact, much evidence of pressure from large aerospace firms for missile contracts and production orders.

In the IRBM field, for example, the Thor-Jupiter controversy was as much a fight between the airframe industry (especially the Douglas Aircraft Company) and other industrial aspirants for a major role in missile development, as between the Air Force and the Army.[67] The Chrysler Corporation, under contract to develop the Army's Jupiter missile, and with major plants in Alabama, heralded the ability of the Jupiter and was joined by the Alabama congressional delegation. Simultaneously Douglas Aircraft pushed the Thor missile, and was joined by the California delegation.[68]

Throughout the late 1950s, Convair (Consolidated-Vultee Aircraft, later a division of the General Dynamics Corporation) worked through the Air Force in attempts to get larger Atlas production orders. In February 1959 Thomas G. Lanphier, vice-president and assistant to the president of Convair, spoke out against the Eisenhower Administration for ordering missiles so slowly.[69] In February 1960 Lanphier resigned from Convair and became a major national critic of the administration's missile policies. Lanphier argued before the House Committee on Sci-

65. Victor Perlo, *Militarism and Industry*, p. 14.
66. Senate Committee on Labor and Public Welfare, Report of the Subcommittee on Employment and Manpower, *Convertibility of Space and Defense Resources to Civilian Needs: A Search for New Employment Potentials* (1964).
67. Michael H. Armacost, *The Politics of Weapons Innovation*, especially chap. 4.
68. Edgar M. Bottome, *The Balance of Terror*, p. 60.
69. *Aviation Week & Space Technology*, 9 February 1959, p. 25; *Missiles & Rockets*, 30 March 1959, p. 15; and *Congressional Record, Senate*, 24 February 1960, p. 3329.

ence and Astronautics in March 1960 that if Convair had been able to begin Atlas production in late 1957, the United States would by then have had a stockpile of some 400 missiles, instead of the mere handful currently operational;[70] he later called for the immediate addition of 100 Atlas and 20 Titan missiles to the U.S. program.[71] Eisenhower added a further 18 Atlas missiles to the authorized program in late March, and Lanphier concluded his missile gap crusade in late May 1960.[72] According to James Killian, there is no doubt that Lanphier's campaign had "an impact on the White House"—and that this was only part of "tremendous lobbying by industry for Atlas missiles."[73]

During the Kennedy Administration, however, there was little evidence of extensive industrial pressure for a further expansion of the U.S. missile program, although Secretary McNamara did state in April 1963 that "economic interests affected by defense decisions . . . inevitably [generated] political pressures on defense officials."[74] Such pressures are, of course, notoriously difficult to document in any event, but two general points might explain their apparent relative absence in the early 1960s.

First, industrial pressure is strong when there are two or more rival programs, as in the case of the Thor-Jupiter controversy and the Atlas-Titan controversy, with rival companies fighting for larger shares of the total program. After 1961, however, the Minuteman had no land-based competitors.

Second, industrial pressure for defense programs is usually strongest in the period before the awarding of production contracts, when companies are competing, and no new prime contracts were given for missile programs after the Boeing Aircraft Company received the Minuteman prime contract in October 1958.

There was a partial exception to this in the winter of 1960–61. By the end of 1960 the mobile Minuteman project had advanced to the point where a procurement and deployment decision

70. *Missiles & Rockets*, 14 March 1960, pp. 19–20; *Aviation Week & Space Technology*, 14 March 1960, pp. 34–35.
71. *Missiles & Rockets*, 4 April 1960, p. 18.
72. *Missiles & Rockets*, 30 May 1960, p. 70.
73. Interview with James R. Killian, 16 January 1973.
74. Samuel A. Tucker, ed., *A Modern Design for Defense Decision*, p. 25.

could be made. In December Boeing put a mock-up mobile Minuteman system on display at one of its Seattle plants, and by inviting the Air Force's Minuteman program director, Colonel Phillips, and the commander of the Air Research and Development Command, Lieutenant-General Schriever, Air Force design engineers, congressmen, railroad representatives, and the trade press, etc., to inspect it, managed to engender much interest and enthusiastic support for the system.[75] Eisenhower's F/Y 1962 defense budget included authorization for three mobile Minuteman squadrons (90 missiles), but this did not necessarily commit the new administration to the mobile program, and the February 1961 edition of the *Boeing Magazine* carried a major promotional article, "Minuteman on Wheels," with the intention of affecting the Kennedy defense reappraisal then under way.[76] At the same time, American Car and Foundry (ACF), the developer of the railroad car transporter and launcher of the mobile Minuteman missiles, placed advertisements for the system in business and trade journals.[77]

Although there is no other evidence of Boeing pressure with regard to the Minuteman, this does not mean that Boeing did not attempt to increase its Minuteman business volume. For example, in spring 1961 Boeing proposed a "growth version" of the Minuteman missile as the launch vehicle for Program SR-199A, an Air Force program for orbital and suborbital "recallable ICBM's."[78] And in June 1963, T. A. Wilson, Boeing vice-president in charge of the Minuteman program, initiated a cost-cutting program with the explicit aim of making the Minuteman "even more attractive to the cost-conscious Department of Defense" and hence of receiving more Minuteman orders.[79] But in

75. *Aviation Week & Space Technology*, 19 December 1960, pp. 21, 30; House Appropriations Committee, *Department of Defense Appropriations for 1962*, part 3, p. 427.

76. *Boeing Magazine*, February 1961, pp. 6–7; see also House Appropriations Committee, *Department of Defense Appropriations for 1962*, part 5, pp. 561–74.

77. See, for example, *Business Week*, 25 March 1961, p. 90.

78. Interview with Larry Booda, 6 February 1973.

79. *Missiles & Rockets*, 24 June 1963, pp. 40, 42, 43. Wilson "estimated an outstanding Boeing effort could add from $200 to $400 million a year in business volume from 1964 to 1967." This would have represented an additional 50 to 100 Minuteman missiles per year, or perhaps as much as a 40 percent increase in the total program.

1961–62 Boeing's lobbying attention was focused primarily on efforts to keep the B-52 manned bomber in production.[80]

One of the first missile decisions of the Kennedy Administration was to double Minuteman production facilities.[81] Boeing could look forward to substantial Minuteman production contracts for many years under Kennedy, and certainly to much larger orders than Eisenhower would ever have made; and by the time the administration had placed the 1,000-missile ceiling on the force, the Minuteman II retrofit program was well under way, assuring Boeing of a continued production run. Under the Kennedy Administration, Boeing really had very little need to lobby for more Minuteman missiles.

There were, on the other hand, pressures of a different sort from other companies affected by other circumstances which related to the missile program. There was, for example, a major public relations campaign conducted by the Douglas Aircraft Company when it became known in December 1962 that Skybolt was to be cancelled. The Skybolt program involved thousands of jobs at Douglas, and Kennedy admitted that Douglas's economic position had been considered when the decision was made to cancel it.[82] Moreover, industry was always actively interested in pushing new missile systems and programs. The major support for the MMRBM concept, for example, appears to have come from industry sources, particularly the West Coast aerospace industries.[83]

80. The B-52 program was far more attractive to Boeing than was the Minuteman program. With regard to airframe manufacturing, for example, the fabrication of 1,000 Minuteman missiles was equivalent to only 15 B-52s (Charles J. V. Murphy, "The Plane Makers Under Stress," *Fortune*, July 1960, p. 11). Boeing was also more interested in the B-52s because of the K-135 tankers which accompanied the bomber fleet. Boeing's two major production centers for the B-52 were Wichita and Seattle, and the company received support from Senators Carlson (Republican, Kansas) and Jackson (Democrat, Washington) in its lobbying for the B-52 (see, for example, Senator Carlson, *Congressional Record, Senate*, 23 June 1962, pp. 11448–49).

81. This decision was made at least partly for antirecession reasons (see *Missiles & Rockets*, 20 March 1961, p. 9). Boeing's two major Minuteman production centers were at Hill Air Force Base, near Ogden, Utah, and at Seattle.

82. *Aviation Week & Space Technology*, 24 December 1962, p. 20; President Kennedy, press conference of 17 December 1962, in *Kennedy and the Press*, ed. Harold W. Chase and Allen H. Lerman, pp. 354–55.

83. Companies which pressured for the MMRBM included, for example,

But these were not pressures which can reasonably be interpreted as being responsible for forcing the U.S. missile program
to higher levels; the impetus for the missile expansion of 1961–
63 must be found elsewhere.

The Missile Program and the U.S. Economy. A slightly different
argument, though one still involving recourse to industrial and
economic factors, is that President Kennedy expanded the U.S.
strategic missile force in order to stimulate the depressed economy he inherited in January 1961. Seymour Melman, for example, has argued that

> having just concluded that an infusion of capital funds was needed
> in order to raise American economic activity to a higher level, the
> White House decided that an outlay of capital for missiles, as well
> as other military forces, was necessary. This particular form of
> economic stimulation was carried out through the period 1961–
> 1963.[84]

On taking office Kennedy certainly saw getting the United
States out of economic recession as one of his principal tasks. He
had made the recession a central issue in his 1960 campaign. It
had deepened throughout 1960, and during the weeks after the
election it continued to worsen; by February 1961 unemployment had reached 8.1 percent of the labor force, or about 5.5
to 6 million able-bodied persons.[85] In his State of the Union message of 30 January 1961, Kennedy discussed the recession and
called for action to stimulate the economy.[86]
During the interregnum, Kennedy had appointed a task force
to inquire into the state of the economy and to recommend
measures for getting it moving again. The task force's report,
prepared by Paul Samuelson, was explicitly adjusted "to fit the

Hughes Aircraft, NORAIR, Goodyear Aircraft, Thiokol, General Precision, etc.
See Julius Duscha, "Arms and the Big Money Men," *Harper's*, March 1964, p. 43;
Missiles & Rockets, 11 December 1961, p. 9, and 6 April 1964, p. 9.
    84. Seymour Melman, *Pentagon Capitalism*, p. 108.
    85. Schlesinger, *A Thousand Days*, chap. 23; Theodore C. Sorensen, *Kennedy*,
chap. 16; Seymour Harris, *Economics of the Kennedy Years*, p. 3; and *Business Week*,
28 January 1961, p. 32.
    86. See text of President Kennedy's address, Department of State *Bulletin*, 13
February 1961, pp. 207–14.

presidential and congressional mood."[87] On defense, the report stated:

> Defense expenditures ought to be determined on their own merits. They are not to be the football of economic stabilization. Nor, as was so often done in the past, ought they to be kept below the optimal level needed for security because of the mistaken notion that the economy is unable to bear any extra burdens. . . . And they should certainly not be maintained at high levels merely for the purpose of substitution for other measures designed to keep employment high. On the other hand, any stepping up of these programs that is deemed desirable for its own sake can only help rather than hinder the health of our economy in the period immediately ahead.[88]

The report singled out increased defense spending as its main recommendation—apart from defense, it refrained from recommending investment in the public sector—and the administration's main resort. Kennedy's economic actions through the spring of 1961 were largely an implementation of this report.[89]

Throughout the Kennedy Administration, there was an explicit recognition that larger defense outlays were a favorable factor in stimulating the economy.[90] President Kennedy himself ruled that defense spending would have to serve as the major economic stimulant, rejecting other alternative measures such as increased public works.[91] And most of his principal economic advisers were personally in favor of expanded defense expenditures.[92]

As Charles H. Hitch, then assistant secretary of defense (comptroller), has pointed out, in early 1961, "requirements for higher military and space expenditures were in harmony with the Administration's economic policy, and in this case fiscal policy was accommodated to the needs of national security."[93]

87. Schlesinger, *A Thousand Days*, p. 547.
88. *New Frontiers of the Kennedy Administration*, ed. Public Affairs Press, p. 31.
89. Schlesinger, *A Thousand Days*, p. 547; and Sorensen, *Kennedy*, p. 439.
90. Seymour E. Harris, *The Economics of the Kennedy Years*, p. 220.
91. Sorensen, *Kennedy*, p. 440.
92. See, for example, Seymour E. Harris, *The Economics of the Political Parties*, pp. 136–37; and *Business Week*, 13 May 1961, pp. 33–34.
93. Charles J. Hitch, in *A Modern Design for Defense Decision*, ed. Samuel A. Tucker, p. 43. Hitch was the principal advocate within the Kennedy Administration of the policy of harmonizing military policy with economic and fiscal

Indeed, in October 1961 the DoD completed a major study of the "effects of the September 1961 Program Packages on employment in major aircraft and missile plants" to ensure that military policy and economic policy were in harmony.[94]

But the administration was quite adamant, publicly and explicitly, that defense expenditures should never be determined solely by economic factors. On the one hand, the Kennedy Administration stressed that arbitrary budget ceilings would never be imposed on the U.S. defense effort. Kennedy himself stated, in his 28 March message, that,

> Our arms must be adequate to meet our commitments and insure [sic] our security, without being bound by arbitrary budget ceilings. This Nation can afford to be strong—it cannot afford to be weak. We shall do what is needed to make and to keep us strong.[95]

And, on the other hand, the administration denied that the state of the economy should ever be a factor in determining the *level* of defense expenditures. Hitch has particularly denied that defense programs were ever stepped up merely for the purpose of keeping the economy buoyant. According to Hitch, "it has been a long-established policy of the Government to avoid using the defense program as a 'prop' for industry."[96] And Sorensen has reported that "John Kennedy did not believe that the economic health of either the country or any community had to depend on excessive or inefficient armaments."[97]

However, the economic policies, programs and spending procedures of the Kennedy Administration did affect the missile program in two definite ways. In the first place, the application of Keynesian economics by liberal practitioners favoring increased defense expenditures was, as compared with the economic policies of all previous administrations, peculiarly amenable to an expanded missile program. As Bellany has written:

policy (see Charles J. Hitch, "Plans, Programs and Budgets in the Department of Defense," pp. 3–4).

94. Eric Stevenson and John Teeple, "Research in Arms Control and Disarmament, 1960–63," mimeographed (a project of the International Affairs Program, The Ford Foundation, 30 September 1963), pp. A2–27.

95. President Kennedy, *Special Message*, 28 March 1961, p. 2.

96. Hitch, in *A Modern Design for Defense Decision*, ed. Tucker, p. 44.

97. Sorensen, *Kennedy*, p. 462.

It is not at all certain that had a Republican Administration been returned in the 1960 elections it would have authorized such a large increase in government spending at such a time; the previous Eisenhower Administrations had certainly no great reputation for Keynesian thinking and indeed had an inbuilt aversion to "spending one's way out" of stagnation.[98]

Secondly, and far more subtly, the programming and spending procedures employed by the Kennedy Administration allowed a missile program much larger than even that administration might later (but within the same planning, programming, and spending period) have wanted. While denying that economic recession would prompt any increase in the overall U.S. defense effort, Hitch, testifying before the Joint Congressional Economic Committee on 10 April 1961, went on to point out that the administration would allocate its (endogenously determined) defense expenditures countercyclically. In discussing the ways defense expenditure could assist in countering the 1960–61 economic recession, Hitch stated:

> There is one other way in which the Defense Department, at the request of the President has recently responded to the needs of the current economic situation. Together with all other Government departments and agencies, we have sought wherever feasible and sensible, to accelerate the placement of contracts for programs already approved. In this case, however, we are simply buying the same things, or doing the same things, somewhat earlier than had originally been planned.[99]

By accelerating the placement of contracts and the commitment of funds for defense programs, $151 million in obligations which would otherwise have been made at the end of F/Y 1962 were moved forward to the last quarter of F/Y 1961 (April–June 1961). This was approximately 23 percent of the $660 million in government-wide accelerated obligations. Hitch also said that, if necessary because of a slack economy, the administration

98. Ian Bellany, in Carsten Holbraad, ed., *Super Powers and World Order* (Canberra: Australian National University Press, 1971), p. 44. Bellany explicitly relates this argument to the Kennedy-McNamara strategic missile build-up.

99. Joint Economic Committee, Congress, *January 1961 Economic Report of the President and the Economic Situation and Outlook (1961)*, p. 615.

might continue its acceleration of defense programs beyond the April–June 1961 period for another "year from now or two years from now."[100] In addition to the $151 million in accelerated obligations, Kennedy's 28 March 1961 special message added a net $1,954 million to the U.S. defense bill, making an injection into the economy of slightly more than $2.1 billion from accelerated and expanded defense programs in the first fiscal quarter of his administration.[101]

In the revised F/Y 1962 defense budget, the U.S. missile program was expanded and accelerated to the maximum extent feasible.[102] There was always the assumption that whatever could be included in the F/Y 1962 defense budget—and the economic conditions favored a maximum program—this would be less than the ultimate requirement. If a changed international situation (mainly the estimate of the Soviet threat) suggested later that a lesser program would suffice, it would have been too late. Moreover, the political calculus would have insisted on at least some further missile procurement. The high rate of procurement during the economically depressed early part of the Kennedy Administration effectively ruled out the possibility of a Minuteman force of anything less than about 800 missiles, no matter what later strategic reevaluations.

It was being reported soon after Kennedy's election that the slackening of business conditions would induce his administration to boost the U.S. defense budget even further than the very sizable increases that Kennedy had indicated were necessary for national-security reasons.[103] And the January–March 1961 defense decisions were very much affected by the current economic conditions. Besides the acceleration of contract-letting, fund obligations, and production payments referred to by Hitch in his 10 April 1961 testimony, such decisions as those to double Minuteman production capacity and facilities, and to accelerate the

100. Ibid., p. 678.   101. Ibid., pp. 615–16.
102. The F/Y 1962 Minuteman program was set at 600 missiles solely on the basis of lead-time funding: six hundred was all the production that was feasible within the period before F/Y 1963 funds would come into use (interview with Dr. Alain Enthoven, 17 August 1970).
103. *Missiles & Rockets*, 19 December 1960, p. 9.

Polaris program, were taken at least partly for antirecession reasons.[104]

Under both Kennedy and Johnson, the unusual interest in economics and the concern for the economy on the part of the presidency must undoubtedly have meant that economic conditions were always taken into account when defense decisions were being made. For example, Johnson decided very soon after he succeeded to the presidency that budget reasons dictated that severe cuts be made in federal expenditures, not excluding defense expenditure,[105] and according to Neal Stanford of the *Christian Science Monitor*, the authorization of only 50 Minuteman missiles in the F/Y 1965 defense budget was a direct consequence of this decision.[106]

It would, of course, be unrealistic to believe that economic considerations never affected defense decisions, particularly in the United States, where large sections of the economy are dependent upon defense programs. Usually it is more or less arbitrary budget limits which, except for the rare periods of budgetary relaxation, attract attention. In the early Kennedy years, a political decision was made that much more could be spent on defense, and with the temporary relaxation of budgetary limits, the acceptance of Keynesian economics, and the prevailing recessionary economic conditions, the missile program was expanded and accelerated. But after a brief period of exuberance the old constraints reappeared.[107] By the time the preparation of the F/Y 1965 and F/Y 1966 defense budgets began, these constraints had become major factors in the missile decisions.

All this is not to confirm Professor Melman's contention, cited at the beginning of this section. The relationship between the prevailing economic situation and the U.S. missile decisions was

104. *Missiles & Rockets*, 20 March 1961, p. 9; "Speeding Up Defense Spending," *Business Week*, 11 February 1961, p. 31; and testimony of Charles J. Hitch, Joint Economic Committee, Congress, *January 1961 Economic Report of the President and the Economic Situation and Outlook (1961)*, p. 678.

105. Lyndon Baines Johnson, *The Vantage Point*, pp. 36–37.

106. Neal Sanford, *Christian Science Monitor*, 3 January 1964.

107. James R. Schlesinger, in Senate Committee on Government Operations, *Planning, Programming, Budgeting* (1970), p. 132.

much more subtle than Melman would suggest, and the direction of the relationship much more circumstantial than necessarily determined. But it does prove fruitful to discuss the Kennedy missile decisions against the background of the depressed
economy which faced Kennedy when he assumed office in January 1961. Through a combination of perceived economic necessities and the self-generated and intramural bureaucratic pressures, the Kennedy-McNamara Administration was induced to
undertake a strategic missile build-up to a level not warranted
by strategic requirements alone.

Conclusion

The study of U.S. national security policy causes much sense of déjà vu. There seems to be some quite uncanny regularity in the development of basic issues requiring resolution by American strategic policy makers. Strategic doctrine revolves around a bi-polar axis, emphasizing on the one hand deterrence by means of an assured capability for massive destruction and, on the other, more war-fighting capabilities. Similarly, much the same arguments are involved each time a generational leap in development and deployment of U.S. strategic forces is under consideration.

James Schlesinger has described something of the cyclical nature of the developments in American strategic doctrine. In a memorandum for Senator Henry M. Jackson's subcommittee on national security and international operations of the Committee on Government Operations, in April 1968, he wrote:

> Shifting sands seems the best way to characterize the strategic rationales of recent years. In 1961 the suicidal implications of massive retaliation were underscored: the United States would be faced with a choice between humiliation or holocaust. Interest then developed in damage-limiting and coercion . . . since 1965 the merits of Assured Destruction have been emphasized—with little attention paid to the suicidal implications found so distressing in prior years.[1]

The interest in damage-limitation and coercion which developed in 1961–64 was, of course, revived by Schlesinger himself on his becoming secretary of defense in 1973.[2] The similarity of the doctrinal developments of the early 1960s to those during and since Schlesinger's tenure as secretary is quite remarkable. The Carter Administration's desire for strategic options in targeting plans and for the capability to destroy a wide variety of military targets in the Soviet Union, including missile silos and strategic bomber bases, and to limit damage to the United States in the event of any nuclear exchange, as detailed in such documents as PRM-10 and PD-18, corresponds closely to that of the Kennedy-McNamara Administration.[3]

The current concerns with the future development of the U.S. strategic nuclear force structure are also closely reminiscent of those of the early 1960s. Whereas the decisions of the Kennedy-McNamara Administration were preceded by widespread fears of a missile gap, those of the late 1970s were foreshadowed by similar fears of the imminent vulnerability of the extant strategic forces to Soviet ICBM developments. The NIE of 21 December 1976, entitled "National Estimate of Soviet Strategic Capabilities and Objectives," greeted President Carter with much the same

1. James R. Schlesinger, "Uses and Abuses of Analysis" in Senate Committee on Government Operations, *Planning, Programming, Budgeting* (1970), p. 133.
2. See Desmond Ball, *Déjà Vu*.
3. For details of current U.S. strategic planning as set out in PRM-10 and PD-18, see the *New York Times*, 26 August 1977; and *Aviation Week & Space Technology*, 6 March 1978, p. 16.

sort of somber assessments of Soviet intentions and strategic nuclear capabilities as those made available to President Kennedy in early 1961.[4]

When the Kennedy Administration entered office in January 1961, it was faced with questions regarding the future character and force levels of each leg of the Triad which would evidently require decisions during its four-year term. The administration reacted in haste. On 28 March 1961 Kennedy announced the decisions to limit the Titan II ICBM force to 54 missiles and to cancel development of the B-70 supersonic bomber; on 22 September McNamara decided to limit the Navy to 41 FBM submarines; and although the decision to limit the Minuteman force to 1,000 missiles was not finally confirmed until November–December 1964, it seems that McNamara had also decided on this by late 1961.

Similar decisions must be made by the present administration. On 30 June 1977 President Carter announced the cancellation of plans to produce the B-1 bomber, the lineage of which can be traced back to the B-70.[5] Consideration must soon be given to the eventual number of Trident submarines to be deployed; at the current building rate, the Trident fleet will reach 31 submarines by the year 2000[6]—744 SLBMs, each with some 10 to 17 warheads. With regard to ICBMs, the MX has reached the stage where full-scale engineering development is underway; deployment decisions will be required at least by the 1980s.

The similarities between the early 1960s and the late 1970s suggest that some of the lessons of the earlier period may well be relevant to the impending strategic ballistic-missile force-level decisions as to how many Trident submarines and MX ICBMs should be deployed.

4. For discussions of the NIE of 21 December 1976, see the *New York Times*, 26 December 1976; and Lawrence Freedman, *U.S. Intelligence and the Soviet Strategic Threat*, pp. 196–98.

5. See A. A. Tinajero and R. P. Cronin, "B-1 Strategic Bomber Program," mimeographed (Congressional Research Service, Library of Congress, Issue Brief No. IB 75040, 1 August 1977), pp. 1–2.

6. Harold Brown, *Department of Defense Annual Report, Fiscal Year 1979*, 2 February 1978, p. 112.

HASTE AND COMPROMISE: THE KENNEDY MISSILE DECISIONS

It is clear both that the strategic ballistic-missile levels of the 1960s were in excess of those required by the United States at that time, and that this misjudgment is not explicable in terms of inadequate intelligence or poor analytic techniques of force-posture development. It was determined, rather, by other, more political factors.

The principals in the decision making on the size and character of the strategic ballistic missile force were, of course, President Kennedy, Secretary of Defense McNamara, and their military and civilian advisers. But, the U.S. national decision-making process being one in which outcomes are shaped largely by an adversary process of "quasi-sovereignties" rather than by presidential directives, there were perspectives, arguments, and interests not at all shared by either Kennedy or McNamara which were influential and important in deciding the final outcome.

These various perspectives, arguments, and interests invariably corresponded to identifiable, formal groups within the bureaucratic structure of the administration—in particular, the military services, the White House staff, and the relevant governmental departments and their suboffices. While there were differences within each of these groups (there were, for example, at least three perceptibly different positions within the Air Force), and while some positions did cut across departmental or institutional lines (the strategic policy and strategic force posture advocated in large sections of the Navy, for example, received widespread support among members of President Kennedy's Science Advisory Committee within the White House staff), the extent to which different positions on the question of the U.S. missile requirement could be identified with institutional groups was undoubtedly remarkable. For example, General Le May has written of "a recognizable consensus among Air Force officers";[7] former White House staff members all show a shared and definite position in their subsequent writings; and the senior officials of the Kennedy-McNamara Department of Defense—

7. Gen. Curtis E. Le May, *America is in Danger*, p. xi.

McNamara, Gilpatric, Nitze, Hitch, Enthoven, and Rowen—appear to have held a reasonably common position.

All of the missile decisions of the Kennedy-McNamara Administration, throughout the years of the missile build-up (1961–64), were, in some senses at least, political. In other words, the outcomes of the decision-making process were not wholly or solely the results of objective and systematic analyses, but rather resulted from a reconciliation both of a diversity of values and goals and of alternative means and policies, with the actual outcomes reflecting, more than anything else, the relative power of the participating groups.[8]

This is not to say, of course, that the numerous analyses on strategic-weapons systems and programs did not figure in the decision-making process. Their conclusions, the cogency of their arguments, and the articulateness of their sponsors were a significant factor in the relative power of the participating groups. They also served to set the bounds and the subjects of the strategic debate, and to establish a "climate of opinion" from which the eventual outcome emerged. Each of the military services, and to some extent the White House staff and the Office of the Secretary of Defense, developed what Hedley Bull has termed "its strategic ideology"—i.e., each developed a strategic doctrine that pointed to the goals it sought to achieve, and each was anxious "to exploit the authority of studies independently undertaken and scientifically followed through." They "at least charted some reasoned course where otherwise there might well have been only drift."[9] But strategic doctrine in the Kennedy-McNamara Administration was never decisive with regard to the missile program; it appears to have served as no more than a rationalization for decisions taken on other grounds.

The first strategic missile decisions of the Kennedy-McNamara Administration, those of January and March 1961, resulted largely from the initiative of President Kennedy himself. In the first case, that of January 30, even the form and character of the new administration's actions were largely decided by the new

8. See Roger Hilsman, "The Foreign Policy Consensus," p. 365.
9. Hedley Bull, "Strategic Studies and Its Critics," pp. 602–5.

president: such action had to be truly symbolic of the urgency with which the new administration was approaching the problems of defense, and capable of being surrounded in stark but liberal rhetoric—while actually being quite cautious from both a military and a monetary standpoint. Obviously, these requirements were not dictated by either military (the presence of genuine defense inadequacies) or strategic (stable relations with the Soviet Union) necessity. Rather, they were political considerations dictated by the necessity, as perceived by President Kennedy, of making a contrast between his and the previous administration. The acceleration of the Polaris FBM submarine program fitted these requirements perfectly.

The second set of strategic-forces decisions made by the new administration, those which were presented in President Kennedy's special message to Congress of 28 March 1961, were also initiated by the president himself in January. And, as Secretary McNamara was to explain, they had a similar political genesis.[10] But in this case, the actual specifics of the decisions were largely determined by the Department of Defense, and, in particular, the Office of the Secretary of Defense (OSD) and the office of the comptroller of that department. Based primarily on the work which McNamara and a series of task forces had done over the previous two months (in which the WSEG No. 50 study of the previous administration was an important input), the decisions had the relatively limited objective of reducing the vulnerability of U.S. strategic forces and of "rationalizing" strategic programs. Yet those decisions of March 1961 determined to a very large extent the character of the U.S. strategic-forces posture over the next decade—and after only two months' study by a new and relatively inexperienced administration.

Both the January and March decisions are directly susceptible to the charge that they were *political*, and, moreover, unnecessarily so, not only in their genesis, but also in their timing and formulation. Whatever weight the argument linking commitments made by Kennedy during the 1960 election campaign to the missile decisions may have, it relates wholly to these two sets

10. See *Newsweek*, 27 March 1961, p. 16.

of decisions. But the charge of irresponsibility can be directed particularly at the decisions presented in the March message, because those decisions were politically, militarily, and strategically so consequential.

The F/Y 1963 defense budget, which was transmitted to Congress in January 1962, and on which the administration had been working since the early spring of 1961, was essentially "a McNamara budget." Although the chiefs of staff and the service secretaries had allegedly (and undoubtedly) done more work on and contributed more to the F/Y 1963 defense budget during the course of its development throughout 1961 than had been the case with any previous defense budget, not only was it true that "the final decisions were made by me [McNamara]," but the outcome was also fairly close to McNamara's own personal position.[11] The F/Y 1963 defense budget can fairly be interpreted as the fiscal representation of the McNamara military posture.

But like all defense budgets the F/Y 1963 defense budget was nevertheless still the product of a great deal of bargaining, negotiation, and intramural appeasement among the many principal individuals and institutions concerned with the development of the U.S. military posture and strategic policy.[12] Prima facie evidence for the existence of such processes exists in the compromise, albeit partly involuntary, which the official F/Y 1963 strategic-forces program represented in the disparate positions on the subject of long-range strategic missile requirements which were held throughout the development of the F/Y 1963 defense budget. The progressive discounting of the various "wish lists" which were contained in the initial program package submissions of the services of July and August 1961 was a concrete facet of such negotiations. Submissions for 50 Polaris FBM submarines in November can also be interpreted as aimed at gaining official approval for the Navy's goal of 45 such submarines; and the changes in the proposed F/Y 1963 Minuteman request in December evince the existence of bargaining. Also,

11. See the exchange between Congressman Sikes and McNamara, House Appropriations Committee, *Department of Defense Appropriations for 1963*, part 2, p. 24.
12. See Aaron Wildavsky, *The Politics of the Budgetary Process*, pp. 4–5.

the cancellation (e.g., of the mobile Minuteman) and propagation (e.g., of the MMRBM) of weapons-systems programs in the research and/or development phase, in the later stages of the preparation of the budget, can be interpreted as bargaining techniques used by the DoD. Finally, the charges of former White House staff members (particularly Schlesinger and Wiesner) provide direct evidence of a political process.

That the outcome of this process was actually very close to the personal position of Secretary McNamara can be attributed to several factors. In the first place, McNamara was tightly in control of his own department, and was ably supported by a deputy secretary (Gilpatric) and several assistant secretaries (Hitch, Enthoven, and Nitze), who had come (to some extent independently) to share his position. He also had the support of President Kennedy, and against the much higher requests of the Air Force, the support of the Army and Navy and the White House staff (including the BoB).

Secondly, McNamara himself was fairly adept at bureaucratic bargaining and the handling of service pressures. In particular, he manipulated weapons systems and programs in order to resist those pressures. The generation of tentative Minuteman force projections (1,200 in the F/Y 1963–67 defense program) was one technique he made much use of. McNamara's planning and working techniques also enhanced his position. His clear, coherent, explicated reasoning made it hard for his opponents to argue against him; they were not able, for several years, to reason their own positions in his language and terms. Being forced to justify their positions on ground rules (such as the language, techniques, and tools of systems analysis) different from those they had used to reach those positions in the first place, and indeed, to integrate these new ground rules into patterns of thought they had evolved over a lifetime, was extraordinarily difficult for the Air Force and Congress. The changing of the ground rules by the McNamara Administration conceded to those who were better versed in them a considerable advantage in the bargaining process.

In any case, the F/Y 1963 strategic-forces program proposed

by the administration already represented a considerable quantitative increase over the previously authorized missile force—the additional 200 Minuteman ICBMs and 12 submarines (192 SLBMs) were 25 percent more than the missile program of March 1961 (and about 50 percent more if the calculation is based on the projected 1,200-missile Minuteman program). And McNamara could cut the Air Force missile requests, as he had at this time no reason to expect any major fight on the manned bomber front.

Most importantly, however, the demise of the missile gap during 1961, and the public reevaluation of the Soviet-American strategic relationship in the fall of 1961, undermined the position of the Air Force. Once that service had accepted the NIE of September 1961, and once Congress and the American public had accepted the administration's confidence in the strategic position of the United States in the fall of 1961, much of the Air Force's case for larger missile forces had been severely eroded.

There is some evidence that by the late summer of 1961 McNamara had realized that he could not hold his own personal position (a maximum of around 800–900 Minuteman ICBMs) much past 1961 or 1962—the successive annual increment which this figure represented for future years over the previously programmed 600-missile Minuteman force being too small to withstand the pressures of the Air Force and its congressional allies—and he prepared to give way to a force of 1,000 Minuteman missiles.

There was, for example, a meeting between McNamara, Hitch, and Enthoven at that time (the late summer of 1961) in which McNamara asked his two closest assistant secretaries how many Minuteman missiles they thought the United States should have. Apparently prepared, Hitch and Enthoven both replied: "One thousand as soon as possible, then wait and see!!" McNamara is said to have then produced a piece of paper on which he had previously written his own figure—of course, 1,000.[13] Other close civilian aides to McNamara in 1961 also believe that

13. Interview with Dr. Alain Enthoven, 17 August 1970.

he had decided on a force of 1,000 Minuteman missiles at about that time.[14] And several senior Air Force generals are, in retrospect, "sure of it" that McNamara had decided on 1,000 long before he set that figure in 1964.[15]

In 1961 McNamara was not, however, prepared to make this concession known outside a small group of his closest civilian assistants and advisers. To do so would have removed its value as bargaining leeway which was to enable him more or less to hold the line in 1962 and 1963 and finally to set the Minuteman ceiling at 1,000 in November 1964 (and publicly announce it in January 1965, with the presentation of the F/Y 1966 defense budget).

Also in 1963 and 1964, McNamara several times used the technique of manipulating the tentative projections to enable him to hold the Minuteman force at no more than 1,000 missiles, while at the same time eliminating other long-range strategic missile systems and programs. The maneuvering over the Skybolt cancellation and its Minuteman replacement is, of course, a good example of this.

This bargaining process, of which a U.S. strategic ballistic missile force of 1,710 long-range missiles was the final outcome, was conducted in an historical, strategic, domestic, and international environment of which the main determinants were outlined in Part 1. However, while the strategic (including the implicit though nevertheless almost universal acceptance of the notion of strategic superiority), historical (the "missile gap" debate, the 1960 presidential campaign, the missile commitments left over by the Eisenhower Administration), and international (the Soviet missile program and the pessimistic general international outlook for the United States in 1960–61) background, together with the bargaining bench marks set by the military services, can explain the relative order of magnitude of the Kennedy-McNamara strategic missile build-up, other, more prosaic and commonplace, but nevertheless real factors are needed to explain the exact level of that build-up, i.e., why,

14. Interviews with, for example, Daniel Ellsberg, 24 August 1970, and Roswell Gilpatric, 20 January 1973.

15. Interview with Gen. Le May, 16 August 1970.

precisely, 41 Polaris FBM submarines and 1,000 Minuteman ICBMs?

The example of the Polaris submarine fleet is illustrative. Why 41 submarines rather than any other number from 40 to 47 (the range suggested by the Hickey study)?[16] According to Dr. Alain Enthoven, the person principally responsible for setting the program figure, the choice of 41 was:

> simply an historical accident. There was no precise calculation of the necessary number of missiles. The Administration had inherited a program of 19 [Polaris submarines] then added ten, and then six and six, for forty-one.[17]

And why precisely 1,000 Minuteman missiles? According to one of the principals involved in setting the program level, 1,000 was simply the result of a "visceral feeling" on the part of McNamara and his aides that that figure was a satisfactory and viable compromise.[18] And the choice of exactly 1,000 (rather than, say, 983 or 1,039, or any other prime number) can be explained in terms of the simple *salience* of that figure, rather than in terms of precise calculation.[19]

The U.S. strategic missile force levels derived then, at least at the limit, from arbitrary judgment and "visceral feelings." Hence, the character of the personnel of the Kennedy-McNamara Administration and their cognitive processes were important factors in the missile build-up.[20]

There were several characteristics which distinguished the personnel of the defense policy-making establishment of the Kennedy Administration. The senior officials of the Pentagon possessed high academic credentials, were dynamic, young (in

16. Interview with Dr. Alain Enthoven, 17 August 1970; testimony of Gen. Wheeler, Senate Armed Services Committee, *Status of U.S. Strategic Power* (1968), part 1, p. 18.

17. Interview with Dr. Alain Enthoven, 17 August 1970. Enthoven himself worked with the Hickey study group.

18. Interview with Gen. Maxwell D. Taylor, 27 July 1970.

19. A position can be defined as "salient" if the chances of it being adopted are greater than the bare logic of abstract random possibilities would ever suggest (see Thomas C. Schelling, *The Strategy of Conflict*, p. 57).

20. For a discussion of the cognitive perspectives of the personnel of the Kennedy-McNamara Administration, see John D. Steinbruner, *The Cybernetic Theory of Decision*.

their thirties and early forties), highly intelligent, and able—
"Whiz Kids," in short, eager to exercise power. To a large extent
they were a closed group (many of them had worked together at
the RAND Corporation), sharing each other's assumptions, perspectives, language, and working techniques. They were, moreover, sometimes conceited and arrogant, and often unwilling to
listen to known alternative opinions (including professional military opinion).

The Kennedy Administration gathered together an extraordinary number of university professors, intellectuals, and liberals,
largely within the White House staff and the State Department,
but also in the DoD. These people radiated hope and optimism;
they had vigor and determination, and they were confident,
even excessively assured, that they could find solutions to the
problems of international relations and of U.S. national security
in terms of American power.

But the lessons of the history of modern presidential government in the United States were ignored. As Neustadt has
written:

> Truman's seven years and Eisenhower's eight suggest a certain
> rhythm in the modern presidency. The first twelve to eighteen
> months become a learning time for the new president who has to
> learn—or unlearn—many things about his job. No matter what
> his prior training, nothing he has done will have prepared him for
> all facets of that job. Some aspects of the learning process will
> persist beyond the first year-and-a-half. Most presidents will go on
> making new discoveries as long as they hold office (until at last
> they learn the bitterness of leaving office). But the intensive learn-
> ing time comes at the start and dominates the first two years.[21]

Certainly, the first eighteen months of the Kennedy Administration were ones of discovery—of the non-existence of a missile
gap; of learning—that the making of defense and national-
security policy was a decidedly more political process than
RAND taught; and of experimentation—the "shifting sands" of
strategy over the first two years. Yet it was during this period
that *all* the principal decisions were taken.

21. R. E. Neustadt, "Kennedy in the Presidency," cited in *The Politics of John
F. Kennedy*, ed. Edmund S. Ions, p. 178.

IMPLICATIONS FOR THE REPLACEMENT DECISIONS

The two most significant conclusions which emerge from this study of the strategic ballistic missile decisions of the Kennedy-McNamara Administration are that they were hasty and the product of political compromise; while the haste was unnecessary and quite avoidable, the politics were perhaps inevitable. These two factors have direct implications for future force developments. First, they emphasize the need for great caution and moderation. And, second, given that the force levels were the product of governmental politics rather than being derived from strategic criteria, replacement levels could be quite different.

The numbers that were decided upon in the early 1960s have come to assume some sanctity. Technologically, the strategic forces deployed during the 1960s are obsolescent. Qualitative improvements of great significance have certainly taken place, particularly with the conversion of 31 of the FBM submarines to carry Poseidon SLBMs and with the replacement of 550 of the earlier Minuteman missiles with the Minuteman III ICBM. However, further qualitative development of these systems is limited. The 41 FBM submarines, the first of which were deployed in 1960, will reach the end of their life-of-type in the early 1980s; and the configuration of the Minuteman missile and its silos rules out many technologically attractive possibilities. Moreover, these systems are becoming increasingly vulnerable to Soviet force developments. The older FBM submarines are relatively slow and noisy, and are unable to keep abreast of Soviet advances in ASW techniques. And the Minuteman force, based in fixed silos, must inevitably succumb to improvements in Soviet missile accuracy.

There is some tendency to opt for the one-to-one replacement of these systems. For example, Secretary Brown has stated that the 31 Trident submarines projected through F/Y 2000 is "based upon the need to replace our [31] aging [Poseidon submarines]."[22]

22. Harold Brown, *Department of Defense Annual Report, Fiscal Year 1979*, p. 113.

The replacement syndrome is always questionable. At the very least, it usually involves the replacement of given systems with ones of higher capability. This is certainly the case with the Trident systems as compared to the Polaris and Poseidon systems and, perhaps even more so, with the MX missile vis-à-vis the Minuteman III. But, more importantly, it begs the question about the need for such replacement. There are the implicit assumptions both that the initial decision was correct and also that its repetition is required in current circumstances.

The prospective decisions provide an opportunity to question these assumptions. The decisions of the early 1960s led to excessively high stockpiles of what are now increasingly vulnerable systems. The replacement strategic forces will be much better able to survive attack; they could also be rather fewer. From this point of view, the impending generational leap in U.S. strategic capabilities would be more reasonable than the last one.

Select Bibliography

GOVERNMENT PUBLICATIONS

The great bulk of the official publications cited in the text can be summarized into two groups. First, there are the *Annual Reports* to Congress of the secretary of defense, beginning with that of Secretary McNamara, *Fiscal Year 1963–67 Defense Program and 1963 Defense Budget*, 19 January 1962. The "threat" sections of the F/Y 1963 through F/Y 1973 classified versions of the *Annual Reports* were declassified in 1975. Second, there are four complete sets of congressional hearings—those of the House Armed Services Committee and the Senate Armed Services Committee, from F/Y 1962 through F/Y 1968, and the subcommittees on defense of the Senate Appropriations Committee and the House Appropriations Committee, from F/Y 1960 through F/Y 1968. The following U.S. government publications have also been cited:

Strategic Systems Project Office, U.S. Navy. *Polaris and Poseidon Chronol-*

ogy. Washington, D.C.: Strategic Systems Project Office, Navy Department, 1973.

Strategic Systems Project Office, U.S. Navy. *Polaris and Poseidon FBM Facts*. Washington, D.C.: Strategic Systems Project Office, Navy Department, 1973.

U.S. Congress, House. *Congressional Record*. 1960 to 1965.

U.S. Congress, Senate. *Congressional Record*. 1960 to 1965.

U.S. Congress, House, Committee on Science and Astronautics, Hearings. *Review of the Space Program*, pt. 1. 86th Cong., 2nd sess., 1960.

U.S. Congress, Senate, Preparedness Investigating Subcommittee of Committee on Armed Services and Committee on Aeronautical and Space Science. *Joint Hearings, Missiles, Space, and Other Major Defense Matters*. 86th Cong., 2nd sess., 1960.

U.S. Congress, House. Document No. 123, *Message from the President of the United States Relative to Recommendations Relating to our Defense Budget*. 87th Cong., 1st sess., 28 March 1961.

U.S. Congress, Senate, Committee on Armed Services, Hearings. *Construction Cost of the Air Force Atlas and Titan Missile Sites*. 87th Cong., 2nd sess., 1963.

U.S. Congress, Senate, Committee on Armed Services, Hearings. *Military Aspects and Implications of Nuclear Test Ban Proposals and Related Matters*, pt. 1. 88th Cong., 1st sess., May–August 1963. Published 1964.

U.S. Congress, Senate, Committee on Armed Services, Hearings. *Military Aspects and Implications of Nuclear Test Ban Proposals and Related Matters*, pt. 2. 88th Cong., 1st sess., August 1963. Published 1964.

U.S. Congress, Senate, Committee on Foreign Relations, Hearings. *Nuclear Test Ban Treaty*. 88th Cong., 1st sess., 1963.

U.S. Congress, Senate, Preparedness Investigating Subcommittee of the Committee on Armed Services. *Hearings on Series of Explosions of Air Force's Atlas F Intercontinental Ballistic Missiles*. 88th Cong., 2nd sess., 1964.

U.S. Congress, House, Committee on Armed Services, Hearings. *Department of Defense Decision to Reduce the Numbers and Types of Manned Bombers in the Strategic Air Command*. 89th Cong., 2nd sess., 1966.

U.S. Congress, House, Committee on Armed Services. *Report on the DOD Decision to Reduce the Numbers and Types of Manned Bombers in the Strategic Air Command*. 89th Cong., 2nd sess., 1966.

U.S. Congress, Senate, Committee on Armed Services, Hearings. *Status of U.S. Strategic Power*, pt. 1. 90th Cong., 2nd sess., 1968.

U.S. Congress, Senate, Committee on Armed Services, Hearings. *Status of U.S. Strategic Power*, pt. 2. 90th Cong., 2nd sess., 1968.

U.S. Congress, Senate, Inquiry of the Subcommittee on National Security and International Operations, Committee on Government Operations. *Planning, Programming, Budgeting*. 91st Cong., 2nd sess., 1970.

BOOKS AND MONOGRAPHS

Abel, Elie. *The Missile Crisis*. New York: Bantam Books, 1966.

Allison, Graham T. *Essence of Decision: Explaining the Cuban Crisis*. Boston: Little, Brown, 1971.

Allison, Graham, and Szanton, Peter. *Remaking Foreign Policy: The Organizational Connection*. New York: Basic Books, 1976.

Alsop, Stewart. *The Centre: The Anatomy of Power in Washington*. London: Hodder & Stoughton, 1968.

Armacost, Michael H. *The Politics of Weapons Innovation: The Thor-Jupiter Controversy*. New York: Columbia University Press, 1969.

Baar, James, and Howard, William E. *Combat Missileman*. New York: Harcourt, Brace, and World, 1961.

————. *Polaris!* New York: Harcourt, Brace and Co., 1960.

Baldwin, Hanson W. *The Great Arms Race*. New York: Praeger, 1958.

Ball, Desmond. *Déjà Vu: The Return to Counterforce in the Nixon Administration*. Santa Monica: California Seminar on Arms Control and Foreign Policy, 1974.

Barnaby, C. F., and Boserup, A., eds. *Implications of Anti-Ballistic Missile Systems*. Pugwash Monograph No. 2. New York: Humanities Press, 1969.

Barnet, Richard J. *The Economy of Death*. New York: Atheneum, 1969.

Beard, Edmund. *Developing the ICBM: A Study in Bureaucratic Politics*. New York: Columbia University Press, 1976.

Bloomfield, Lincoln P.; Clemens, Walter C.; and Griffiths, Franklyn. *Khrushchev and the Arms Race*. Cambridge, Mass.: MIT Press, 1966.

Borklund, C. W. *The Department of Defense*. New York: Praeger, 1968.

Bottome, Edgar M. *The Balance of Terror: A Guide to the Arms Race.* Boston: Beacon Press, 1971.

———. *The Missile Gap: A Study of the Formulation of Military and Political Policy.* Cranbury, N.J.: Fairleigh Dickinson University Press, 1971.

Brennan, Donald G., ed. *Arms Control, Disarmament, and National Security.* New York: Braziller, 1961.

Brodie, Bernard. *A Review of William W. Kaufmann's "The McNamara Strategy."* Santa Monica: RAND Corp., P-3077, March 1965.

———. *Escalation of the Nuclear Option.* Princeton, N.J.: Princeton University Press, 1966.

———. *Strategy in the Missile Age.* Princeton, N.J.: Princeton University Press, 1965.

Brown, William M. *Limiting Damage from Nuclear War.* Santa Monica: RAND Corp., RM-6043-PR, October 1969.

Buchan, Alastair. *NATO in the 1960s.* New York: Praeger, rev. ed., 1963.

Chapman, John L. *Atlas: The Story of a Missile.* New York: Harper, 1960.

Chase, Harold W., and Lerman, Allen H., eds. *Kennedy and the Press.* New York: Crowell, 1965.

Chayes, Abram, and Wiesner, Jerome B., eds. *ABM: An Evaluation of the Decision to Deploy an Antiballistic Missile System.* New York: Signet Books, 1969.

Cox, Donald W. *America's New Policy Makers: The Scientist's Rise to Power.* Philadelphia: Chilton Books, 1964.

David, Paul T., ed. *The Presidential Election and Transition, 1960–1961.* Washington, D.C.: Brookings Institution, 1961.

Dinerstein, H. S. *War and the Soviet Union.* New York: Praeger, rev. ed., 1962.

Donovan, Col. James A. *Militarism, U.S.A.* New York: Charles Scribner's Sons, 1970.

Dougherty, James E., and Lehman, J. F., Jr., eds. *Arms Control for the Late Sixties.* New York: Van Nostrand Reinhold Co., 1967.

Duscha, Julius. *Arms, Money and Politics.* New York: Ives Washburn, 1965.

Edwards, David V. *Arms Control in International Politics.* New York: Holt, Rinehart and Winston, 1969.

Eisenhower, Dwight David. *The White House Years: Waging the Peace, 1956–1961*. Garden City, N.Y.: Doubleday, 1965.

Englebardt, Stanley L. *Strategic Defenses*. New York: Crowell, 1966.

Enke, Stephen, ed. *Defense Management*. Englewood Cliffs, N.J.: Prentice-Hall, 1967.

Enthoven, Alain C., and Smith, K. Wayne. *How Much is Enough?: Shaping the Defense Program, 1961–1969*. New York: Harper & Row, 1971.

Frankel, Joseph. *The Making of Foreign Policy*. London: Oxford University Press, 1963.

Freedman, Lawrence. *U.S. Intelligence and the Soviet Strategic Threat*. London: The Macmillan Press Ltd., 1977.

Fryklund, Richard. *100 Million Lives: Maximum Survival in a Nuclear War*. New York: Macmillan Co., 1962.

Gantz, Lt. Col. Kenneth F., ed. *The United States Air Force Report on the Ballistic Missile*. Garden City, N.Y.: Doubleday, 1958.

Gavin, Gen. James M. *War and Peace in the Space Age*. New York: Harper, 1958.

Ginsburgh, Col. Robert N. *U.S. Military Strategy in the Sixties*. New York: Norton, 1965.

Goldwater, Barry M. *Why Not Victory?: A Fresh Look at American Foreign Policy*. New York: McGraw-Hill, 1962.

Goulding, Phil. G. *Confirm or Deny: Informing the People on National Security*. New York: Harper & Row, 1970.

Goure, Leon. *Civil Defense in the Soviet Union*. Berkeley and Los Angeles: University of California Press, 1962.

Greenwood, Ted. *Making the MIRV: A Study in Defense Decision-Making*. Cambridge, Mass.: Ballinger, 1975.

Hadley, Arthur T. *The Nation's Safety and Arms Control*. New York: Viking, 1961.

Halle, Louis J. *The Cold War as History*. London: Chatto & Windus, 1970.

Halperin, Morton H. *Contemporary Military Strategy*. Boston: Little, Brown, 1967.

———. *Defense Strategies for the Seventies*. Boston: Little, Brown, 1971.

———. *National Security Policy-Making: Analyses, Cases and Proposals*. Lexington, Mass.: Lexington Books, 1975.

Hammond, Paul Y. *Resource Limits, Political and Military Risk Taking, and the Generation of Military Requirements*. Santa Monica: RAND Corp., P-3421-1, September 1966.

Harris, Seymour E., *The Economics of the Political Parties*. New York: Macmillan Co., 1962.

————. *Economics of the Kennedy Years and a Look Ahead*. New York: Harper & Row, 1964.

Hartt, Julian. *The Mighty Thor: Missile in Readiness*. New York: Duell, Sloan and Pearce, 1961.

Hilsman, Roger. *To Move a Nation*. New York: Delta Books, 1964.

————. *The Politics of Policy Making in Defense and Foreign Affairs*. New York: Harper & Row, 1971.

Hitch, Charles J. *Decision-Making for Defense*. Berkeley and Los Angeles: University of California Press, 1969.

Holst, Johan J., and Schneider, William, eds. *Why ABM?* New York: Pergamon Press, 1969.

Hoopes, Townshend. *The Limits of Intervention*. New York: David McKay, 1969.

Horelick, Arnold L., and Rush, Myron. *Strategic Power and Soviet Foreign Policy*. Chicago: University of Chicago Press, 1966.

Huntington, Samuel P. *The Common Defense*. New York: Columbia University Press, 1966.

Ions, Edmund S., ed. *The Politics of John F. Kennedy*. London: Routledge & Kegan Paul, 1964.

Johnson, Lyndon Baines. *The Vantage Point: Perspectives on the Presidency, 1963–69*. London: Weidenfeld & Nicolson, 1971.

Kahn, Herman. *On Thermonuclear War*. New York: Free Press, 2nd ed., 1969.

Kaplan, Morton A., ed. *Great Issues of International Politics*. Chicago: Aldine, 1970.

Kaufmann, William W. *The McNamara Strategy*. New York: Harper & Row, 1964.

Kennedy, John F. *Profiles in Courage*. New York: Harper, 1956.

————. *The Strategy of Peace*. Edited by Allan Nevins. New York: Popular Library, 1961.

Kennedy, Robert F. *13 Days: The Cuban Missile Crisis, October, 1962*. London: Pan Books, 1969.

Key, V. O., Jr. *Politics, Parties and Pressure Groups*. 5th ed. New York: Crowell, 1964.

Kintner, William R. *Peace and the Strategy Conflict*. New York: Praeger, 1967.

Kissinger, Henry A. *The Necessity for Choice*. Garden City, N.Y.: Doubleday, 1960.

———. *American Foreign Policy*. London: Weidenfeld & Nicolson, 1969.

———, ed. *Problems of National Security*. New York: Praeger, 1965.

Kistiakowsky, George B. *A Scientist at the White House: The Private Diary of President Eisenhower's Special Assistant for Science and Technology*. Cambridge, Mass.: Harvard University Press, 1976.

Klass, Philip J. *Secret Sentries in Space*. New York: Random House, 1971.

Knorr, Klaus, ed. *NATO and American Security*. Princeton, N.J.: Princeton University Press, 1959.

Korb, Lawrence J. "The Role of the Joint Chiefs of Staff in the Defense Budget Process from 1947 to 1967." Ph.D thesis, State University of New York at Albany, 1969.

———. *The Joint Chiefs of Staff: The First Twenty-Five Years*. Bloomington, Ind.: Indiana University Press, 1976.

Kuenne, Robert E. *The Polaris Missile Strike*. Columbus: Ohio State University Press, 1966.

Laird, Melvin R. *A House Divided: America's Security Gap*. Chicago: Henry Regnery Co., 1962.

Lapp, Ralph E. *Arms Beyond Doubt: The Tyranny of Weapons Technology*. New York: Cowles Book Co., 1970.

———. *Kill or Overkill: The Strategy of Annihilation*. London: Weidenfeld & Nicolson, 1962.

———. *The Weapons Culture*. Baltimore: Penguin Books, 1969.

Laurus, Joel. *Nuclear Weapons, Safety, and the Common Defense*. Columbus: Ohio State University Press, 1967.

Le May, Gen. Curtis E. *America is in Danger*. New York: Funk & Wagnalls, 1968.

————., with Kantor, MacKinlay. *Mission with Le May, My Story*. Garden City, N.Y.: Doubleday, 1965.

Lindblom, Charles E. *The Policy-Making Process*. Englewood Cliffs, N.J.: Prentice-Hall, 1968.

Lowe, George E. *The Age of Deterrence*. Boston: Little, Brown, 1964.

Lyons, Gene M., and Morton, Louis. *Schools for Strategy*. New York: Praeger, 1965.

McBride, James H. *The Test Ban Treaty*. Chicago: Henry Regnery Co., 1967.

MacCloskey, Monro. *The United States Air Force*. New York: Praeger, 1967.

McNamara, Robert S. *The Essence of Security: Reflections in Office*. London: Hodder & Stoughton, 1968.

McSherry, James E. *Khrushchev and Kennedy in Retrospect*. Palo Alto, Calif.: Open-Door Press, 1971.

Manchester, William. *Portrait of a President: John F. Kennedy in Profile*. Boston: Little, Brown, rev. ed., 1967.

Melman, Seymour. *Pentagon Capitalism: The Political Economy of War*. New York: McGraw-Hill, 1970.

————, ed. *A Strategy for American Security*. New York: Lee Services, 1963.

Mollenhoff, Clark R. *The Pentagon*. New York: G. P. Putnam's Sons, 1967.

Morgenstern, Oskar. *The Question of National Defense*. New York: Vintage Books, 1960.

Moulton, Harland B. "American Strategic Power: Two Decades of Nuclear Strategy and Weapon Systems 1945–1965." Ph.D. thesis, University of Minnesota, 1969.

Neal, Roy. *Ace in the Hole: The Story of the Minuteman Missile*. New York: Doubleday, 1962.

Neustadt, Richard E. *Alliance Politics*. New York: Columbia University Press, 1970.

Nieburg, H. L. *In the Name of Science*. Chicago: Quadrangle Books, 1966.

Nixon, Richard M. *Six Crises*. New York: Pyramid Books, 1968.

Novick, David. *Program Budgeting: Long-Range Planning in the Depart-

ment of Defense. Santa Monica: RAND Corp., RM-3359-ASDC, November 1962.

Parson, Nels A., Jr. *Missiles and the Revolution in Warfare*. Cambridge, Mass.: Harvard University Press, 1962.

Peeters, Paul. *Massive Retaliation: The Policy and Its Critics*. Chicago: Henry Regnery Co., 1959.

Penkovsky, Oleg. *The Penkovsky Papers*. New York: Avon Books, 1965.

Perlo, Victor. *Militarism and Industry: Arms Profiteering in the Missile Age*. London: Lawrence & Wishart, 1963.

Perry, Robert L. *The Ballistic Missile Decisions*. Santa Monica: RAND Corp., P-3686, October 1967.

Pitman, George R. *Arms Races and Stable Deterrence*. Security Studies Paper No. 18. Los Angeles: Arms Control & International Studies Center, University of California, 1969.

Polsky, Nelson W., and Wildavsky, Aaron B. *Presidential Elections*. New York: Charles Scribner's Sons, 1964.

Porter, Kirk H., and Johnson, Donald Bruce. *National Party Platforms, 1840–1964*. Urbana, Ill.: University of Illinois Press, 1966.

Power, Gen. Thomas S. *Design for Survival*. New York: Coward-McCann, 1965.

Powers, Francis Gary. *Operation Overflight*. New York: Holt, Rinehart and Winston, 1970.

Public Affairs Press. *The New Frontiersmen: Profiles of the Men Around Kennedy*. Washington, D.C.: Public Affairs Press, 1961.

———. *New Frontiers of the Kennedy Administration: The Texts of the Task Force Reports Prepared for the President*. Washington, D.C.: Public Affairs Press, 1961.

Quester, George H. *Nuclear Diplomacy: The First Twenty-Five Years*. Boston: Dunnellin, 1971.

Ransom, Harry Howe. *Can American Democracy Survive Cold War?* Garden City, N.Y.: Doubleday, 1963.

———. *The Intelligence Establishment*. Cambridge, Mass.: Harvard University Press, 1970.

Rathjens, George. *The Future of the Strategic Arms Race: Options for the 1970s*. New York: Carnegie Endowment for International Peace, 1969.

Raymond, Jack. *Power at the Pentagon*. London: Heinemann, 1964.

Rees, Ed. *The Manned Missile: The Story of the B-70*. New York: Duell, Sloan and Pearce, 1960.

Rockefeller Panel, The. *Prospect for America: The Rockefeller Panel Reports*. Garden City, N.Y.: Doubleday, 1961.

Roberts, Chalmers M. *The Nuclear Years: The Arms Race and Arms Control, 1945–1970*. New York: Praeger, 1970.

Rodberg, Leonard S., and Shearer, Derek, eds. *The Pentagon Watchers*. Garden City, N.Y.: Anchor Books, 1970.

Roherty, James M. *Decisions of Robert S. McNamara*. Coral Gables, Florida: University of Miami Press, 1970.

Ronblom, H. K. *Wennerstrom the Spy*. London: Hodder & Stoughton, 1966.

Rostow, Walt W. *The Diffusion of Power, 1957–1972*. New York: Macmillan Co., 1972.

Salinger, Pierre. *With Kennedy*. New York: Avon Books, 1966.

Sapolsky, Harvey M. *The Polaris System Development*. Cambridge, Mass.: Harvard University Press, 1972.

Schelling, Thomas C. *The Strategy of Conflict*. New York: Oxford University Press, 1963.

———, and Halperin, Morton H. *Strategy and Arms Control*. New York: Twentieth Century Fund, 1961.

Schilling, Warner R.; Hammond, Paul Y.; and Snyder, Glen H. *Strategy, Politics and Defence Budgets*. New York: Columbia University Press, 1962.

Schlesinger, Arthur M., Jr. *Kennedy or Nixon? Does It Make Any Difference?* New York: Macmillan Co., 1960.

———. *A Thousand Days: John F. Kennedy in the White House*. London: André Deutsch, 1965.

———. *The Bitter Heritage: Vietnam and American Democracy*. London: André Deutsch, 1967.

Schlesinger, James R. *Arms Interactions and Arms Control*. Santa Monica: RAND Corp., P-3881, September 1968.

Schwiebert, Ernest G. *A History of the U.S. Air Force Ballistic Missiles*. New York: Praeger, 1965.

Sidey, Hugh. *John F. Kennedy: Portrait of a President*. Harmondsworth, Middlesex, England: Penguin Books, 1965.

Singer, J. David. *Deterrence, Arms Control and Disarmament*. Columbus: Ohio State University Press, 1962.

Smith, Bruce L. R. *The RAND Corporation*. Cambridge, Mass.: Harvard University Press, 1966.

Sorensen, Theodore C. *Decision-Making in the White House*. New York: Columbia University Press, 1963.

————. *Kennedy*. London: Pan Books, 1966.

————. *The Kennedy Legacy*. New York: Macmillan Co., 1969.

Spanier, John. *American Foreign Policy Since World War II*. New York: Praeger, 2nd ed., 1962.

Stebbins, Richard P. *The United States in World Affairs, 1962*. New York: Vintage Books, 1963.

————. *The United States in World Affairs, 1963*. New York: Harper & Row, 1964.

Steinbruner, John D. *The Cybernetic Theory of Decision: New Dimensions of Political Analysis*. Princeton, N.J.: Princeton University Press, 1974.

Stewart, William A. *Counterforce, Damage-Limiting and Deterrence*. Santa Monica: RAND Corp., P-3385, July 1967.

Stone, Jeremy J. *Containing the Arms Race*. Cambridge, Mass.: MIT Press, 1966.

Taylor, Gen. Maxwell D. *The Uncertain Trumpet*. New York: Harper, 1960.

————. *Responsibility and Response*. New York: Harper & Row, 1967.

Tompkins, John S. *The Weapons of World War III*. London: Robert Hale, 1966.

Trewhitt, Henry L. *McNamara: His Ordeal in the Pentagon*. New York: Harper & Row, 1971.

Tucker, Samuel A., ed. *A Modern Design for Defense Decision: A McNamara-Hitch-Enthoven Anthology*. Washington, D.C.: Industrial College of the Armed Forces, 1966.

Tully, Andrew. *The Super Spies*. New York: Morrow, 1969.

Twining, Gen. Nathan F. *Neither Liberty Nor Safety*. New York: Holt, Rinehart and Winston, 1966.

Whiteside, Thomas. *An Agent in Place: The Wennerstrom Affair*. New York: Viking, 1966.

Wildavsky, Aaron. *The Politics of the Budgetary Process*. Boston: Little, Brown, 1964.

Wilson, Andrew. *War Gaming*. Baltimore: Penguin Books, 1970.

Wise, David, and Ross, Thomas B. *The U-2 Affair*. New York: Random House, 1962.

————. *The Invisible Government*. New York: Random House, 1964.

Wohlstetter, A. J.; Hoffman, F. S.; Lutz, R. J.; and Rowen, H. S. *Selection and Use of Strategic Air Bases*. Santa Monica: RAND Corp., R-266, April 1954.

Wynne, Greville. *The Man from Moscow: The Story of Wynne and Penkovsky*. London: Arrow Books, 1968.

Yarmolinsky, Adam. *The Military Establishment: Its Impact on American Society*. New York: Harper & Row, 1971.

York, Herbert F. *Race to Oblivion: A Participant's View of the Arms Race*. New York: Simon & Schuster, 1970.

ARTICLES

In addition to the specific references below, articles have been cited from the following newspapers and periodicals: *Aerospace International*; *Air Force & Space Digest*; *Aviation Week & Space Technology*; *Boeing Magazine*; *Bulletin of the Atomic Scientists*; *Business Week*; *Chicago Tribune*; *Christian Science Monitor*; *Congressional Quarterly Weekly Report*; Department of State *Bulletin*; *Foreign Affairs*; *Fortune*; *Herald Tribune*; *Military Review*; *Missiles & Rockets*; *NATO's Fifteen Nations*; *New Republic*; *Newsweek*; *New York Review of Books*; *New York Times*; *San Francisco Examiner*; *Saturday Evening Post*; *Space/Aeronautics*; *The Reporter*; *Time*; *U.S. News & World Report*; *Washington Post*; *Washington Star*.

Art, Robert J. "Bureaucratic Politics and American Foreign Policy: A Critique." *Policy Sciences* 4 (December 1973): 467–90.

Ball, Desmond John. "The Blind Men and the Elephant: A Critique of Bureaucratic Politics Theory." *Australian Outlook* 28 (April 1974): 71–92.

Brown, Harold. "Planning Our Military Forces." *Foreign Affairs* 45 (January 1967): 227–90.

Bull, Hedley. "Strategic Studies and Its Critics." *World Politics* 20 (July 1968): 593–605.

Bundy, McGeorge. "The Presidency and the Peace." *Foreign Affairs* 42 (April 1964): 353–65.

———. "To Cap the Volcano." *Foreign Affairs* 48 (October 1969): 1–20.

Burke, Adm. Arleigh. "Polaris." Unpublished paper, no date.

Carleton, William G. "Kennedy in History: An Early Appraisal." *Antioch Review* 24 (1964): 277–99.

Erskine, Helen Gaudet. "The Polls: Defense, Peace, and Space." *Public Opinion Quarterly* 25 (Fall 1961): 478–89.

Foster, William C. "Prospects for Arms Control." *Foreign Affairs* 47 (April 1969): 413–21.

Friedman, Saul. "The RAND Corporation and Our Policy-Makers." *The Atlantic Monthly*, September 1963, pp. 61–68.

Gibney, Frank. "When the West Had a Man in the Kremlin." *Washington Post*, 31 October 1965, p. E1.

Gilpatric, Roswell L. "Our Defense Needs: The Long View." *Foreign Affairs* 42 (April 1964): 366–78.

Gordon, T. J., and Haywood, Harold. "Initial Experiments with the Cross Impact Method of Forecasting." *Futures* 1 (December 1968): 100–16.

Graham, Lt. Gen. Daniel O. "The Soviet Military Budget Controversy." *Air Force Magazine*, May 1976, pp. 33–37.

Gray, Colin S. "The Arms Race Phenomenon." *World Politics* 24 (October 1971): 39–79.

Halperin, Morton H. "The Gaither Committee and the Policy Process." *World Politics* 13 (April 1961): 360–84.

———. "The Military Problem: Choosing Our Weapons." *The New Republic*, 2 October 1961, pp. 34–36.

———. "The President and the Military." *Foreign Affairs* 50 (January 1972): 310–24.

Hilsman, Roger. "The Foreign Policy Consensus: An Interim Research Report." *Journal of Conflict Resolution* 3 (December 1959): 361–82.

Hitch, Charles J. "Plans, Programs and Budgets in the Department of Defense." *Operations Research* 11 (January–February 1963): 1–17.

Kennedy, John F. "The State of the Union." Department of State *Bulletin* 44 (13 February 1961): 207–14.

Kurth, James R. "A Widening Gyre: The Logic of American Weapons Procurement." *Public Policy* 19 (Summer 1971): 373–404.

Lall, Betty Goetz. "Superiority and Innovation in U.S. Defense Forces." *Bulletin of the Atomic Scientists* 23 (May 1967): 11–13.

Lapp, Ralph E. "Can SALT Stop MIRV?" *The New York Times Magazine*, 1 February 1970, p. 14.

Lazo, Dr. Mario. "Decision for Disaster." *Reader's Digest*, Australian edition, October 1964, pp. 170–99.

Licklider, Roy E. "The Missile Gap Controversy." *Political Science Quarterly* 85 (December 1970): 600–15.

Lowe, George E. "The Only Option?" *U.S. Naval Institute Proceedings* 97 (April 1971): 18–26.

McNamara, Robert S. "The Dynamics of Nuclear Strategy." Department of State *Bulletin* 57 (9 October 1967): 443–51.

Midgaard, Knut. "Arms Races, Arms Control and Disarmament." *Cooperation and Conflict*, no. 1 (1970): 20–51.

Murphy, Charles J. V. "Defense: The Converging Decisions." *Fortune*, October 1958, p. 119.

———. "The Education of a Defense Secretary." *Fortune*, May 1962, p. 102.

———. "Khrushchev's Paper Bear." *Fortune*, December 1964, p. 114.

Nacht, Michael L. "The Delicate Balance of Error." *Foreign Policy*, no. 19 (Summer 1975): 163–77.

Neustadt, R. E. "Kennedy in the Presidency: A Premature Appraisal." *Political Science Quarterly* 79 (September 1964): 321–34.

———. "White House and Whitehall." *The Public Interest*, no. 2 (Winter 1966): 55–69.

Nitze, Paul H. "Limited Wars or Massive Retaliation." *The Reporter*, 5 September 1957, pp. 40–42.

Powers, Francis Gary. "Francis Gary Powers Tells His Story." *New York Times Magazine*, 19 April 1970, p. 36.

Stone, I. F. "McNamara and the Militarists." *The New York Review of Books*, 7 November 1968, pp. 5–10.

————. "Theater of Delusion." *The New York Review of Books*, 23 April 1970, pp. 15–24.

————. "The Test Ban Comedy." *The New York Review of Books*, 7 May 1970, pp. 14–22.

Symington, Stuart. "Where the Missile Gap Went." *The Reporter*, 15 February 1962, pp. 21–23.

Wiesner, Jerome B. "Arms Control: Current Prospects and Problems." *Bulletin of the Atomic Scientists* 26 (May 1970): 6–8.

Wohlstetter, A. J. "The Delicate Balance of Terror." *Foreign Affairs* 37 (January 1959): 211–34.

————. "Scientists, Seers, and Strategy." *Foreign Affairs* 41 (April 1963): 466–78.

————. "Vietnam and Bureaucracy." In *Great Issues of International Politics*, edited by Morton A. Kaplan. Chicago: Aldine Publishing Company, 1970.

————. "Racing Forward or Ambling Back." *Survey* 22 (Summer/Autumn 1976): 163–214.

Wyden, Peter. "The Chances of Accidental War." *Saturday Evening Post*, 3 June 1961, p. 17.

Yarmolinsky, Adam. "Some Lessons of Vietnam." *The Round Table*, January 1972, pp. 85–92.

York, Herbert F. "Military Technology and National Security." *Scientific American*, August 1969, pp. 17–29.

————. "A Personal View of the Arms Race." *Bulletin of the Atomic Scientists* 26 (March 1970): 27–31.

INTERVIEWS

During the summer of 1970, the winter of 1972–73, the fall of 1975, and the fall of 1977, I interviewed some fifty former senior military and civilian persons within or associated at first hand with the Kennedy-McNamara defense establishment. Their names and former relevant positions, and the places and dates of the interviews are as follows:

Bell, David E. Director, Bureau of the Budget, 1961–63. Ford Foundation, New York, 20 Dec. 1972.

Booda, Larry L. Military editor, *Aviation Week*, 1960–64. Arlington, Virginia, 6 Feb. 1973.

Brennan, Donald G. DoD consultant. Hudson Institute, New York, 2 July 1970.

Brodie, Bernard. DoD consultant. University of California, Los Angeles, 14 Aug. 1970.

Brooks, Harvey. President's Science Advisory Committee (PSAC); Fletcher Committee on Minuteman, 1961. Harvard University, 15 Jan. 1973.

Bundy, McGeorge. President Kennedy's special assistant for national security affairs. Ford Foundation, New York, 18 Dec. 1972.

Burke, Adm. Arleigh. Chief of naval operations, JCS. Center for Strategic Studies, Washington, D.C., 29 July 1970.

Dean, Dr. L. Weapons Systems Evaluation Group (WSEG Report No. 50). Lambda Corporation, Arlington, Va., 27 July 1970.

Doty, Paul. President's Science Advisory Committee (PSAC); Foster arms control task force, early 1961. Harvard University, 23 Feb. 1973.

Ellsberg, Daniel. DoD consultant; Partridge Committee, 1961. RAND Corporation, Los Angeles, 24 Aug. 1970, and Cambridge, Mass., 8 Oct. 1972.

Enthoven, Dr. Alain C. Deputy comptroller and deputy assistant secretary of defense. Los Angeles, Litton Industries, 17 Aug. 1970.

Everett, Hugh. Weapons Systems Evaluation Group (WSEG Report No. 50). Lambda Corporation, Arlington, Va., 1 Feb. 1973.

Fryklund, Richard. Pentagon correspondent, *Washington Star*, and assistant secretary of defense. RAND Corporation, Washington, D.C., 20 July 1970, and 2 Feb. 1973.

Gilpatric, Roswell L. Deputy secretary of defense, 1961–63. New York, 20 Jan. 1973.

Glass, Henry. Aide to Secretary McNamara. Pentagon, Washington, D.C., 29 July 1970.

Goldberg, Alfred. RAND Historian. RAND Corporation, Washington, D.C., 20 July 1970, 12 Feb. 1973, and 26 Nov. 1975.

Gordon, Kermit. Director, Bureau of the Budget. Brookings Institution, Washington, D.C., 8 Feb. 1973.

Halperin, Morton H. DoD consultant, and deputy assistant secretary of defense (ISA). RAND Corporation, Santa Monica, Calif., 20 Aug. 1970.

Harlan, Neil A. Assistant secretary of the Air Force for financial management. Washington, D.C., 21 July 1970.

Hilsman, Roger. Director, Bureau of Intelligence and Research, U.S. State Department. Columbia University, New York, 27 May 1970, and 12 June 1970.

Hitch, Charles J. Assistant secretary of defense (comptroller). Berkeley, Calif., 11 Aug. 1970.

Hoag, Malcolm W. Consultant to ISA (DoD). RAND Corporation, Santa Monica, Calif., 19 Aug. 1970.

Hoffman, F. S. DoD consultant. RAND Corporation, Santa Monica, Calif., 25 Aug. 1970.

Kaufmann, William W. Consultant to Secretary McNamara. MIT, Cambridge, Mass., 9 July 1970, 28 Jan. 1973, and 22 Feb. 1973.

Kaysen, Carl. Deputy special assistant for national security affairs. Institute for Advanced Study, Princeton, N.J., 19 Dec. 1972.

Keeny, Spurgeon M. Office of Science and Technology, Executive Office of the President. Arms Control and Disarmament Agency, Washington, D.C., 7 Feb. 1973.

Kent, Maj. Gen. Glenn A. Office of Chief of Staff for Studies and Analysis, USAF. Pentagon, Washington, D.C., 16 July 1970.

Killalea, Neil. Weapons Systems Evaluation Group (WSEG Report No. 50). Lambda Corporation, Arlington, Va., 1 Feb. 1973.

Killian, Dr. James R. President's Science Advisory Committee (PSAC); and chairman, President's Foreign Intelligence Advisory Board, 1961–63. MIT, Cambridge, Mass., 16 Jan. 1973.

Kilmarx, Robert A. Air Force Intelligence. Center for Strategic Studies, Washington, D.C., 22 July 1970.

Kistiakowsky, George B. Special assistant to the president for science and technology, 1958–61. Harvard University, 20 Feb. 1973.

Le May, Gen. Curtis E. Chief of staff, USAF. Los Angeles, 16 Aug. 1970.

Lukeman, Maj. Gen. Robert P. Office of Chief of Staff for Studies and Analysis, USAF. Pentagon, Washington, D.C., 5 Feb. 1973, and 12 Feb. 1973.

McCrae, Dr. Vincent. Staff, Office of Science and Technology, Executive Office of the President. By telephone, through Jerome B. Wiesner, 20 Feb. 1973.

McGarvey, David. Consultant to OSD. The RAND Corporation, Santa Monica, Calif., 29 Oct. 1975.

Marshall, Andrew W. Gaither committee (1957); DoD consultant. Executive Office of the President, Washington, D.C., 13 Feb. 1973; Pentagon, 7 Sept. 1977.

Martin, Col. Donald F. Office of Chief of Staff for Plans and Programs, USAF. Washington, D.C., 29 July 1970.

Nitze, Paul H. Deputy assistant secretary of defense (ISA); secretary of the navy; deputy secretary of defense. Pentagon, Washington, D.C., 7 Feb. 1973.

Paul, Norman S. Assistant to the secretary of defense for legislative affairs, 1961–62. Washington, D.C., 9 Feb. 1973.

Pugh, Dr. George. Weapons Systems Evaluation Group (WSEG Report No. 50). Lambda Corporation, Arlington, Va., 24 July 1970, and 1 Feb. 1973.

Raskin, Marcus G. Member of President Kennedy's Special Staff of the National Security Council, 1961–62. Institute for Policy Studies, Washington, D.C., 6 Feb. 1973.

Rathjens, George. Deputy director, ARPA. MIT, Cambridge, Mass., 11 July 1970, and 8 Dec. 1972.

Richardson, Gen. Robert C. Office of Chief of Staff for Plans and Programs. USAF. Alexandria, Va., 25 July 1970.

Rowen, Henry S. Assistant Secretary of Defense for ISA. RAND Corporation, Santa Monica, Calif., 25 Aug. 1970.

Scoville, Herbert. Assistant director for science and technology, CIA, 1955–61; and deputy director for research, CIA, 1961–63. McLean, Va., 9 Feb. 1973.

Shapley, Willis H. Deputy director of National Security Division, Bureau of the Budget. National Aeronautics and Space Administration, Washington, D.C., 8 Feb. 1973.

Smith, Gen. Frederic H. Vice-chief of staff, USAF. Washington, D.C., 28 July 1970.

Stern, Dr. Marvin. Assistant director, DDR&E. Los Angeles, 21 Aug. 1970.

Taylor, Gen. Maxwell D. Presidential military advisor for foreign and military political and intelligence operations; and chairman, joint chiefs of staff. Chevy Chase, Md., 27 July 1970.

Veatch, Ellis H. Director of National Security Division, Bureau of the Budget, Office of Management and Budget. New Executive Office Building, Washington, D.C., 6 Feb. 1973.

Wiesner, Jerome B. Special assistant to the president for science and technology. MIT, Cambridge, Mass., 20 Feb. 1973.

Wohlstetter, Dr. Albert J. Consultant to ISA, OSD, and Systems Analysis (DoD). Los Angeles, 16 Aug. 1970, and Chicago, 18 Nov. 1972.

Yarmolinsky, Adam. Special assistant to the secretary and deputy secretary of defense. Harvard University, 10 July 1970.

York, Dr. Herbert F. Director of defense research & engineering, 1958–61. San Diego, 15 Aug. 1977.

Zuckert, Eugene M. Secretary of the U.S. Air Force. Washington, D.C., 21 July 1970.

Index

Navy, 67–68; opposed by the White House staff, 84–87; vs. "overkill" theory, 79–81; rationalization of provided by strategic policies, 211; reduction in, 144, 150; role of U.S. intelligence on Soviet strength in, 7, 8, 9–11, 13–15, 19–21, 54–58, 140, 142, 154, 158, 165–178; "worst case analysis" conducive to, 139–140
— explanations of, xv, xxiv–xxvi, 165–263, 274; aerospace industry in, 252–257; bargaining with the military, xxvi, 221, 234, 240–252, 271–275 (*see also* Bargaining); cancelled Skybolt ALBMs replaced by Minuteman missiles, 150, 214, 224–231, 251, 274; commitments made during Kennedy's 1960 presidential campaign, xxv, 5, 17, 233, 234–240, 270–271; comparison of Kennedy's and McNamara's responsibility for, 245–247; compromise on the 1,000-Minuteman force, 251–252, 273–274, 275; concept of U.S. strategic superiority in, 180–186; congressional pressures, 246, 247–249; as a consequence of confrontations on the B-70 manned bomber, 213, 214–224, 245, 249; economic recession in, 121–122, 256n, 257–263; intelligence estimates of Soviet strategic forces in, xxiv, 165–178, 268; military-industrial capitalism, 234, 252–263; military pressures on McNamara, 250–251; "no-cities" counterforce strategy in, 195, 200, 201; pressures by the Air Force, 245–252 *passim*, 272, 273; strategic policy in, 194, 205–211. *See also* Political explanations of the strategic missile build-up
—historical background of, xxii–xxiii, 3–104, 274; conclusions of arms-control studies, 82–84; demise of the missile gap, 88–104; domestic politics in, 7, 10, 12–13; groups and individuals opposed to, 78–87; and Kennedy's presidential campaign, 5, 15–22, 126, 188, 234–

240, 257, 270–271; missile gap controversy in, 4–22; missile program of the Eisenhower Administration, 41–42, 43–46; numbers of U.S. and Soviet ICBMs assessed, 42, 46–47; opposed by the White House staff, 84–87; vs. "overkill theory," 79–82; qualitative development, 48–53; quantitative development, 46–48; Soviet missile program, 43, 53–58; strategic studies before 1961, 5, 25–240

Kent, Glenn A., General, 202, 209n
Kent study, 202–204, 208–209. *See also* Damage limitation strategic policy
Key, V. O., 236
Keynesian economics, 259, 262
Khrushchev, N., 183; increased military spending announced by, 131; "minimum deterrence" adopted by, 170; and U.S. first-strike position, 198
Kilday, Paul J., Congressman, 243
Killian, James, 30, 31n, 85; on lobbying by industry, 254
Kilmarx, Robert A., 244
Kissinger, Henry: in arms-control study group, 82; consultant to the Kennedy Administration, 31; influence of A. Wohlstetter evaluated by, 40; *The Necessity for Choice* by, 188; Rockefeller Brothers' Report directed by, 30
Kistiakowsky, George, 85; technical argument against mobile Minuteman presented by, 123
Korth, Secretary of the Navy, 66, 67
Kuenne, Robert, 141n
Kurth, James R., xvii

Lall, Betty Goetz, 83n
Lanphier, Thomas G.: missile production advocated by, 253–254
Lapp, Ralph: and political explanations of the missile build-up, xxv, 235
Launchers: defined, 48; Soviet, 56–57

Designer: David Bullen
Compositor: G & S Typesetters
Printer: Braun-Brumfield
Binder: Braun-Brumfield
Text: VIP Baskerville
Display: VIP Helvetica
Cloth: Holliston Roxite C 56548 Vellum
Paper: 50 lb. P&S Offset B32